THE KEY

Applied Mathematics 30

THE KEY

THE KEY series of student study guides is specifically designed to assist students in preparing for unit tests, provincial achievement tests, and diploma examinations. Each **KEY** includes questions, answers, detailed solutions, and practice tests. The complete solutions show problem-solving methods, explain key concepts, and highlight potential errors.

TABLE OF CORRELATIONS

Castle Rock Research has designed **THE KEY** by correlating every question and its solution to Alberta Education's curriculum outcomes. Each unit of review begins with a Table of Correlations that lists the General and Specific Outcomes from the Alberta curriculum along with Related Questions that correspond to the outcomes. Usually the emphasis placed on outcomes, concepts, and skills within each unit varies. Students and teachers can quickly identify the relevant importance of each outcome and concept in the unit as determined by the number of related questions provided in **THE KEY**.

For grades 3, 6, 9, and 12, the weighting of each unit and concept is determined by analyzing the blueprint for the respective provincial achievement tests and diploma examinations. Based on this analysis, the Related Questions for outcomes and concepts are organized on a proportionate basis. For grades other than 3, 6, 9, and 12, the breakdown of each course is determined by consulting with experienced teachers and by reviewing curriculum guides and textbooks.

The Table of Correlations is a critical component of **THE KEY**. For students, it offers a visual cue for effectively organizing study time. For teachers, the Table of Correlations indicates the instructional focus for each content strand, serves as a curriculum checklist, and focuses on the outcomes and concepts that are the most important in the unit and the particular course of study. Students become "test wise" by becoming familiar with exam and question formats used most often in provincial examinations.

© 2003 – 2008 by Castle Rock Research Corp.
All rights reserved. No part of this book covered by the copyright hereon
may be reproduced or used in any form or by any means graphic,
electronic, or mechanical, including photocopying, recording, taping, or
information storage and retrieval systems without the express permission
of the publisher.

Canadian Cataloguing in Publication Data

Rao, Gautam, 1961 –
THE KEY – Applied Mathematics 30 (2008 Edition)

   1.   Mathematics – Juvenile Literature. I. Title

Published by
Castle Rock Research Corp.
2340 Manulife Place
10180 – 101 Street
Edmonton, AB T5J 3S4

5 6 7 FP 07 06 05

Printed in Canada

Publisher
Gautam Rao

Contributors
Aaron Stavne
Jeremy Klassen

Dedicated to the memory of Dr. V. S. Rao

THE KEY – Applied Mathematics 30

THE KEY is a study guide specifically designed to assist students in preparing for unit tests and provincial diploma examinations. It is a compilation of questions and answers from previous diploma examinations, complete with detailed solutions for all questions. Questions have been grouped by concepts so that students can use the resource throughout the year to study for all unit tests and to prepare for their provincial diploma exams. To accurately reflect the Applied Mathematics 30 curriculum, additional questions have been created by Castle Rock Research to supplement the questions from previous diploma exams. Newly added questions are marked with a key icon so that students can distinguish them from actual diploma exam questions. *THE KEY* is organized into the following sections.

I *KEY Factors Contributing to School Success* provides students with examples of study and review strategies. Information is included on learning styles, study schedules, and developing review notes.

II *Unit Review* includes questions from 1999, 2000 and 2001 January and June diploma exams. All questions are classified according to the units studied in class and are correlated to the specific concept(s) being tested. In Unit Review, questions considered to be more difficult are labelled as *Challenger* questions. *THE KEY* **provides detailed solutions for all questions.**

III *Unit Tests* have been created for each unit to provide students with a sample test that covers the breadth of the curriculum. These tests are comprised of the relevant diploma exam questions from January and June 2001 and teacher generated questions.

IV *KEY Strategies for Success on Exams* explores topics such as common exam question formats and strategies for responding, directing words most commonly used, how to begin the exam, and managing test anxiety.

V *Diploma Examination* section contains the diploma examination that was administered in January 2002. The questions presented here are distinct from the questions in the previous section. It is recommended that students work through the exam carefully because it is reflective of the exam format and level of difficulty that students are likely to encounter on their final. **Complete solutions are provided for all questions in this section.**

THE KEY *Study Guides* are available for Biology 30, Chemistry 30, Physics 30, English 30-1, English 30-2, Applied Mathematics 30, Pure Mathematics 30, Social Studies 30, and Social Studies 33. A complete list of the *THE KEY* *Study Guides* for Grades 3 to 12 is included at the back of this book.

At Castle Rock Research, we strive to produce a resource that is error-free. If you should find an error, please contact us so that future editions can be corrected.

CONTENTS

KEY STRATEGIES FOR SUCCESS ON EXAMS

DIPLOMA EXAMINATION

ANSWERS AND SOLUTIONS – DIPLOMA EXAMINATION

APPENDICES

NOTES

KEY FACTORS CONTRIBUTING TO SCHOOL SUCCESS

Copyright Protected

NOTES

Not for Reproduction

 *KEY* FACTORS CONTRIBUTING TO
SCHOOL SUCCESS

You want to do well in school. There are many factors that contribute to your success. While you may not have control over the number or types of assignments and tests that you need to complete, there are many factors that you can control to improve your academic success in any subject area. The following are examples of these factors.

- **REGULAR CLASS ATTENDANCE** – helps you to master the subject content, identify key concepts, take notes and receive important handouts, ask your teacher questions, clarify information, use school resources, and meet students with whom you can study

- **POSITIVE ATTITUDE AND PERSONAL DISCIPLINE** – helps you to come to classes on time, prepared to work and learn, complete all assignments to the best of your ability, and contribute to a positive learning environment

- **SELF-MOTIVATION AND PERSONAL DISCIPLINE** – helps you to set personal learning goals, take small steps continually moving toward achieving your goals, and to "stick it out when the going gets tough"

- **ACCESSING ASSISTANCE WHEN YOU NEED IT** – helps you to improve or clarify your understanding of the concept or new learning before moving on to the next phase

- **MANAGING YOUR TIME EFFICIENTLY** – helps you to reduce anxiety and focus your study and review efforts on the most important concepts

- **DEVELOPING 'TEST WISENESS'** – helps to increase your confidence in writing exams if you are familiar with the typical exam format, common errors to avoid, and know how the concepts in a subject area are usually tested

- **KNOWING YOUR PERSONAL LEARNING STYLE** – helps you to maximize your learning by using effective study techniques, developing meaningful study notes, and make the most efficient use of your study time

Copyright Protected

📖 KNOW YOUR LEARNING STYLE

You have a unique learning style. Knowing your learning style – how you learn best – can help you to maximize your time in class and during your exam preparation. There are seven common learning styles. Read the following descriptions to see which one most closely describes your learning preferences.

- **LINGUISTIC LEARNER** (sometimes referred to as an auditory learner) – learns best by saying, hearing and seeing words; is good at memorizing things such as dates, places, names and facts

- **LOGICAL/MATHEMATICAL LEARNER** – learns best by categorizing, classifying and working with abstract relationships; is good at mathematics, problem solving and reasoning

- **SPATIAL LEARNER** (sometimes referred to as a visual learner) – learns best by visualizing, seeing, working with pictures; is good at puzzles, imaging things, and reading maps and charts

- **MUSICAL LEARNER** – learns best by hearing, rhythm, melody, and music; is good at remembering tones, rhythms and melodies, picking up sounds

- **BODILY/KINESTHETIC LEARNER** – learns best by touching, moving, and processing knowledge through bodily sensations; is good at physical activities

- **INTERPERSONAL LEARNER** – learns best by sharing, comparing, relating, cooperating; is good at organizing, communicating, leading, and understanding others

- **INTRAPERSONAL LEARNER** – learns best by working alone, individualized projects, and self-paced instruction

(Adapted from http://snow.utoronto.ca/Learn2/mod3/mistyles.html)

Your learning style may not fit "cleanly" into one specific category but may be a combination of two or more styles. Knowing your personal learning style allows you to organize your study notes in a manner that provides you with the most meaning. For example, if you are a spatial or visual learner, you may find mind mapping and webbing are effective ways to organize subject concepts, information, and study notes. If you are a linguistic learner, you may need to write and then "say out loud" the steps in a process, the formula, or actions that lead up to a significant event. If you are a kinesthetic learner you may need to use your finger to trace over a diagram to remember it or to "tap out" the steps in solving a problem or "feel" yourself writing or typing the formula.

Not for Reproduction

📖 SCHEDULING STUDY TIME

Effective time management skills are an essential component to your academic success. The more effectively you manage your time the more likely you are to achieve your goals such as completing all of your assignments on time or finishing all of the questions on a unit test or year-end exam. Developing a study schedule helps to ensure you have adequate time to review the subject content and prepare for the exam.

You should review your class notes regularly to ensure you have a clear understanding of the new material. Reviewing your lessons on a regular basis helps you to learn and remember the ideas and concepts. It also reduces the quantity of material that you must study prior to a unit test or year-end exam. If this practice is not part of your study habits, establishing a study schedule will help you to make the best use of your time. The following are brief descriptions of three types of study schedules.

- **LONG-TERM STUDY SCHEDULE** – begins early in the school year or semester and well in advance of an exam; is the **most effective** manner for improving your understanding and retention of the concepts, and increasing self-confidence; involves regular, nightly review of class notes, handouts and text material

- **SHORT-TERM STUDY SCHEDULE** – begins **five to seven days prior to an exam**; must organize the volume of material to be covered beginning with the most difficult concepts; each study session starts with a brief review of what was studied the day before

- **CRAMMING** – occurs the night before an exam; is the **least effective** form of studying or exam preparation; focuses on memorizing and reviewing critical information such as facts, dates, formulas; do not introduce new material; has the potential to increase exam anxiety by discovering something you do not know

Regardless of the type of study schedule you use, you may want to consider the following to maximize your study time and effort:

- establish a regular time and place for doing your studying

- minimize distractions and interruptions during your study time

- plan a ten minute break for every hour that you study

- organize the material so you begin with the most challenging content first

- divide the subject content into smaller manageable "chunks" to review

- develop a marking system for your study notes to identify key and secondary concepts, concepts that you are confident about, those that require additional attention or about which you have questions

- reward yourself for sticking to your schedule and/or completing each review section

- alternate the subjects and type of study activities to maintain your interest and motivation

- make a daily task list with the headings "must do", "should do", and "could do"

- begin each session by quickly reviewing what you studied the day before

- maintain your usual routine of eating, sleeping, and exercising to help you concentrate for extended periods of time

📖 *KEY* STRATEGIES FOR REVIEWING

Reviewing textbook material, class notes, and handouts should be an ongoing activity and becomes more critical in preparing for exams. You may find some of the following strategies useful in completing your review during your scheduled study time.

READING OR SKIMMING FOR KEY INFORMATION

- Before reading the chapter, preview it by noting headings, charts and graphs, chapter questions.

- Turn each heading and sub-heading into a question before you start to read.

- Read the complete introduction to identify the key information that is addressed in the chapter.

- Read the first sentence of the next paragraph for the main idea.

- Skim the paragraph noting key words, phrases, and information.

- Read the last sentence of the paragraph.

- Repeat the process for each paragraph and section until you have skimmed the entire chapter.

- Read the complete conclusion to summarize each chapter's contents.

- Answer the questions you created.

- Answer the chapter questions.

Not for Reproduction

CREATING STUDY NOTES

Mind Mapping or Webbing

- Use the key words, ideas, or concepts from your reading or class notes to create a *mind map or web* (a diagram or visual representation of the information). A mind map or web is sometimes referred to as a knowledge map.

- Write the key word, concept, theory, or formula in the centre of your page.

- Write and link related facts, ideas, events, and information to the central concept using lines.

- Use coloured markers, underlining, or other symbols to emphasize things such as relationships, information of primary and secondary importance.

- The following example of a mind map or web illustrates how this technique can be used to develop an essay.

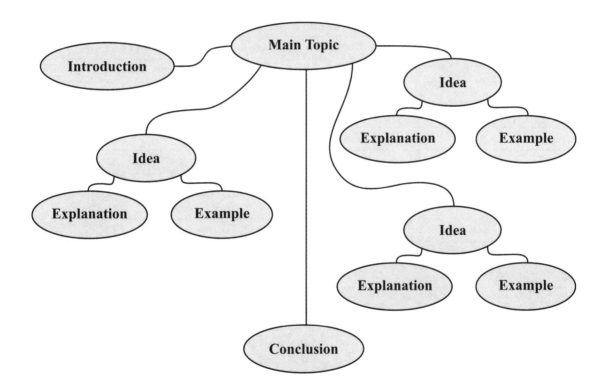

Charts

♦ Use charts to organize your information and relate theories, concepts, definitions, applications, and other important details.

♦ Collect and enter the information in key categories.

♦ Use the completed chart as a composite picture of the concept or information.

The following is an example of how a chart can be used to help you organize information when exploring an issue in subjects such as Social Studies, the Sciences, or Humanities.

Define Key Words		
1.		
2.		
3.		
Explore the Issue		
Yes to the Issue	**No** to the Issue	**Maybe** to the Issue
1.	1.	1.
2.	2.	2.
3.	3.	3.
Case Studies and **Examples**		
1.	1.	
2.	2.	
3.	3.	
Defense of Your Point of View		
1.		
2.		
3.		

Index Cards

♦ Write a key event, fact, concept, theory, word, or question on one side of the index card.

♦ On the reverse side, write the date, place, important actions and key individuals involved in the event, significance of the fact, salient features of the concept, essence and application of the theory, definition of the word or answer to the question.

♦ Use the cards to quickly review important information.

International System of Units (SI)

International System of Units (SI)

SI base unit

Base quantity	Name	Symbol
length	metre	m
mass	kilogram	kg
time	second	s
amount of substance	mole	mol

Derived Measures

Measures	Unit	Symbol
volume	cubic metre	m^3

SI Prefixes

Factor	Name	Symbol
10^6	mega	M
10^3	kilo	k
10^{-2}	centi	c
10^{-3}	milli	m
10^{-6}	micro	μ

Symbols

♦ Develop your own symbols to use when reviewing your material to identify information you need in preparing for your exam. For example, an exclamation mark (!) may signify something that "must be learned well" because it is a key concept that is likely to appear on unit tests and the year-end exam. A question mark (?) may identify something you are unsure of while a star or asterisk (*) may identify important information for formulating an argument.

A check mark (✓) or an (✗) can be used to show that you agree or disagree with the statement, sentence or paragraph.

Copyright Protected

Crib Notes

- Develop brief notes that are a critical summary of the essential concepts, dates, events, theories, formulas, supporting facts, or steps in a process that are most likely to be on the exam.

- Use your crib notes as your "last minute" review before you go in to write your exam. You cannot take crib notes into an exam.

MEMORIZING

- **ASSOCIATION** relates the new learning to something you already know. For example, in distinguishing between the spelling of 'dessert' and 'desert', you know 'sand' has only one 's' and so should desert.

- **MNEMONIC DEVICES** are sentences you create to remember a list or group of items. For example, the first letters of the words in the sentence "**E**very **G**ood **B**oy **D**eserves **F**udge" helps you to remember the names of the lines on the treble clef staff (E, G, B, D, and F) in music.

- **ACRONYMS** are words formed from the first letters of the words in a group. For example, **HOMES** helps you to remember the names of the five Great Lakes (**H**uron, **O**ntario, **M**ichigan, **E**rie, and **S**uperior).

- **VISUALIZING** requires you to use your mind's eye to "see" the chart, list, map, diagram, or sentence as it exists in your textbook, notes, on the board, computer screen or in the display.

APPLIED MATHEMATICS 30

Unit Review has been developed to aid students in their study throughout the term. Students can prepare for unit exams while gaining exposure to previous Diploma Exam questions. The *Unit Review* section of **THE KEY** contains questions from previous Diploma Exams administered in 2002 (January). Additional teacher-generated questions have been created to supplement the *Unit Review* section. These questions are marked with a key icon so students can distinguish teacher generated questions from previous diploma examination questions.

All questions have been organized by content strand to correspond to the units in Applied Mathematics 30. Students will find questions for *Matrices and Pathways; Statistics and Probability; Finance; Cyclic, Recursive and Fractal Patterns; Vectors;* and *Design*. A **Table of Correlations** at the beginning of each unit lists the curriculum outcomes and the *Multiple Choice*, *Numerical Response* and *Written Response* questions which specifically test those concepts.

THE KEY contains detailed solutions for all questions. Solutions show the processes and/or ideas used in arriving at the correct answers **and** may *help* students gain a better understanding of the concepts that are being tested.

In *Unit Review*, certain questions have been categorized as *Challenger Questions*. *Challenger Questions* represent the more difficult questions that a student is likely to encounter, as illustrated in the following example.

CHALLENGER QUESTION	40.7

16. John invested *P* dollars at 3% compounded annually for a 20-year period. The amount of money that John will have at the end of each year is increased from the amount at the end of the previous year by a factor of

   A. 0.03   **B.** *P*

   C. 1.03   **D.** 1.03*P*

The *Difficulty* rating is based on the percentage of students that answered the question correctly when it appeared on the Diploma Exam. In the example, only 40.7% of students answered it correctly (Source: Alberta Education Examiner's Reports). *Challenger Questions* for Applied Mathematics 30 include those with less than a 60% achievement rate as indicated by *Difficulty*.

MATRICES AND PATHWAYS

Table of Correlations		
Topic	**Outcomes**	**Questions**
Solve problems based on the counting of sets, using techniques such as the fundamental counting principle, permutations, and combinations.	*It is expected that students will:* 1.1 Solve pathway problems, interpreting and applying any constraints	1, 2, 3
	1.2 Use the Fundamental Counting Principle to determine the number of different ways to perform multi-step operations	4, 5, NR1, 6, NR2, 7
Describe and apply operations on matrices to solve problems, using technology as required.	1.3 Perform, using technology only for larger matrices, the matrix operations of addition, subtraction, matrix multiplication, and multiplication by a scalar.	8, 9, 10, 11, 12, 13, 14, NR3
	1.4 Model and solve consumer and network problems, performing matrix operations and using algebraic solution strategies as needed.	15, 16, 17, NR4

Copyright Protected

Not for Reproduction

MATRICES AND PATHWAYS

Students will solve problems based on the counting of sets, using techniques such as the fundamental counting principle, permutations, and combinations.

1.1 Solve pathway problems, interpreting and applying any constraints.

PATHWAYS

In solving pathway problems, movement must always be toward the goal in order to ensure a minimum number of routes.

We can use Pascal's Triangle as a model for solving two-dimensional pathway problems. Notice the pattern in the following diagram:

Each value in Pascal's Triangle is equal to the sum of the two values above it to the left and the right. As shown in the diagram, notice that $4 + 6 = 10$.

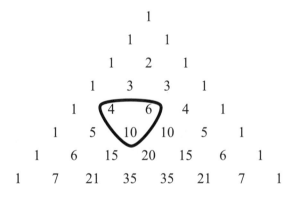

For simple grid pathway problems, we follow the pattern in Pascal's Triangle to determine the number of pathways from the starting point to each individual node, or intersection point, in the grid.

In order to move from point A to point B in the following diagram, we need to move either right or down so that we are always moving closer to the goal—B. This means that the number of different paths to any specific intersection point will equal the sum of the number of paths to the intersection point above it and to the left of it.

If there is no node above or to the left of a particular intersection point, assume that there is a zero there.

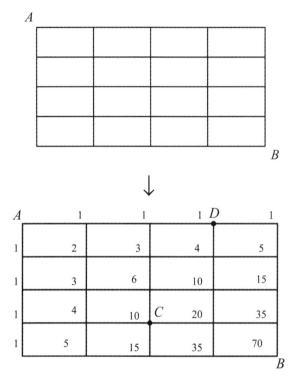

In the diagram above, the total number of paths from point A to point C is 10 because there are 6 paths to the intersection point above it and 4 paths to the intersection point left of it.

The number of paths to point D is 1; there is one path to the intersection point left of it, but there is no intersection point above it. The total number of pathways from point A to point B is 70.

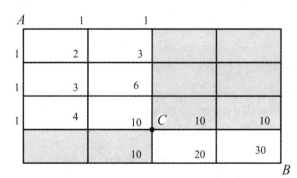

Copyright Protected

If there was a restriction in the above example that the pathway from point *A* to point *B* must pass through point *C*, then we would ignore all parts of the grid below and to the left of point *C* as well as all the parts of the grid above and to the right of point *C*.

There are 30 pathways from *A* to *B* that must pass through *C*.

More difficult problems can be handled in the same manner.

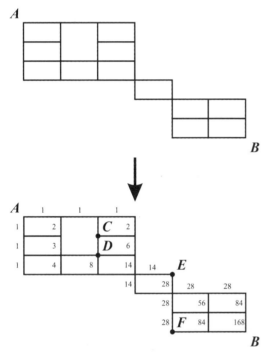

Note that the number of different pathways to intersection *C* is 1. It is not connected to the intersection to its left, so we assume that the value to its left is zero. Intersection *D* does have an intersection above it and to the left of it so to find the number of pathways to *D*, add these two values. Note that some intersections, such as *E* and *F*, are connected to only one intersection to the left or above, so we assume zeros in the other positions. There are 168 different pathways leading from *A* to *B*.

Pathway problems may also be represented as network diagrams like the one below that shows an airline's flight routes and connections for five cities. Using this network diagram, determine the number of routes that one can fly from Edmonton to Vancouver.

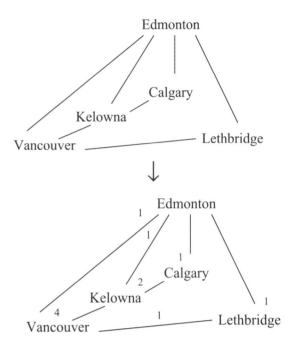

To solve this problem, remember that all routes must start at Edmonton and continue toward Vancouver. According to the diagram, there is only 1 route from Edmonton to each of the other 4 cities, but there are 2 routes from Edmonton to Kelowna: one direct and one through Calgary. If we add the number of routes from the cities connected to Vancouver, we see that there are a total of 4 routes from Edmonton to Vancouver.

Related Questions: 1, 2, 3

1.2   Use the Fundamental Counting Principle to determine the number of different ways to perform multi-step operations.

THE FUNDAMENTAL COUNTING PRINCIPLE

The Fundamental Counting Principle states that if a project can be broken into stages, the total number of ways in which the project can be completed is equivalent to the product of the number of choices at each stage.

Not for Reproduction

Example: Suppose that Jerry is shopping for a vehicle. He decides on a particular model that comes in three different editions and five different colours. How many different vehicles does Jerry have to choose from?

Jerry has a choice of 3 editions and for each of these editions, there are 5 different colours, to solve, multiply the number of these options together.
The product of 3 and 5 is 15, so he can choose from 15 different vehicles.

This can be illustrated with a tree diagram as shown below.

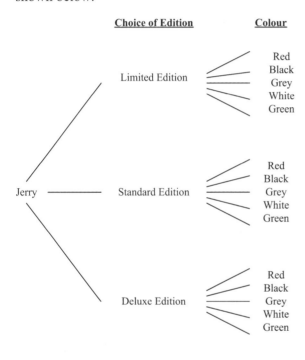

Each branch of the tree corresponds to a specific combination of choices.

The Fundamental Counting Principle is often used to answer questions about the number of possibilities of organizing items, with or without restrictions.

Without restrictions
We can use the Fundamental Counting Principle to arrange 5 people standing in a row.
Identify the possible number of people for every position starting with 5 choices for the first position, 4 for the next, and so on, until everyone is positioned.

$\underline{5} \times \underline{4} \times \underline{3} \times \underline{2} \times \underline{1} = 120$

There are 120 arrangements of 5 people standing in a row.

With restrictions
When answering ordering questions that include restrictions, begin with the restrictions.
For example, consider the word TRIANGLE. How many different arrangements of these letters can be made can be made that begin and end with a vowel? There are 3 options for the beginning vowel (first restriction), and once that is chosen, there are 2 choices for the final position (second restriction). After these have been chosen, arrange the remaining letters as before.

$\underline{3} \times \underline{6} \times \underline{5} \times \underline{4} \times \underline{3} \times \underline{2} \times \underline{1} \times \underline{2} = 4\ 320$

Other restrictions could include taking a limited number of choices from the given options. For example, how many different arrangements of the consonants in the word TRIANGLE are possible? Since there are only 5 consonants, we determine the number of arrangements of 5 different consonants.

$\underline{5} \times \underline{4} \times \underline{3} \times \underline{2} \times \underline{1} = 120$

Finally, we may be asked to arrange objects where repetitions are allowed. For example, how many different passwords consisting of any 2 letters followed by any 3 numbers are possible. Because we are allowing for repetitions, there are 26 options for each letter and 10 options (0 to 9) for each number.

$\underline{26} \times \underline{26} \times \underline{10} \times \underline{10} \times \underline{10} = 676\ 000$

In questions about the specific digits of a number, repetitions are always allowed unless otherwise specified.

Related Questions: 4, 5, NR1, 6, NR2, 7

Students will describe and apply operations on matrices to solve problems, using technology as required.

1.3   Perform, using technology only for larger matrices, the matrix operations of addition, subtraction, matrix multiplication, and multiplication by a scalar.

MATRIX OPERATIONS

A matrix is a rectangular array of values called elements. When describing the dimensions of a matrix, we begin by identifying its number of rows and then its number of columns.

For example, matrix $A = \begin{bmatrix} a_{11} & a_{12} & a_{13} \\ a_{21} & a_{22} & a_{23} \end{bmatrix}$ is a

2×3 matrix because it has 2 rows and 3 columns. Notice that we use a lower case a with subscripts to represent the individual elements, or values, in matrix A. The subscripts represent the row and the column in which the variable is positioned.

If $A = \begin{bmatrix} 5 & -6 & 0 \\ 1 & 2 & -11 \\ 9 & 0 & -4 \end{bmatrix}$

then $a_{23} = -11$, $a_{31} = 9$, $a_{12} = -6$, etc.

To add or subtract matrices, they must have the same size and shape. When adding or subtracting matrices, we combine the corresponding elements from each matrix. The resultant matrix will be the same size and shape as the two original matrices.

For example, if

$A = \begin{bmatrix} -1 & 5 \\ 9 & 11 \\ 6 & -3 \end{bmatrix}$ and $B = \begin{bmatrix} 10 & 2 \\ -3 & 0 \\ 8 & 7 \end{bmatrix}$

then…

$A + B = \begin{bmatrix} -1 & 5 \\ 9 & 11 \\ 6 & -3 \end{bmatrix} + \begin{bmatrix} 10 & 2 \\ -3 & 0 \\ 8 & 7 \end{bmatrix}$

$= \begin{bmatrix} -1 + 10 & 5 + 2 \\ 9 + -3 & 11 + 0 \\ 6 + 8 & -3 + 7 \end{bmatrix}$

$= \begin{bmatrix} 9 & 7 \\ 6 & 11 \\ 14 & 4 \end{bmatrix}$

A scalar is a constant value. To multiply a matrix by a constant, we multiply each element of the matrix by the constant in order to create a new matrix.

For example, to multiply matrix $A = \begin{bmatrix} 1 & 5 \\ 4 & 3 \end{bmatrix}$ by 2, we do as follows:

$2A = 2 \begin{bmatrix} 1 & 5 \\ 4 & 3 \end{bmatrix}$

$= \begin{bmatrix} 2(1) & 2(5) \\ 2(4) & 2(3) \end{bmatrix}$

$= \begin{bmatrix} 2 & 10 \\ 8 & 6 \end{bmatrix}$

Notice that the resulting matrix has the same dimensions as matrix A.

Multiplying one matrix by another is possible only if the first matrix has the same number of columns as the number of rows in the second matrix. The dimensions of the product—the resulting matrix—will be equal to the number of rows in the first matrix and the number of columns in the second matrix.

For example, it is possible to multiply

$A = \begin{bmatrix} 3 & 7 \\ 0 & 1 \\ 5 & 4 \end{bmatrix}$ by $B = \begin{bmatrix} -3 & 8 \\ 2 & 1 \end{bmatrix}$

because there are 2 columns in [A] and 2 rows in [B].

To multiply two matrices, we multiply each element along a row of the first matrix by each element along a column of the second matrix and add up the results. Take note of which row number you are using from the first matrix and which column number you are using from the second matrix, because these determine the location of your result in the final product.

If $A = \begin{bmatrix} 3 & 7 \\ 0 & 1 \\ 5 & 4 \end{bmatrix}$ and $B = \begin{bmatrix} -3 & 8 \\ 2 & 1 \end{bmatrix}$, then

$$A \times B = \begin{bmatrix} (3)(-3) + (7)(2) & (3)(8) + (7)(1) \\ (0)(-3) + (1)(2) & (0)(-3) + (1)(2) \\ (5)(-3) + (4)(2) & (5)(8) + (4)(1) \end{bmatrix}$$

$$= \begin{bmatrix} 5 & 31 \\ 2 & 1 \\ -7 & 44 \end{bmatrix}$$

The element in the third row and second column of the product is a combination of the third row of A and the second column of B.

The product is a 3×2 matrix because the first matrix has 3 rows and the second matrix has 2 columns. Notice that it is impossible to multiply $[B] \times [A]$ because the number of columns in $[B]$ is not the same as the number of rows in $[A]$. As a result, matrix multiplication is **not** generally commutative.

All of the above operations and many more can be performed using a graphic display calculator.

Related Questions: 8, 9, 10, 11, 12, 13, 14, NR3

1.4   Model and solve consumer and network problems, performing matrix operations and using algebraic solution strategies as needed.

APPLICATIONS

Matrices can be used to solve consumer problems.

Example: Mr. Smith sells spruce, pine, elm, and poplar trees at his tree nursery. A spruce tree sells for $40, a pine for $35, an elm for $29, and a poplar for $15.

Mr. Smith sells an average of 15 spruce, 12 pine, 20 elm, and 7 poplar each day.

- Make a row matrix to represent the selling price for each type of tree
- Create a column matrix to represent the average number of each type of tree that he sells in a day
- Use matrix multiplication to determine his revenue in a day
- What is his revenue in a week?

Solution:
A row matrix is a matrix with only one row. In this case, we list the price of every tree, as follows:

$$\text{Price} = \begin{array}{cccc} \text{Sp} & \text{Pi} & \text{El} & \text{Po} \\ \end{array}$$
$$\text{Price} = \begin{bmatrix} 40 & 35 & 29 & 15 \end{bmatrix}$$

A column matrix is a matrix consisting of only one column. In this case, we list the number of trees sold, as follows:

$$\text{Tree type} = \begin{array}{c} \text{Sp} \\ \text{Pi} \\ \text{El} \\ \text{Po} \end{array} \begin{bmatrix} 15 \\ 12 \\ 20 \\ 7 \end{bmatrix}$$

To determine the revenue in one day, we want to get a single answer, meaning that our final matrix should be a one-by-one matrix. To achieve this, we multiply the price matrix, which has one row, by the matrix containing the number of trees, which has one column. The product matrix will also have one row and one column.

$$\text{Price} \times \text{Number} = \begin{bmatrix} 40 & 35 & 29 & 15 \end{bmatrix} \begin{bmatrix} 15 \\ 12 \\ 20 \\ 7 \end{bmatrix}$$

$$= \begin{bmatrix} (40)(15) + (35)(12) + (29)(20) + (15)(7) \end{bmatrix}$$
$$= \begin{bmatrix} 1\ 705 \end{bmatrix}$$

Therefore, Mr. Smith's revenue at the end of one day is $1 705.

To determine his revenue for one week, we can multiply his revenue for one day by 7. |The result would be $11 935. We can also adjust our number matrix to determine the number of trees of each type that he sells in a week by multiplying by a scalar.

$$7 \times \begin{bmatrix} 15 \\ 12 \\ 20 \\ 7 \end{bmatrix} = \begin{bmatrix} 105 \\ 84 \\ 140 \\ 49 \end{bmatrix}$$

This new matrix tells us that he sells 105 spruce, 84 pine, 140 elm, and 49 poplar in one week. Now, multiply this by the price matrix to determine total revenue.

$$\begin{bmatrix} 40 & 35 & 29 & 15 \end{bmatrix} \begin{bmatrix} 105 \\ 84 \\ 140 \\ 49 \end{bmatrix}$$

$$= \begin{bmatrix} (40)(105) + (35)(84) + (29)(140) + (15)(49) \end{bmatrix}$$

$$= \begin{bmatrix} 11\ 935 \end{bmatrix}$$

The results are the same.

Matrices can also be used to solve network problems.

The diagram illustrates the connecting flights that exist between the given cities.

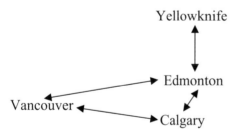

To create a matrix representing this network, we let the rows represent which city you are flying from and the columns to represent where you are flying to. If a connection exists between the two cities, we use a one for that element, if not, we use a zero.

$$A = \text{From} \begin{array}{c} \\ V \\ C \\ E \\ Y \end{array} \begin{array}{cccc} V & C & E & Y \\ \begin{bmatrix} 0 & 1 & 1 & 0 \\ 1 & 0 & 1 & 0 \\ 1 & 1 & 0 & 1 \\ 0 & 0 & 1 & 0 \end{bmatrix} \end{array}$$

To determine the number of connections between two cities that have exactly one stopover, we simply square the matrix.

$$A^2 = \begin{array}{c} \\ V \\ C \\ E \\ Y \end{array} \begin{array}{cccc} V & C & E & Y \\ \begin{bmatrix} 2 & 1 & 1 & 1 \\ 1 & 2 & 1 & 1 \\ 1 & 1 & 3 & 0 \\ 1 & 1 & 0 & 1 \end{bmatrix} \end{array}$$

Element a_{24} tells us that there is one way we can travel from Calgary to Yellowknife with one stopover. Element a_{34} tells us that there are no trips between Edmonton to Yellowknife that include one stopover.

To determine the number of possible trips with n stopovers, we raise the matrix to $n - 1$.

If the question asks how many routes between Vancouver and Edmonton have at most 2 stopovers, we would simply add the matrices representing no stopovers, one stopover, and 2 stopovers.

$$A + A^2 + A^3 = \begin{bmatrix} 4 & 5 & 6 & 2 \\ 5 & 4 & 6 & 2 \\ 6 & 6 & 5 & 4 \\ 2 & 2 & 4 & 1 \end{bmatrix}$$

From here we read off the appropriate element. There are 6 routes from Vancouver to Edmonton that have at least 2 stopovers.

Matrices can also be used to answer transition problems.

Transition problems deal with how a population changes. We start by identifying the original state of the population in a matrix called the probability matrix, P_0. The subscript zero identifies to us that this is the original scenario. We then multiply this by a transition matrix. The transition matrix identifies what percentage of the population is moving from one position to the other over a given period of time.

Because we are talking about the whole population, the sum of the values in the rows of a transition matrix must add to one.

$P_0 \times T =$ the distribution of the population after one period of time

$P_0 \times T^2 =$ the distribution of the population after two periods of time

$P_0 \times T^n =$ the distribution of the population after n periods of time

Example: After introducing two new creamers at a coffee shop, it was observed that 60% of the customers liked the French Vanilla creamer in their coffee while 40% preferred the Hazelnut creamer. Research showed that every month 35% of the people who preferred the French Vanilla switched to Hazelnut and 45% of the people who preferred Hazelnut switched to French Vanilla.

• Write the initial probability matrix

• Write the transition matrix

• Determine what percentages of the population are drinking the creamers after 1 month

• Determine what percentages of the population are drinking the creamers after 2 months

• Determine the long-term trend in this population

Solution:
The initial probability matrix is

$$\begin{array}{cc} \text{FV} & \text{H} \end{array}$$
$$P_0 = \begin{bmatrix} 0.6 & 0.4 \end{bmatrix}$$

The transition matrix is

$$T = \text{From} \begin{array}{c} \\ \text{FV} \\ \text{H} \end{array} \begin{array}{cc} \text{FV} & \text{H} \end{array} \begin{bmatrix} 0.65 & 0.35 \\ 0.45 & 0.55 \end{bmatrix}$$

The rows must add to one

To determine the distribution after one month, we multiply the initial probability matrix by the transition matrix.

$$P_0 \times T = \begin{bmatrix} 0.6 & 0.4 \end{bmatrix} \times \begin{bmatrix} 0.65 & 0.35 \\ 0.45 & 0.55 \end{bmatrix}$$
$$= \begin{bmatrix} 0.57 & 0.43 \end{bmatrix}$$

After one month, 57% of the population will use French Vanilla and 43% will use Hazelnut.

To determine the distribution after one month, we repeat the process, but we multiply by the transition matrix squared.

$$P_0 \times T^2 = \begin{bmatrix} 0.6 & 0.4 \end{bmatrix} \times \begin{bmatrix} 0.65 & 0.35 \\ 0.45 & 0.55 \end{bmatrix}^2$$
$$= \begin{bmatrix} 0.564 & 0.436 \end{bmatrix}$$

After two months, 56.4% of the population will use French Vanilla and 43.6% will use Hazelnut.

To determine the long term distribution of the population, simply pick a sufficiently large exponent for T, such as 100.

$$P_0 \times T^{100} = \begin{bmatrix} 0.6 & 0.4 \end{bmatrix} \times \begin{bmatrix} 0.65 & 0.35 \\ 0.45 & 0.55 \end{bmatrix}^{100}$$
$$= \begin{bmatrix} 0.5625 & 0.4375 \end{bmatrix}$$

We see that over time, 56.25% of the population will use French Vanilla and 43.75% will use Hazelnut.

Related Questions: 15, 16, 17, NR4

Copyright Protected

*Use the following information to answer
the first question.*

A children's game consists of a maze through
which a marble travels downward, as shown
below.

Marble entrances

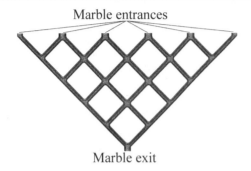

Marble exit

CHALLENGER QUESTION 55.

1. If the marble can enter through any of the
   6 entrances, then the total number of
   different paths that a marble can take
   through the maze is

   A. 21

   B. 30

   C. 32

   D. 120

   Source: January 2001

---

*Use the following information to answer
the next question.*

John attends Highview School, and he walks
there every day from his house. A map of the
streets in the area is shown below.

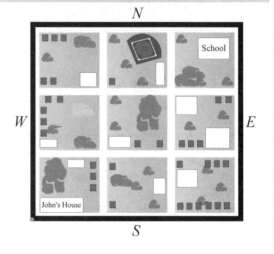

2. How many different routes can
   John take from his school to his
   house, if he can only walk from
   west to east, and from south to
   north along the streets shown?

   A. 10

   B. 15

   C. 20

   D. 40

Not for Reproduction

Use the following information to answer the next question.

Mary works at a restaurant called "La Grange." When she drives from her home to the restaurant, she only travels from west to east and north to south along the paths shown in the diagram below.

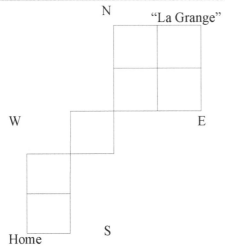

3. How many different routes are there for Mary get to work?

A. 24

B. 36

C. 45

D. 54

Use the following information to answer the next question.

The Hawaiian alphabet has only twelve letters:
Vowels   *a, e, i, o, u*
Consonants *h, k, l, m, n, p, w*

4. The number of 3-letter "words" that can be made using the Hawaiian alphabet if every "word" must have the pattern of consonant-vowel-consonant, and if letters can be repeated, is

A. 19   B. 175

C. 245   D. 1 728

Source: January 2001

CHALLENGER QUESTION   41.

5. Jaycen and Kate are the first and second students in a line of 7 students. The number of different orders in which the remainder of the students can line up behind them is

A. 120

B. 240

C. 3 125

D. 5 040

Source: June 2001

Numerical Response

1. The number of 3-digit numbers **less than 400** that can be formed if the last digit is either 4 or 5 is _____ .

Source: January 1999

6. How many two–letter combinations start with a consonant and end with a vowel, given that the letter *y* is considered a consonant?

A. 25

B. 105

C. 130

D. 625

Numerical Response

2. An airline company requires flight attendants to wear a pair of slacks, a shirt, a tie, and a blazer. The flight attendants have a choice of 3 different pairs of slacks, 5 different shirts, 4 different ties, and 2 different blazers. The maximum number of different outfits that a flight attendant could create using the items provided is _____ outfits.

Source: June 1999

Use the following information to answer the next question.

The manager of a sports store wants 5 different tents to be illustrated on one page of a sales flyer. The illustrations will be positioned one above the other.

Dome Tent

Scout Tent

Rain Tent

Hiking Tent

Spacious Tent

7. In the flyer, the Dome, Rain, and Spacious tents are blue, the Scout tent is beige, and the Hiking tent is yellow. The blue tents can appear in any order; however, the manager does not want to have one blue tent immediately after another blue tent. If this is the only restriction, then how many different positions are possible?

   A. 2

   B. 12

   C. 20

   D. 60

Source: January 1999

Use the following information to answer the next two questions.

Deanna wishes to buy flowers for a Valentine's Day promotion at her school. She needs carnations, roses, baby's breath, and greenery. She obtains the following quotes.

	Rose	Carnation	Baby's Breath	Greenery
Rosie's Flowers	$3.50	$1.50	$2.99	$1.75
The Flower Shop	$4.25	$1.25	$2.49	$1.99
Flowers Everywhere	$3.25	$1.30	$2.55	$2.50

She intends to choose only one shop to fill the entire order.

CHALLENGER QUESTION	54.5

8. Deanna wants to set up a 3 × 4 matrix to represent the price of flowers, and a second matrix to represent the required quantity of each flower. What dimensions must the second matrix have?

   A. 3 × 1

   B. 4 × 1

   C. 3 × 4

   D. 4 × 3

Source: June 2001

9. To determine which shop has the lowest cost for the entire order, Deanna should perform a

   A. matrix addition

   B. matrix subtraction

   C. matrix multiplication

   D. multiplication by a scalar

Source: June 2001

Use the following information to answer the next question.

A soccer league collected the following statistics over eight games.

	Win	Tie	Loss
Bulldog	4	3	1
Titans	7	1	0
Rovers	2	2	4

Each team earns 2 points for a win, 1 point for a tie, and 0 points for a loss.

10. Which of the following matrix operations could be used to determine the points earned by each team after eight games?

A. $\begin{bmatrix} 4 & 3 & 1 \\ 7 & 1 & 0 \\ 2 & 2 & 4 \end{bmatrix} \times \begin{bmatrix} 2 \\ 1 \\ 0 \end{bmatrix}$

B. $\begin{bmatrix} 2 \\ 1 \\ 0 \end{bmatrix} \times \begin{bmatrix} 4 & 3 & 1 \\ 7 & 1 & 0 \\ 2 & 2 & 4 \end{bmatrix}$

C. $\begin{bmatrix} 4 & 3 & 1 \\ 7 & 1 & 0 \\ 2 & 2 & 4 \end{bmatrix} \times \begin{bmatrix} 2 & 1 & 0 \end{bmatrix}$

D. $\begin{bmatrix} 2 & 1 & 0 \end{bmatrix} \times \begin{bmatrix} 4 & 3 & 1 \\ 7 & 1 & 0 \\ 2 & 2 & 4 \end{bmatrix}$

Source: June 2001

Use the following equation to answer the next question.

$$\begin{bmatrix} 1 & 5 & 2 \\ -1 & 0 & 1 \\ 3 & 2 & 4 \end{bmatrix} + \begin{bmatrix} 6 & 1 & 3 \\ x & 1 & 2 \\ 4 & 1 & 3 \end{bmatrix} = \begin{bmatrix} 7 & 6 & 5 \\ -2 & 1 & 3 \\ 7 & 3 & 7 \end{bmatrix}$$

11. The value of x is

A. −2   B. −1

C. 1   D. 2

Use the following equation to answer the next question.

$$\begin{bmatrix} 1 & 2 & 4 \\ 2 & 6 & 0 \end{bmatrix} \times \begin{bmatrix} 1 \\ -1 \\ 7 \end{bmatrix} = ?$$

12. The product of the above matrices is

A. $\begin{bmatrix} -4 \\ 27 \end{bmatrix}$

B. $\begin{bmatrix} -4 & 27 \end{bmatrix}$

C. $\begin{bmatrix} 27 \\ -4 \end{bmatrix}$

D. $\begin{bmatrix} 27 & -4 \end{bmatrix}$

Use the following equation to answer the next question.

$$\begin{bmatrix} a & b \\ c & d \end{bmatrix} - 2\begin{bmatrix} 4 & 5 \\ 6 & 7 \end{bmatrix} = \begin{bmatrix} -4 & -3 \\ 0 & -11 \end{bmatrix}$$

13. The value of c is
A. −12
B. −6
C. 6
D. 12

Use the following equation to answer the next question

$$\begin{bmatrix} 2 & 4 & 5 \\ 8 & 3 & 2 \end{bmatrix} + 4\begin{bmatrix} 7 & 3 & 5 \\ 2 & x & 1 \end{bmatrix} = \begin{bmatrix} 30 & 16 & 25 \\ 16 & 11 & 6 \end{bmatrix}$$

14. Solve for x in the matrix operation.
A. −8
B. 2
C. 8
D. 7

Copyright Protected

Use the following information to answer the next question.

$$\begin{bmatrix} 2 & 0 & 3 \\ 5 & 0 & -2 \\ 3 & -1 & -2 \\ 1 & 0 & 4 \end{bmatrix} \times \begin{bmatrix} 1 \\ -5 \\ 2 \end{bmatrix} = B$$

Numerical Response

3. In matrix B above, the entries that result from the matrix multiplication, in order from top to bottom, are _____, _____, _____, and _____.

Source: January 2001

Use the following information to answer the next question.

Three major countries produce cars to be purchased in Canada: Canada, Japan, and Germany. A poll of car owners in Canada revealed that of people who presently own a Canadian-produced car, 51% would purchase another Canadian-produced car the next time they purchase a car. Of people who presently own a Japanese-produced car, 30% would purchase a Canadian-produced car the next time they purchase a car. The following matrix shows detailed results of the poll.

	CA	JA	GR	Other
CA	0.51	0.32	0.12	0.05
JA	0.30	0.50	0.12	0.08
GR	0.35	0.15	0.40	0.10
Other	0.20	0.25	0.15	0.40

15. The entry in row 3 and column 2 indicates that

A. 15% of people who presently own a Japanese-produced car would purchase a German-produced car the next time they purchase a car

B. 12% of people who presently own a German-produced car would purchase a Japanese-produced car the next time they purchase a car

C. 15% of people who presently own a German-produced car would purchase a Japanese-produced car the next time they purchase a car

D. 12% of people who presently own a Japanese-produced car would purchase a German-produced car the next time they purchase a car

Source: January 2001

Use the following information to answer the next question.

A manufacturing company stores items in a number of warehouses, as modeled in the matrix below.

Warehouse	I	II	III	IV	V
A	40	23	9	24	13
B	20	5	12	10	14
C	10	28	38	61	12
D	15	41	62	14	10

16. The sum of the values in column II represents the total number of

A. items in warehouse B

B. items in all warehouses

C. item II in warehouse B

D. item II in all warehouses

Source: January 2001

Not for Reproduction

Use the following information to answer the next question.

As Norma walks into her office tower, she is facing north. She walks due east from the front door to the elevator. She takes the elevator up 10 floors, then walks due north to her office.

17. Which of the following 3-D diagrams could be used to model Norma's path?

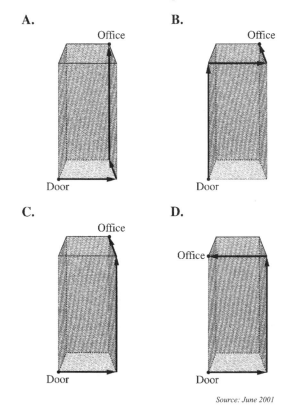

A. Office / Door

B. Office / Door

C. Office / Door

D. Office / Door

Source: June 2001

Use the following information to answer the next question.

A student is drawing a diagram on an Etch-A-Sketch, as shown below. The stylus is at point *A*, but the student wants to add more detail at point *B*. To prevent ruining his diagram, he can only move the stylus along previously drawn lines.

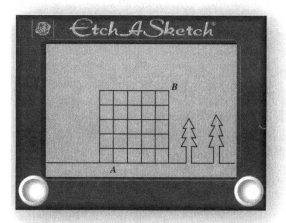

CHALLENGER QUESTION   22.6

Numerical Response

4. If the student moves the stylus only up or to the right from point *A* to point *B,* then the number of paths he may follow is

_____ .

Source: June 2001

Written Response

Use the following information to answer the next question.

Tim took a summer job with a company in Edmonton. The company also has offices in Regina and Winnipeg. The company ships supplies and product by airplane from and to its three offices. It can ship directly between Edmonton and Regina, and Regina and Winnipeg, but has no direct freight transport between Edmonton and Winnipeg. Tim decides to set up a network matrix for freight transport between the cities. He uses "1" to denote direct freight transport between two cities and "0" to denote no direct freight transport between two cities.

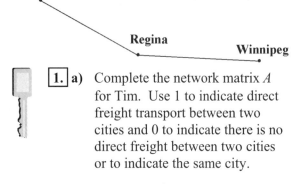

1. a) Complete the network matrix A for Tim. Use 1 to indicate direct freight transport between two cities and 0 to indicate there is no direct freight between two cities or to indicate the same city.

$$\begin{array}{c} \text{Matrix } A \\ \begin{array}{ccc} R & E & W \end{array} \\ \begin{array}{c} R \\ E \\ W \end{array} \left[\phantom{\begin{array}{ccc} 0 & 0 & 0 \\ 0 & 0 & 0 \\ 0 & 0 & 0 \end{array}} \right] \end{array}$$

b) Matrix A^2 can represent the network matrix for one-way routes and round trip routes that have exactly one stop-over. A stop-over occurs when the plane stops in a city on its way to its final destination. Evaluate matrix A^2.

26

UNIT TEST 1—MATRICES AND PATHWAYS

1. Let $A = \begin{bmatrix} 2 & -4 \\ 5 & 1 \end{bmatrix}$, $B = \begin{bmatrix} 0 & 2 \\ -3 & 8 \end{bmatrix}$ and

   $C = \begin{bmatrix} 6 & 1 \\ 1 & -3 \end{bmatrix}_{x \to \infty}^{\lim}$, then $(A + B) - C$ is

   equivalent to

   A. $\begin{bmatrix} -4 & -3 \\ 1 & 6 \end{bmatrix}$ B. $\begin{bmatrix} -4 & -3 \\ 1 & 12 \end{bmatrix}$

   C. $\begin{bmatrix} 8 & -5 \\ 9 & 10 \end{bmatrix}$ D. $\begin{bmatrix} 4 & 7 \\ -7 & 4 \end{bmatrix}$

Numerical Response

1. Assuming that $A = \begin{bmatrix} 7 & -11 & 5 \\ 8 & 4 & -3 \\ 1 & 1 & 9 \end{bmatrix}$ and

$k = 2$ then a new matrix, B, is defined by scalar multiplication as $B = kA$. In the new matrix, B, the element b_{23} is _____.

2. If $A = \begin{bmatrix} 2 & 1 \\ 0 & -1 \\ 3 & 4 \end{bmatrix}$, $B = \begin{bmatrix} 3 & 9 & 1 \\ 5 & -5 & 2 \end{bmatrix}$,

   $C = \begin{bmatrix} 7 & 2 \\ 4 & 4 \end{bmatrix}$ and $D = \begin{bmatrix} -3 \\ 10 \\ 9 \end{bmatrix}$ then which of

   the following represents pairs that can be multiplied together?

   A. AB

   B. BC

   C. CA

   D. AD

3. When we define matrix C as $C = AB$, where

   $A = \begin{bmatrix} a & b \\ c & d \end{bmatrix}$ and $B = \begin{bmatrix} e & f & g \\ h & i & j \end{bmatrix}$, then the

   element c_{12} is equivalent to

   A. $ce + dh$

   B. $cf + di$

   C. $af + bi$

   D. $ae + bh$

Use the following information to answer the next three questions.

A certain manufacturer produces wrenches, screwdrivers and hammers. The manufacturer sells these for $5, $4 and $8 respectively. A hardware store purchases 550 wrenches, 700 screwdrivers and 430 hammers.

4. Which of the following represents the correct matrix operation for determining the total revenue the manufacturer collected?

   A. $\begin{bmatrix} 550 \\ 700 \\ 430 \end{bmatrix} \begin{bmatrix} 5 \\ 4 \\ 8 \end{bmatrix}$

   B. $\begin{bmatrix} 5 & 4 & 8 \end{bmatrix} \begin{bmatrix} 550 & 700 & 430 \end{bmatrix}$

   C. $\begin{bmatrix} 550 \\ 700 \\ 430 \end{bmatrix} \begin{bmatrix} 5 & 4 & 8 \end{bmatrix}$

   D. $\begin{bmatrix} 5 & 4 & 8 \end{bmatrix} \begin{bmatrix} 550 \\ 700 \\ 430 \end{bmatrix}$

5. If the manufacturer wants to increase the price of each product by 10%, which of the following operations will produce the new prices?

A. $0.1 \begin{bmatrix} 5 \\ 4 \\ 8 \end{bmatrix}$

B. $1.1 \begin{bmatrix} 5 \\ 4 \\ 8 \end{bmatrix}$

C. $0.9 \begin{bmatrix} 5 \\ 4 \\ 8 \end{bmatrix}$

D. $1.9 \begin{bmatrix} 5 \\ 4 \\ 8 \end{bmatrix}$

Use the following information to answer the next two questions.

Market research has shown that 65% of the customers at a local donut shop like glazed and 35% like cream filled. After a month it has been found that 25% of the glazed donut eaters switched to cream filled and 40% of the cream filled eaters switch to the glazed. This pattern continues every month.

Numerical Response

2. The percentage of customers, to the nearest tenth of a percent, that are eating glazed and cream filled donuts after one month are _____ and _____ respectively.

6. If the shop maintains a clientele of about 2 000 customers, how many are eating cream filled donuts after three months?

A. 766   **B.** 1 234

C. 1 239   **D.** 761

Use the following information to answer the next question.

Peter lives at point *A* in the following diagram, and he needs to deliver a package to Shauna at point *B*.

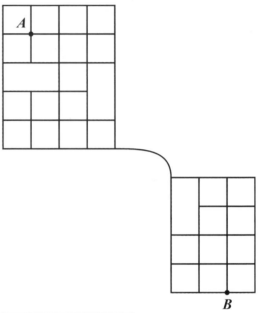

Numerical Response

3. The number of different pathways that Peter can choose from is _____.
(Remember that Peter must always move towards Shauna.)

Use the following information to answer the next question.

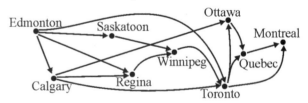

7. How many different routes are possible to travel from Edmonton, Alberta to Montreal, Quebec given the existing connections illustrated in the following diagram?

A. 16   **B.** 11

C. 8   **D.** 14

Copyright Protected

8. How many different ways can the letters in the word "TRIANGLE" be ordered?

A. 36

B. 40 320

C. 8

D. 5 040

Use the following information to answer the next question.

A physical trainer has given Matt a list of activities to help him get fit, and he has told Matt that he needs to pick one activity from each category. There were 4 different warm up stretches, 3 different cardio exercises, 3 strength training exercises and 5 cool down stretches.

9. How many different programs can Matt put together if he chooses one from each category?

A. 15

B. 540

C. 27

D. 180

Numerical Response

4. A license plate consists of 3 letters, the first of which cannot be O, and then 3 numbers, the first of which cannot be 0. There are _____ possible plates.

Written Response

Use the following information to answer the next question.

If three retail stores purchase products from the manufacturer according to the following chart:

	Wrenches	Screwdrivers	Hammers
Store A	350	570	1 100
Store B	1 200	200	610
Store C	800	975	420

1. Use matrix multiplication to help the manufacturer determine how much revenue is made from each store.

Use the following information to answer the next two questions.

The following illustrates a network of friends. The connections indicate that the two people know each other.

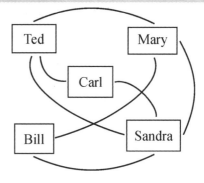

2. Identify the network matrix that corresponds with the given information.

3. How many connections are there in this network that would be described as wither friends or friends of a friend? (i.e. there is either a direct connection or there is an intermediate person between the two)

Copyright Protected

STATISTICS AND PROBABILITY

Table of Correlations		
Topic	**Outcomes**	**Questions**
Use normal and binomial probability distributions to solve problems involving uncertainty.	*It is expected that students will:*	
	2.1 Find the population standard deviation of a data set, using technology.	1, 2, 3, NR1
	2.2 Use z-scores to solve problems related to the normal distribution.	4, 5, 6, 7, NR2, 8, 9, 10
	2.3 Use the normal approximation to the binomial distribution to solve problems involving confidence intervals for large-sample binomial experiments.	11
Model the probability of a compound event, and solve problems based on the combining of simpler probabilities.	2.4 Construct a sample space for two or three events.	2, 13
	2.5 Classify events as independent or dependent.	14, 15, 16, 17
	2.6 Use expressions for P(A and B) to solve problems involving independent and dependent events.	18, 19, 20
	2.7 Solve problems using the probabilities of mutually exclusive and complementary events.	NR3, 21, 22, NR4, 23, NR5, 24

Not for Reproduction

STATISTICS AND PROBABILITY

Students will use normal and binomial probability distributions to solve problems involving uncertainty.

2.1   Find the population standard deviation of a data set, using technology.

STANDARD DEVIATION

A *population* is any complete collection of items that is being studied, and a *sample* is a portion of the population from which we can make inferences regarding the entire population.

When analyzing a population, we may use *measures of central tendency* and *measures of dispersion*.

The measures of central tendency include the *mean*, the *median,* and the *mode*.

For a set with an odd number of data values, the *median* is the middle value when all the data values are arranged in order. For a set with an even number of data values, the median is the mean of the middle two values when they are arranged in order. The *mode* for a set of data values is the value or values that occur with the greatest frequency.

The *mean* of a set of data values is equivalent to the sum of the values divided by the total number of values. We use two symbols to represent the mean. We use $\overline{x}$ when we are finding the mean of a sample, and we use μ to represent the mean of an entire population.

The measures of dispersion include the *range* and the *standard deviation*.

The *range* is the difference between the largest and smallest data values.

The *standard deviation* is essentially the average distance that all the data values are away from the mean. We use the symbol σ to represent the standard deviation of a population, and *s* to represent the standard deviation of a sample.

For this course, the discussions are restricted to entire populations.

Most scientific and graphic display calculators possess features that allow the user to input data and from it, calculate the measures of central tendency and measures of dispersion.

Data can be given to you as a list or in the form of a frequency table. Be aware of this when you are using the calculator.

A frequency table is a table that aligns specific data values with the number of times it appears in the population.

Example

A class was surveyed and asked what their shoe sizes were. The results were tabulated as follows:

Shoe sizes in class	Number of students
6	3
7	5
8	8
9	4
10	2

The information in this table is shorthand for the following list of shoe sizes:

6, 6, 6, 7, 7, 7, 7, 7, 8, 8, 8, 8, 8, 8, 8, 8, 9, 9, 9, 9, 10, 10

Using technology, we determine that $\mu = 7.9$ and $\sigma = 1.1$, rounded to the nearest tenth.

A histogram is a graph that can compare groups of values using rectangles whose size represents the number of values for each group. The width of the rectangles along the *x*-axis is constant so that the height of the rectangle communicates the number of values in that group.

This example can be represented as a histogram

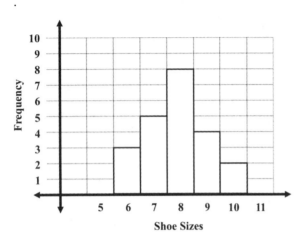

Shoe Sizes

Notice that the majority of the people have shoe sizes at the mean value of the population, and then the numbers trail off to the sides of the mean.

To understand how the standard deviation affects the graph, we can compare two histograms.

Graph A

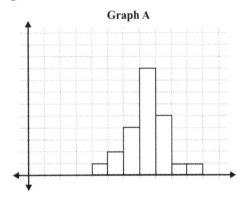

Graph B

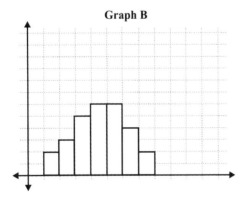

The mean for graph A is larger than the mean for graph B. We can see this because the centre of the data is further along the x-axis in graph A than in graph B.

The standard deviation for graph A is smaller than that of graph B. This is because in graph A the majority of the data is gathered quite close to the mean, and there are few data values that are a distance from the mean. In graph B, there are fewer data values and the mean and more data values can be found further away from the mean. To summarize, there is more spread in the data in graph B than there is in graph A. If these histograms represented the spread of marks on an exam, a small standard deviation indicates that the class had generally the same level of understanding of the material whereas a large standard deviation indicates a large discrepancy between the students who understand the material and those who do not.

If we to increase all of the values in the population by a specified amount, the mean would also increase by the specified amount, but the standard deviation would remain unchanged. This is because the position that each data value is in, with comparison to the mean, has not changes, i.e., the shape of the histogram has not changed.

Related Questions: 1, 2, 3, NR1

2.2   Use z-scores to solve problems related to the normal distribution.

THE NORMAL DISTRIBUTION

A probability distribution is a list of all the possible outcomes of an experiment with their associated probabilities. One way that this can be done is by using a histogram.

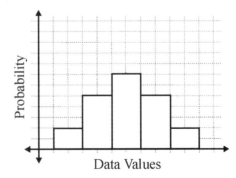

Data Values

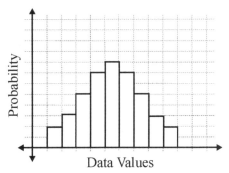

As the total number of data values increases, the bars in the histogram get smaller and the shape of the distribution becomes more defined. There are many kinds of probability distributions, each with a different shape, but the most common one is the Normal Distribution, which has the following shape:

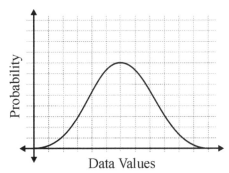

This is the **Normal Distribution Curve** or the **Bell-Shaped Curve**.

What makes the Normal Distribution unique is that the mean, median, and mode of a population that is normally distributed are all the same value. The total area under the curve is one, with 50% of the data less than the mean and 50% of the data above the mean. The area under the Normal Distribution, between any two data values, represents the probability that a data value picked at random is between the two given values.

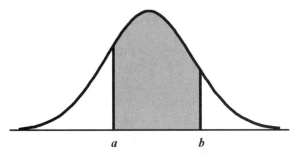

$P(a \le x \le b) =$ area under the curve between a and b.

Another important feature of the normal distribution is that no matter what population we are analyzing, the standard deviation breaks up the distribution in exactly the same way.

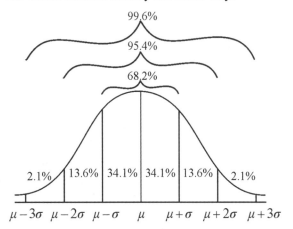

Using the standard deviation to divide up the distribution, as shown above, we can see that 68.2% of the population is within one standard deviation of the mean, 95.4% of the population is within 2 standard deviations of the mean, and 99.6% of the population is within 3 standard deviations of the mean.

Normal Distributions can have an endless combination of means and standard deviations, which makes it difficult to compare two populations. Because the relationship between the probabilities under the curve and the standard deviation remains constant for any normal distribution, it makes more sense to convert data values into the number of standard deviations it is away from the mean.

This is called the data value's *z-score*, and it is calculated as follows:

$$z = \frac{x - \mu}{\sigma}, \text{ where } x \text{ is the specific data value}$$

Using the above formula, we see that the *z*-score for the mean is 0. It also forces the standard deviation to be 1. This creates what is called the *Standard Normal Distribution*.

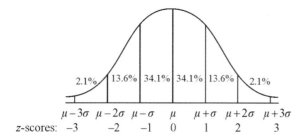

2.1% | 13.6% | 34.1% | 34.1% | 13.6% | 2.1%

$\mu-3\sigma$ $\mu-2\sigma$ $\mu-\sigma$ μ $\mu+\sigma$ $\mu+2\sigma$ $\mu+3\sigma$

z-scores: −3   −2   −1   0   1   2   3

Notice that the probability distribution is the same, but that now we are using *z*-scores along the *x*-axis instead of data values. For a standard normal curve, the area under the curve is still one and the mean still cuts the curve exactly in half, but now we talk about how many standard deviations we are away from the mean. Negative values indicate that a value is below the mean and positive values indicate that a value is above the mean.

We can use *z*-scores to compare two populations. For example, Mike got 76% on a math exam on which his class averaged 70% with a standard deviation of 5%. His friend Bill got 80% on a similar exam, where his class averaged 74% with a standard deviation of 8%. Who did better?

At first glance, Bill did better, because his mark is higher. But, when we ask who did better, we are really asking about how these two ranked in the general group. As these two groups have different means and standard deviations, we need to standardize and find their respective *z*-scores.

Mike: $z = \dfrac{76-70}{5}$ **Bill:** $z = \dfrac{80-74}{8}$

$= 1.2$ $= 0.75$

Because Mike's *z*-score is higher, he did better than Bill in terms of the general group.

Given the *z*-score formula, we must be able to manipulate the equation.

Example

If the mean of a data set is 20 and the *z*-score for a data value of 23 is 1.75, what is the standard deviation?

Solution

$$z = \frac{x-\mu}{\sigma}$$

$$1.75 = \frac{23-20}{\sigma}$$

$$1.75\sigma = 3$$

$$\sigma = \frac{3}{1.75}$$

$$= 1.71$$

Example

If the standard deviation of a set of data values is 5 and the *z*-score for a data value of 33 is −2.46, what is the mean?

Solution

$$z = \frac{x-\mu}{\sigma}$$

$$-2.46 = \frac{33-\mu}{5}$$

$$(-2.46)(5) = 33-\mu$$

$$-12.3-33 = -\mu$$

$$-45.3 = -\mu$$

$$45.3 = \mu$$

Example

If the mean of a set of data is 43 with a standard deviation of 4, then what data value has a *z*-score of 1.94?

Solution

$$z = \frac{x-\mu}{\sigma}$$

$$1.94 = \frac{x-43}{4}$$

$$(1.94)(4) = x-43$$

$$7.76 = x-43$$

$$50.76 = x$$

We can also use *z*-scores to answer questions about probabilities. This typically requires a familiarity with the statistical features on your calculator, or a familiarity with the *z*-score charts. You will need to make yourself comfortable with your calculator. Here, we will discuss the chart.

Copyright Protected

Not for Reproduction

There may be some discrepancies between answers arrived at using a calculator and the chart because the chart is limited to *z*-scores rounded to the nearest hundredth.

As a result, it is often necessary to simply pick the closest value in the chart to the one calculated.

Example

A factory produces 8 000 containers of ice cream a day. The mean mass of a container of ice cream is 2 kg with a standard deviation of 0.2 kg.

Find the *z*-score of a container that has a mass of 1.7 kg.

Solution

$$z = \frac{1.7 - 2}{0.2}$$
$$= -1.5$$

Example

What is the probability that a container of ice cream chosen at random will have a mass less than 1.7 kg?

Solution

To answer this question, it is helpful to sketch the normal curve.

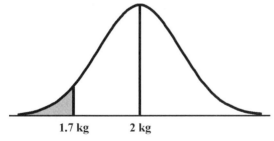

1.7 kg   2 kg

Recall that the *z*-score of 1.7 kg is –1.5. To find the area to the left of this *z*-score, we use the notation *A*(–1.50).

To use the chart, look up –1.5 in the left column and 0.00 in the top row. The value we find in the intersection of this row and column is the area under the curve to the left of the given *z*-score.

In this case, *A*(–1.50) = 0.066 8, meaning that 6.68% of the cases produced will have masses less than 1.7 kg.

Example

What is the probability that a container will have a mass greater than 2.5 kg?

Solution

First look at the sketch.

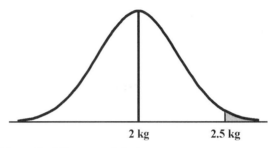

2 kg   2.5 kg

Now, find the associated *z*-score:

$$z = \frac{2.5 - 2}{0.2}$$
$$= 2.5$$

The area under the curve is 1. Since *A*(2.5) produces the area to the left of 2.5, we use $1 - A(2.5)$ to find the area to the right.

$$A(2.5) = 0.993\ 8$$
$$1 - A(2.5) = 1 - 0.993\ 8$$
$$= 0.006\ 2$$

0.62% of the containers will have a mass greater than 2.5 kg.

Example

How many containers can be expected to have a mass between 1.8 kg and 2.3 kg? Again, refer to the sketch.

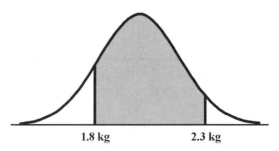

1.8 kg   2.3 kg

Solution

To find the area in between the two given value, we must again find their *z*-scores.

$$z = \frac{2.3 - 2}{0.2} \qquad z = \frac{1.8 - 2}{0.2}$$
$$= 1.5 \qquad\qquad = -1$$

Now, using the chart, we find the total area to the left of 1.5 and then we subtract from it the total area to the left of −1.

$$A(1.5) - A(-1)$$
$$= 0.933\,2 - 0.158\,7$$
$$= 0.774\,5$$

Thus, 77.45% of the data is between 1.8 kg and 2.3 kg.

To find the number of containers, we multiply by the total produced.

$$N = 8\,000(0.774\,5)$$
$$N = 6\,196$$

Therefore, 6 196 containers have a mass between 1.8 kg and 2.3 kg.

Example

What is the smallest mass a container can have so that its mass is in the top 25% of production?

Solution

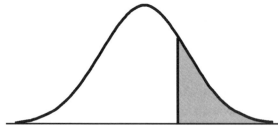

In this case, we are given a probability or area under the curve and we need to find the appropriate data value. The charts only give areas to the left of a data value but we are given the area to the right. To find the necessary area, subtract what we are given from one.

$$A(z) = 1 - 0.25$$
$$A(z) = 0.75$$

Now, to read the chart, we simply find 0.75 as an area and then look to the left most column and the upper most row to find the *z*-score.

From the chart, the closest *z*-score is *z* = 0.67.

At this point, we use the *z*-score to find the missing data value, rounded to the nearest tenth.

$$z = \frac{x - \mu}{\sigma}$$
$$0.67 = \frac{x - 2}{0.2}$$
$$(0.67)(0.2) = x - 2$$
$$(0.67)(0.2) + 2 = x$$
$$2.1 = x$$

Therefore, to be in the top 25%, the ice cream container has to have a mass of at least 2.1 kg.

Related Questions: 4, 5, 6, 7, NR2, 8, 9, 10

2.3   *Use the normal approximation to the binomial distribution to solve problems involving confidence intervals for large-sample binomial experiments.*

THE BINOMIAL DISTRIBUTION

A binomial experiment is one in which the outcomes can either be classified as a success or a failure and the probabilities of successes and failures are known. There are a fixed number of trials in the experiment all of which are independent. In this particular probability distribution, we are finding the probability of a certain number of successful trials out of the total number of trials.

Example

What is the probability of rolling exactly 3 twos when rolling 5 dice?

Solution

This is a binomial experiment because we either observe a 2 on a die (success) or we don't (failure). There is a fixed number of trials (the 5 dice) and the probabilities of a success and failure are known.

Copyright Protected

Not for Reproduction

$P(2) = \dfrac{1}{6}$ and $P(\text{not a } 2) = \dfrac{5}{6}$

In addition, these trials are independent because the outcome of one die does not affect the outcome of another die.

Finally, this is a binomial experiment because we are interested in the probability of a certain number of successful trials out of the total number of trials, that is,

$P\left(\dfrac{3 \text{ successful rolls}}{5 \text{ rolls}}\right)$

The binomial distribution has a different structure than the normal distribution, but if the sample space is large enough, we can use the normal distribution as an approximation. The sample space is considered large enough when $np > 5$ and if $n(1 - p) > 5$, where n is the total number of trials in the experiment, p is the probability of success, and $1 - p$ is the probability of failure.

Once we know if the normal approximation is appropriate, we need to find the mean and standard deviation for the experiment. This is done with the following formulas:

$\mu = np$ and $\sigma = \sqrt{np(1 - p)}$

Example

Suppose an exam consists of 30 multiple-choice questions, each of which has 4 possible answers. Is this binomial experiment large enough to use a normal approximation and if so, what are the mean and standard deviation?

Solution

First, identify the variables:

$n = 30,\ p = \dfrac{1}{4},\ 1 - p = \dfrac{3}{4}$

Thus, $np = 30\left(\dfrac{1}{4}\right) = 7.5$

$n(1 - p) = 30\left(\dfrac{3}{4}\right) = 22.5$

We see that the normal approximation is appropriate.

Therefore we can calculate the mean and standard deviation as follows:

$\mu = np,$ and $\sigma = \sqrt{np(1 - p)}$

$= 30\left(\dfrac{1}{4}\right)$ $= \sqrt{30\left(\dfrac{1}{4}\right)\left(\dfrac{3}{4}\right)}$

$= 7.5$ $= 2.4$

A *confidence interval* is a range of data values chosen such that we have a specified certainty that any data value chosen at random will be in that range. For this course, we look specifically at the symmetric 95% confidence interval. It is illustrated as follows:

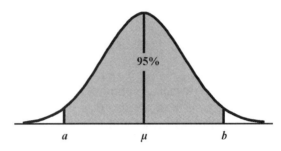

The 95% confidence interval is the range of data values from a to b. It is symmetric because it is equally distributed around the mean. This means that the remaining 5% of the data is equally distributed in the area to the left of a and to the right of b. This means that 2.5% of the data is to the left of a, and knowing this we can look this probability up in our z-score chart to determine that the z-score of a must be -1.96. Since the shape is symmetric, we can conclude that b has a z-score of 1.96. Knowing this, and applying some algebra, we can determine how to find a symmetric 95% confidence interval for any set of data.

Assuming we know the mean and standard deviation, we only need to find the data value, x.

$\pm 1.96 = \dfrac{x - \mu}{\sigma}$

$\pm 1.96\sigma = x - \mu$

$\mu \pm 1.96\sigma = x$

Copyright Protected

Therefore, the 95% confidence interval for a set of data will be the range of values between $\mu - 1.96\sigma$ and $\mu + 1.96\sigma$.

Example

Using the information from the previous example, construct a 95% confidence interval indicating how many questions, when guessed at, are expected to be correct.

Solution

The mean was $\mu = 7.5$ and the standard deviation was $\sigma = 2.4$. Therefore, we can be 95% confident that, by guessing, we will get between,

$\mu - 1.96\sigma$ and $\mu + 1.96\sigma$

$7.5 - 1.96(2.4)$ $\quad$ $7.5 + 1.96(2.4)$

2.796 $\quad\quad\quad\quad$ 12.204

Now, because we cannot complete fractional questions and we want to guarantee at least 95% of the data is included, we will round the bottom value down and the top value up. Our 95% confidence interval is from 2 questions correct to 13 questions correct.

Related Question: 11

Students will model the probability of a compound event, and solve problems based on the combining of simpler probabilities.

2.4   Construct a sample space for two or three events.

SAMPLE SPACES

There are two types of probability: Experimental Probability and Theoretical Probability.

$$\text{Experimental Probablity} = \frac{\text{successful trials}}{\text{total number of trials}}$$

$$\text{Theoretical Probability} = \frac{\text{favourable outcomes}}{\text{total possible outcomes}}$$

In the case of experimental probability, we perform an experiment a certain number of times and we keep track of the number of successful results. The probability is then calculated as indicated above.

The probabilities obtained may vary every time we try to calculate it in this manner, but we assume that as the number of experiments increase, the probabilities should approach the theoretical probability. A sample space is a listing of all possible outcomes to an experiment.

It may be in the form of a list, a chart, a tree diagram, or a lattice diagram.

Example

Create a sample space to illustrate all the results of rolling two dice.

As a chart:

	1	2	3	4	5	6
1	(1,1)	(1,2)	(1,3)	(1,4)	(1,5)	(1,6)
2	(2,1)	(2,2)	(2,3)	(2,4)	(2,5)	(2,6)
3	(3,1)	(3,2)	(3,3)	(3,4)	(3,5)	(3,6)
4	(4,1)	(4,2)	(4,3)	(4,4)	(4,5)	(4,6)
5	(5,1)	(5,2)	(5,3)	(5,4)	(5,5)	(5,6)
6	(6,1)	(6,2)	(6,3)	(6,4)	(6,5)	(6,6)

or, as a lattice diagram:

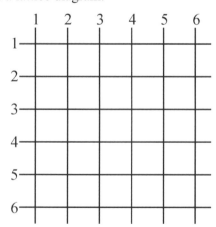

Solution

Notice that the sample space contains 36 events. To answer questions of probability, we need only identify and count the number of favourable events.

Example

What is the probability that the sum of two standard dice is greater than 8?

To answer this, we simply count the number of events in the sample space such that their sum is greater than 8.

$$P(\text{sum} > 8) = \frac{10}{36} = \frac{5}{18}$$

Example

Create a sample space to illustrate the results when spinning a spinner that can point at 4 numbers combined with flipping a coin.

Solution

As a tree diagram:

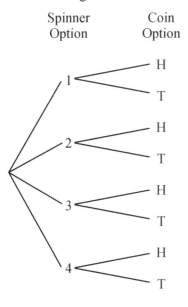

Spinner Option   Coin Option

The size of the sample space is equal to the number of branches in the final step. In the above example, the sample space has 8 events.

What is the probability of rolling a heads and spinning an even number?

We need only count up the applicable events in the sample space: $P(H \text{ and even}) = \frac{2}{8} = \frac{1}{4}$

If we are careful, we may also just list off the sample space. Create the sample space for flipping a coin 3 times.

{HHH, HHT, HTH, HTT, THH, THT, TTH, TTT}

What is the probability of flipping exactly 2 tails out of 3 flips?

Once again, we need only count up the results over the total outcomes: $P(\text{exactly } 2\, T) = \frac{3}{8}$

Related Questions: 12, 13

2.5 Classify events as independent or dependent.

INDEPENDENT OR DEPENDENT EVENTS

When the events of an experiment are independent, each trial has no impact on the sample space of subsequent trials.

For example, when rolling a die and flipping a coin, the result of the die rolling has no impact on the result of flipping the coin. These events are independent.

When the events of an experiment are dependent, each trial changes the sample space for subsequent trials.

For example, when the letters of the word MATH are on tiles in a bag and we pick out letters one at a time without replacing them in the bag, then each choice has an impact on the following choices. There are 4 choices for the first letter, but once that letter is chosen, it is no longer available. This reduces the sample space for the next letter.

In many scenarios, when choices are being made from a specific collection of items, the choices are independent when the item chosen is afterwards replaced.

The choices are dependent when the items are not replaced before the next choice.

Copyright Protected

For example, if we are drawing cards from a deck and subsequently replacing them, then the size of the sample space remains 52 for every choice. This makes the events independent. If the cards are not replaced after choosing, then the size of the sample space diminishes by one after every choice. This makes the events dependent.

Related Questions: 14, 15, 16, 17

2.6   Use expressions for P(A and B) to solve problems involving independent and dependent events.

P(A AND B)

If the events A and B are independent then the probability that A and B will occur is equivalent to the product of their respective probabilities.

$$P(A \text{ and } B) = P(A) \times P(B)$$

Example

What is the probability that when a coin is flipped and a die is rolled that the result is a head and an even number?

Solution

$$P(H \text{ and } even) = P(H) \times P(even)$$

$$P(H \text{ and } even) = \frac{1}{2} \times \frac{3}{6}$$

$$P(H \text{ and } even) = \frac{3}{12} = \frac{1}{4}$$

You must also be prepared to find the probability of a given event knowing the probability of another event and their combined probability.

Example

There is a bag with several marbles inside and the marbles are drawn with replacement.

The probability of drawing a red marble is $\frac{3}{10}$, and the probability of drawing a red and then a blue is $\frac{3}{25}$. What is the probability of drawing a blue marble?

Solution

$$P(R \text{ and } B) = P(R) \times P(B)$$

$$\frac{3}{25} = \frac{3}{5}P(B)$$

$$\frac{3}{25} \div \frac{3}{5} = P(B)$$

$$\frac{1}{5} = P(B)$$

If events A and B are dependent, then the probability that A and B both occur is equivalent to the product of the probability of event A and the probability of event B given that A has already occurred.

$$P(A \text{ and } B) = P(A) \times P(B|A)$$

The factor $P(B|A)$ refers to the probability of B in light of how event A has altered the sample space.

Example

What is the probability of drawing a heart and then a spade from a deck of cards if the cards drawn are not replaced into the deck?

Solution

$$P(H \text{ and } S) = P(H) \times P(S|H)$$

$$P(H \text{ and } S) = \frac{13}{52} \times \frac{13}{51}$$

$$P(H \text{ and } S) = \frac{13}{204}$$

$P(S|H) = \frac{13}{51}$ because there are still 13 spades in the deck, assuming that the first card was a heart. But now, since the first card was chosen, there are only 51 cards remaining in the deck.

Related Questions: 18, 19, 20

2.7 *Solve problems using the probabilities of mutually exclusive and complementary events.*

MUTUALLY EXCLUSIVE AND COMPLEMENTARY EVENTS

Mutually exclusive events do not share any outcomes in common.

For example, in a deck of cards, the set of hearts and the set of spades are mutually exclusive sets, because there is no card that is both a heart and a spade. On the other hand, the set of hearts and the set of Queens are not mutually exclusive because there is a card that is both a heart and a queen.

Questions related to mutually exclusive events typically ask what is the probability of either event A or event B happening. The result is the sum of their respective probabilities.

$$P(A \text{ or } B) = P(A) + P(B)$$

Example

Suppose a bag contains 3 red marbles, 5 blue marbles, and 2 green marbles. What is the probability that a marble drawn at random is either blue or green?

Solution

$$P(B \text{ or } G) = P(B) + P(G)$$

$$P(B \text{ or } G) = \frac{5}{10} + \frac{2}{10}$$

$$P(B \text{ or } G) = \frac{7}{10}$$

We know that these events are mutually exclusive because there is no marble that is both blue and green.

When the sum of the probabilities of two mutually exclusive events is one, these events are called complementary. In other words, when two mutually exclusive events combine to create the entire sample space, they are complementary.

For example, if a bag contains 6 red marbles and 4 blue marble, then the probabilities of choosing a red or a blue are complementary.

$$P(R \text{ or } B) = P(R) + P(B)$$

$$P(R \text{ or } B) = \frac{6}{10} + \frac{4}{10}$$

$$P(R \text{ or } B) = \frac{10}{10} = 1$$

Complementary events can be described as A and not A. In the above example, the two complementary events here can be considered red and not red. Because the sum of complementary probabilities is one, we can use this to solve problems.

For example, the probability that Michele makes a basket from the foul line is 0.7. What is the complement to this event and what is its probability?

The only other option is that Michele misses the basket, therefore the complement to making the basket is missing it. Since these are complementary events, their sum must be one. Therefore, to find the probability of missing the basket we simply subtract her probability of making it from one.

$$P(\text{missing the basket}) = 1 - P(\text{making the basket})$$

$$P(\text{missing the basket}) = 1 - 0.7$$

$$P(\text{missing the basket}) = 0.3$$

The result is that she has a 0.3 probability of missing the basket.

Related Questions: NR3, 21, 22, NR4, 23, NR5, 24

---

1. A billiard cue manufacturer randomly selects a box of 10 cues and weighs each cue in it. In ounces, the cues weigh 16.9, 16.9, 17.3, 16.8, 17.2, 16.9, 17.5, 16.8, 17.1, and 17.3. The mean and standard deviation of these weights are, respectively,

   A. 16.9 oz and 0.2 oz

   B. 16.9 oz and 0.7 oz

   C. 17.1 oz and 0.2 oz

   D. 17.1 oz and 0.7 oz

   Source: June 2001

Use the following information to answer the next question.

Henry played 24 golf games on the same course during each of two seasons. In the first season, his mean score was 78 with a standard deviation of 2.1. In the second season, his mean score was 74 with a standard deviation of 3.8.

2. The **standard deviation** of Henry's scores for the two seasons indicates that his

   A. scores were more consistent in the first season

   B. scores were more consistent in the second season

   C. average score was better in the first season

   D. average score was better in the second season

   Source: June 2001

Use the following information to answer the next question.

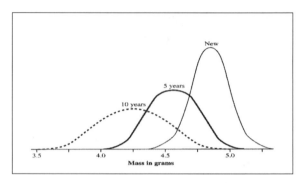

The curves in this graph show the variations in the mass of some dimes that were minted and put into circulation at the same time. One curve shows the distribution of the mass of the dimes, when the dimes were new, and the other two curves show the distributions of the mass of the dimes when they had been in circulation for five years and for ten years.

3. According to this graph, as time passes, the standard deviation of the mass of the dimes

   A. decreases

   B. increases

   C. remains the same

   D. cannot be approximated from the graph

   Source: January 1999

Not for Reproduction

The graphs of four normal distributions are shown below. The graphs are drawn using the same scale.

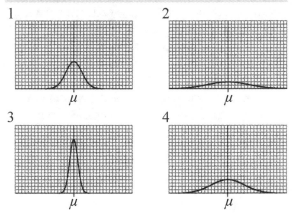

Numerical Response

1. These graphs, listed in order of **increasing** standard deviation, are

_____, _____, _____, and _____.
smallest   largest

Source: June 1999

CHALLENGER QUESTION	49.2

4. At a concert, a random sample of ticket buyers revealed that the amount of time they had waited in line to purchase their tickets was normally distributed with a mean of 185 minutes and a standard deviation of 15 minutes.

What percentage of people stood in line for 180 minutes or less?

A. 33%

B. 37%

C. 63%

D. 67%

Source: January 2001

During a quality control test, 20 batteries are picked at random from an assembly line. The symmetric 95% confidence interval for the average life span of each battery is 116.6 h to 219.4 h.

5. Which of the following graphs has a shaded region indicating this symmetric 95% confidence interval?

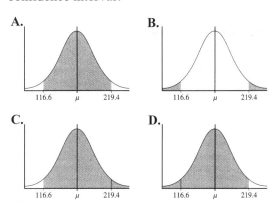

Source: January 2001

CHALLENGER QUESTION	41.8

6. A billiard cue manufacturer claims that the cues he produces have a mean mass of 16.9 oz with a standard deviation of 0.3 oz. If he randomly selects a cue, then the probability that its weight is exactly 16.8 oz **or** less is

A. 0.33   B. 0.37

C. 0.40   D. 0.63

Source: June 2001

Copyright Protected

CHALLENGER QUESTION 38.8

7. In a standard normal distribution, the probability that a particular z-score falls within 0.7 standard deviations of the mean $(-0.7 < z < 0.7)$ is

A. 0.242   B. 0.300

C. 0.516   D. 0.758

Source: June 2001

Numerical Response

2. The marks on a final examination in Biology 20 are normally distributed. Susan scored 68%, which is equivalent to a z-score of 1.25. If the standard deviation of the Biology 20 final examination marks is 4%, then the mean, correct to the nearest tenth of a percentage, is _____ %.

Source: January 1999

8. The manufacturer of "Greenline" lawnmowers gathers information on how soon after purchase the mowers require their first repair.
The data is normally distributed with a mean of 7.5 years and a standard deviation of 2 years. If 35 000 "Greenline" mowers are sold in one year, then the number of those "Greenline" mowers expected to require repairs in the first 5 years is

A. 3 696 mowers

B. 13 804 mowers

D. 31 304 mowers

C. 21 196 mowers

Source: June 1999

Use the following information to answer the next question.

The height of women between ages 18 and 24 is normally distributed with a mean of 162 cm and a standard deviation of 6 cm, as shown below. The height of men between ages 18 and 24 is also normally distributed, but with a mean of 175 cm and standard deviation of 6 cm.

9. If the distribution of the height of the men is put on the same axis as the distribution of the height of the women, then the curve would be

A. a different shape: taller and narrower

B. a different shape: shorter and wider

C. the same shape, shifted to the right

D. the same shape, shifted to the left

Source: January 2000

10. Test scores for an examination are normally distributed with a mean of 67.4% and a standard deviation of 10.5%.
The probability that a particular student gets less than 80% on the examination is

A. 0.115 1

B. 0.384 9

C. 0.512 0

D. 0.884 9

Source: January 1999

Use the following information to answer the next question.

In a particular city with 50 000 high school students, 21 500 were found to be in favour of starting school earlier in the day in order to finish earlier. Josh surveys 100 randomly selected students from this population to determine if they are in favour of this proposal.

CHALLENGER QUESTION   34.2

11. The symmetric 95% confidence interval for the number of students that Josh finds to be in favour of the proposal is

A. 3 to 83   B. 33 to 53

C. 36 to 50   D. 41 to 45

Source: June 2001

12. A particular type of car comes in 4 different colours; red, blue, black, and white. It also comes in 3 different styles. Mark picks a red car with a basic style. What are the number of elements in the sample space for choosing this particular type of car?

A. 3   B. 4

C. 7   D. 12

Use the following information to answer the next question.

A 6-sided green die has two sides labelled with a 1, two sides labelled with a 2, and two sides labelled with a 3.
A red die has 6 sides.
Each side of the red die is labelled with one of the numbers 1, 2, 3, 4, 5, and 6, with each number used only once.

13. The sample space for rolling each of these dice once would **not** include rolling a

A. 2 on each die

B. 1 on the green die and a 3 on the red die

C. 2 on the green die and a 5 on the red die

D. 4 on the green die and a 6 on the red die

Source: January 2001

CHALLENGER QUESTION   57.7

14. An example of dependent events is drawing a red marble out of one jar and drawing a

A. red marble out of another jar

B. green marble out of another jar

C. red marble out of the same jar, after replacing the first marble

D. green marble out of the same jar, without replacing the first marble

Source: January 2001

Copyright Protected

15. Given two random cards, selected without replacement from a standard deck of playing cards, what is the probability that one is the 5 of hearts and the other is the 2 of hearts?

A. $\dfrac{1}{2\,704}$ B. $\dfrac{1}{2\,652}$

C. $\dfrac{1}{1\,352}$ D. $\dfrac{1}{1\,326}$

16. A Monte Carlo roulette wheel has 18 red numbers, 18 black numbers, and green number (0). A spin in which the ball lands on a red number or a black number is an example of

A. an independent event

B. a complementary event

C. a mutually exclusive event

D. a sample space

17. Three cards are drawn at random from a deck of 52 cards. What is the probability that all three cards are aces?

A. 0.000 181   B. 0.000 362

C. 0.001 81   D. 0.003 62

18. After the first turn backgammon, a player rolls two dice and uses the values independently (so, rolling "2 and 1" is treated the same as rolling "1 and 2"). How many distinct rolls are there?

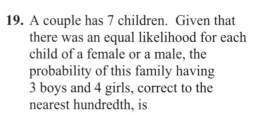

A. 15

B. 18

C. 21

D. 36

19. A couple has 7 children. Given that there was an equal likelihood for each child of a female or a male, the probability of this family having 3 boys and 4 girls, correct to the nearest hundredth, is

A. 0.19   B. 0.27

C. 0.73   D. 0.81

Use the following information to answer the next question.

Two bags contain coloured marbles. Bag A contains 2 white and 2 green marbles. Bag B contains 3 white, 5 red, and 4 green marbles.

20. If one marble is drawn from each of the bags, the probability of drawing one white marble and one green marble is

A. $\dfrac{1}{8}$ B. $\dfrac{1}{6}$

C. $\dfrac{5}{24}$ D. $\dfrac{7}{24}$

Use the following information to answer the next question.

Malaga, Spain lies in a region of Europe known as the Costa Del Sol (Coast of the Sun). The probability of sunshine on any given day in this region is approximately 0.89.

Numerical Response

3. In a non-leap year of 365 days, the average number of days of the year that a tourist could expect to experience weather **other** than sunshine, to the nearest whole number, is _____ .

Source: January 2001

CHALLENGER QUESTION   28.8

21. In a particular town, 70% of the students are bused to school. In a random sample of 1 000 students, the mean of the number of students bused to school is expected to be 700, with a standard deviation of 14.49. The probability that in any given sample of 1 000 students, 720 or more students are bused to school is

A. 0.08 B. 0.38

C. 0.62 D. 0.92

Source: January 2001

Use the following information to answer the next question.

Three of the major countries that produce cars to be purchased in Canada are Canada, Japan, and Germany. A poll of car owners in Canada revealed that of people who presently own a Canadian-produced car, 51% would purchase another Canadian-produced car the next time they purchase a car.
Of people who presently own a Japanese-produced car, 30% would purchase a Canadian produced car the next time they purchase a car.

The following matrix shows detailed results of the poll.

	CA	JA	GR	Other
CA	0.50	0.32	0.12	0.06
JA	0.30	0.50	0.12	0.08
GR	0.35	0.15	0.40	0.10
Other	0.20	0.25	0.15	0.40

CHALLENGER QUESTION   47.0

22. The probability that a current owner of a Canadian-produced car will **not** buy a Japanese-produced or German-produced car on his or her next purchase is

A. 0.44

B. 0.56

C. 0.65

D. 0.71

Source: January 2001

CHALLENGER QUESTION   45.0

Numerical Response

4. The probability of **not** rolling a 4 or a 6 on one roll of a 6-sided fair die with sides numbered 1 through 6, to the nearest hundredth, is _____.

Source: June 2001

Copyright Protected

Use the following information to answer the next question.

Matrix *A* and Matrix *B* have a product, Matrix *C*, as shown below.

Matrix *A*   Matrix *B*

$$\begin{bmatrix} 8 & 7 & 4 \\ 3 & 1 & 2 \\ 5 & 6 & 9 \end{bmatrix} \times \begin{bmatrix} 2 & 1 & 0 & 4 \\ 1 & 2 & 3 & 2 \\ 4 & 2 & 1 & 5 \end{bmatrix} = \text{Matrix } C$$

23. The probability that a randomly chosen element in Matrix *C* is an even number is

A. 0.33

B. 0.38

C. 0.42

D. 0.67

Source: June 2001

Use the following information to answer the next question.

There are six red balls and seven black balls in a bag.

Numerical Response

5. If two balls are chosen without replacement out of the balls, what is the probability, correct to two decimal places, that both are red balls or both are black balls? _____.

24. One letter is chosen from all the letters in the word **T O R O N T O**. What is the probability that this one letter is a **T** or an **O**?

A. $\dfrac{1}{7}$ B. $\dfrac{2}{7}$

C. $\dfrac{3}{7}$ D. $\dfrac{5}{7}$

Written Response

Use the following information to answer the next question.

In humans, earlobe shape is genetically determined by a particular pair of genes. A person may have two dominant genes (*EE*), two recessive genes (*ee*), or a dominant and a recessive gene (*Ee*).

If a person has one or two dominant genes, then he or she will have a detached earlobe.

Attached earlobe   Detached earlobe

1. **a)** Complete the chart to show the sample space for an offspring of parents who each carry one dominant (E) gene for the detached earlobe.

		Mother	
		E	e
Father	E		
	e		

b) What is the probability that an offspring from these parents will have detached earlobes?

Not for Reproduction

Use the following additional information to answer the next part of the question.

Approximately 39% of **all** people have attached earlobes.

c) Calculate the mean and standard deviation for the number of people in a sample of 8 748 that have attached earlobes. Round your answers to the nearest hundredth.

d) Calculate the symmetric 95% confidence interval for the number of people in this sample that have attached earlobes.

Source: June 2001

2. Pollsters estimate that the number of decided voters in favour of a particular proposition is 70% and the number opposed is 30%.

a) What is the expected mean and standard deviation of "yes" voters if the sample size is 400?

b) Construct a symmetric confidence interval of 95%, in this sample, for the expected number and percentage of "yes" voters.

c) If the sample size is 200 instead of 400, what is the 95% confidence interval for the expected percentage of "yes" voters? Compare this with the interval for 400 sample size.

Copyright Protected

NOTES

UNIT TEST 2—STATISTICS AND PROBABILITY

Not for Reproduction

Use the following information to answer the next question.

The following chart represents the heights of the children in a pre-school class.

Student	Height (cm)
Lucas	104
David	106
Stephanie	98
Thomas	101
Erica	96
Eric	104
Danielle	109
Susan	99
Paul	102
Chris	102

Numerical Response

1. The standard deviation for the height of the children in the preschool, to the nearest hundredth, is _____ .

Use the following information to answer the next question.

The following information was gathered from two classes writing an exam on statistics.

	Class A	Class B
Mean	72%	68%
Standard Deviation	8%	5%

1. The standard deviation tells us that

A. class A scored more consistently.

B. class B scored more consistently.

C. class A had a better average mark.

D. class B had a better average mark.

Use the following information to answer the next question.

A distribution company has purchased 650 crates of apples. It has been determined that the mean number of apples in each crate is 77 with a standard deviation of 9.

2. The number of crates that can be expected to have more than 90 apples is

A. 48

B. 80

C. 570

D. 602

Use the following information to answer the next question.

Of the 3 000 valves produced by a company in a day, quality control tells us that the mean number of defective valves produced is 20 with a standard deviation of 4.

3. The probability that on a given day the company produces a batch of valves with less than 18 defective valves is

A. 0.758 0

B. 0.242 0

C. 0.691 5

D. 0.308 5

Use the following information to answer the next question.

> The average driving speed on the highway is 115.5 km/h with a standard deviation of 9.3 km/h.

4. The minimum speed that a car needs to drive, to the nearest tenth, to be in the fastest 15% of the traffic is

   A. 105.9 km/h   B. 129.0 km/h

   C. 125.1 km/h   D. 110.4 km/h

Use the following information to answer the next question.

> A manufacturer of telephones has discovered that the mean lifespan of their telephones is 4 years with a standard deviation of 1.75 years.

Numerical Response

2. To guarantee that the manufacturer only has to replace a maximum of 10% of their products the warrantee, to the nearest tenth of a year, should be _____.

Use the following information to answer the next two questions.

> Tom is doing a study of the predominance of right-handedness in his home-town which has a population of 850 000. He has discovered that about 9.8% of the population is left-handed.

5. The mean, to the nearest whole, and the standard deviation, to the nearest hundredth, for the population of left-handed people in his home-town respectively are

   A. $\mu = 833\,000$ people, $\sigma = 274.11$ people

   B. $\mu = 766\,700$ people, $\sigma = 7\,513.66$ people

   C. $\mu = 83\,300$ people, $\sigma = 274.11$ people

   D. $\mu = 83\,300$ people, $\sigma = 7\,513.66$ people

6. The 95% confidence interval for left-handed people in his city is between

   A. 82 762 people to 83 838 people

   B. 82 763 people to 83 837 people

   C. 83 048 people to 83 552 people

   D. 83 047 people to 83 553 people

Use the following information to answer the next question.

> A certain school district needs to choose a math teacher to send to a national conference. All the math teachers in the district are very eager to be chosen, but only one will be. The district must first choose whether the representative will come from school A, B, C, D, E or F. In addition, each school has three math teachers who are vying for the position.

7. The size of the sample space that the district has to choose from is

   A. 9

   B. 18

   C. 6

   D. 36

Use the following information to answer the next question.

> For a certain game there is a set of 48 cards. There are 12 red cards, 12 blue cards, 12 green cards, and 12 yellow cards. Each of these sets of twelve is numbered 1 through 12. A card from this deck is drawn and then a second is drawn without replacement.

8. The event of drawing the first and second cards is classified as

   A. independent

   B. dependent

   C. mutually exclusive

   D. non-mutually exclusive

Use the following information to answer the next question.

A school runs a contest in which each month a student's name is chosen at random to have lunch with the principal, at the principal's expense. Each month, every student has an equal probability of being chosen, regardless if he or she has been chosen previously.

9. The events of choosing a student each month can be classified as

  A. independent

  B. dependent

  C. mutually exclusive

  D. non-mutually exclusive

Use the following information to answer the next question.

A man is coming into Canada from the US. He bought some fruit in the US to eat on his trip home. He has 4 apples and 7 oranges in the bag. Unfortunately he is not allowed to bring fruit across the border. The guard asks him to reach into the bag and pull out its contents. He pulls out one fruit and then a second.

10. The probability that the first fruit is an apple and the second is an orange is

  A. $\dfrac{1}{2}$

  B. $\dfrac{11}{21}$

  C. $\dfrac{28}{121}$

  D. $\dfrac{14}{55}$

Use the following information to answer the next question.

A low-pressure system is moving in, and for the next 3 days meteorologists are saying that the probability of rain on each day is about $\dfrac{5}{7}$.

11. The probability that it rains on all three days is determined using

  A. $\dfrac{5^3}{7^3}$

  B. $\dfrac{5^3}{7}$

  C. $\dfrac{15}{7}$

  D. $\dfrac{5}{7}$

Use the following information to answer the next question.

Two events, A and B, are independent.

The probability of A is $P(A) = \dfrac{3}{4}$.

The probability of A and B is $P(A \text{ and } B) = \dfrac{15}{24}$.

Numerical Response

3. The probability of event B, $P(B)$, to the nearest hundredth is _____.

12. Complementary events are events where

  A. their sample spaces have events in common

  B. the first event changes the sample space for the second event

  C. their probabilities add up to one

  D. the probability of them both occurring is the product of their individual probabilities

Copyright Protected

Use the following information to answer the next question.

Darlene has invited many people over for her birthday party. They all play a game in which Darlene gets blindfolded, spun around, and then she has to reach out, grab a guest and guess whom it is.

Numerical Response

4. If the probability that she grabs a boy is 0.39, then the probability that she grabs a girl is _____.

Use the following information to answer the next question.

A diagram consists of the following shapes and colours.

13. The probability that a shape chosen at random is either black or a circle is

    A. $\dfrac{4}{27}$

    B. $\dfrac{7}{9}$

    C. $\dfrac{7}{18}$

    D. $\dfrac{1}{3}$

Use the following information to answer the next question.

Two sets of numbers are defined as

$A = \{2,3,5,7,11,13,17,19\}$
$B = \{1,4,9,16\}$

Where set A is the set of all the prime numbers less than 20, and B is the set of all perfect square numbers less than 20.

14. If the numbers 1 through 20 are written on a series of chips which are then put into a bag and then one chip is drawn randomly, the probability of drawing a chip from either set A or B is

    A. 1

    B. $\dfrac{1}{2}$

    C. $\dfrac{1}{5}$

    D. $\dfrac{3}{5}$

Written Response

Use the following information to answer the next question.

A company that produces bags of chips can make about 3 000 bags in an hour. On average, 21 of these bags produced in an hour must be rejected because their mass is either too small or too large.

1. What are the minimum and maximum number of bags that quality control can be 95% sure will need to be rejected within each hour?

Use the following information to answer the next two questions.

A simple game is played where two players each have 5 cards numbered one through five. The two decide who will go first. The first person guesses as to whether the sum of the two cards they will be even or odd. After this, they each simultaneously turn over one of their cards. If the person who guessed is correct, he or she gets to guess again. If the person is wrong, the other player gets a turn. The first person to win three times in a row wins the game.

2. List the sample space for a single event, or a single turn in the described game.

3. Identify the probability of the sum being odd or even. What is the wisest prediction for this game?

FINANCE

Table of Correlations		
Topic	**Outcomes**	**Questions**
Design or use a spreadsheet to make and justify financial decisions.	*It is expected that students will:*	
	3.1 design a financial spreadsheet template to allow users to input their own variables	1, 2, 3, 4, 5, 6, NR1, 7
	3.2 analyze the costs and benefits of renting or buying an increasing asset, such as a home	8, 9, 10, 11, NR2, 12, 13, 14
	3.3 analyze the costs and benefits of leasing or buying a decreasing asset, such as a vehicle or a computer	
	3.4 analyze an investment portfolio, applying such concepts as interest rate, rate of return and total return	15, 16, 17, 18, 19, 20, 21, 22, 23

Not for Reproduction

FINANCE

Students will design or use a spreadsheet to make and justify financial decisions.

3.1   *Design a financial spreadsheet template to allow users to input their own variables.*

SPREADSHEET APPLICATIONS

A familiarity with spreadsheets is assumed in this chapter. Our present goal is to be able to create a spreadsheet for specific applications. How this is accomplished will vary from question to question.

Recall these formulae from Pure and/or Applied Mathematics 20:

Simple Interest: $I = Prt$, where I is the amount of interest earned on the principal amount, P, at a rate of r over the period of time, t.

Note that r and t should be given in terms of the same units of time measure.

Compound Interest: $A = P\left(1 + \dfrac{i}{n}\right)^{nt}$, where A is the accumulated amount of money on a principle amount P at a rate of i compounded n times a year for t years.

Here are four examples of the types of questions that can be expected.

1. You own a computer store and you want to create a spreadsheet that can be used to create invoices for work that you do. Your first customer wants you to upgrade his motherboard, replace the RAM, install a new video card, and install a DVD rewriter. The spreadsheet you create should automatically calculate what the customer would owe you after inputting the item descriptions and their costs.

Solution

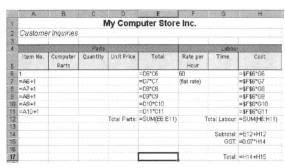

Now, if a new motherboard costs $229.99, each of the 3 required RAM sticks costs $65.50, the new video card costs $89.95, and the DVD rewriter costs $185.50, then these numbers and the required quantities get entered into the appropriate spaces in the spreadsheet.

After this, you decide how much time you will charge in labour for each item that needs to get installed.

Notice that in the cost column we are using *absolute references*. The dollar signs in the cell reference ($F$6) lock this reference in so that it will not change when copied down. The cell reference G6 in cell H6 was a relative reference and changed accordingly as we copied the formula down.

In the given spreadsheet, the fixed value here is the hourly rate. The values that are entered by the user are the quantities of items purchased and their unit prices. The user also enters in the amount of time required for each installation. The computed values will include the costs of the items ordered, the charge for labour on each item, and all of the totals.

	A	B	C	D	E	F	G	H
1			**My Computer Store Inc.**					
2	Customer Inquiries							
3								
4			Parts				Labour	
5	Item No.	Computer Parts	Quantity	Unit Price	Total	Rate per Hour	Time	Cost
6	1	mother-board	1	$ 229.99	$ 229.99	$ 60.00	$ 0.75	$ 45.00
7	2	RAM	3	$ 65.50	$ 196.50	(flat rate)	0	$ -
8	3	video card	1	$ 89.95	$ 89.95		0.3	$ 18.00
9	4	DVD RW	1	$ 185.50	$ 185.50		0.5	$ 30.00
10	5				$ -			$ -
11	6				$ -			$ -
12				Total Parts:	$ 701.94		Total Labour:	$ 93.00
13								
14							Subtotal:	$ 794.94
15							GST:	$ 55.65
16								
17							Total:	$ 850.59

2. You want to invest $5 000.00 with a bank that will offer you 6.5% annually. Create a spreadsheet to follow the growth of the investment over 5 years.

Solution

	A	B	C	D	E
1	Year	Opening Balance	Interest Rate	Interest Earned	Closing Balance
2	1	5000	0.065	=B2*C2	=B2+D2
3	=A2+1	=E2	=C2	=B3*C3	=B3+D3
4	=A3+1	=E3	=C3	=B4*C4	=B4+D4
5	=A4+1	=E4	=C4	=B5*C5	=B5+D5
6	=A5+1	=E5	=C5	=B6*C6	=B6+D6

Notice that the opening balance of subsequent rows is equivalent to the closing balance of the previous row. Here, the inputted values are the initial amount of the investment and the interest rate. All the remaining values are calculated values. Column D is the equivalent of the simple interest equation.

	A	B	C	D	E
1	Year	Opening Balance	Interest Rate	Interest Earned	Closing Balance
2	1	$ 5,000.00	6.5%	$ 325.00	$5,325.00
3	2	$ 5,325.00	6.5%	$ 346.13	$5,671.13
4	3	$ 5,671.13	6.5%	$ 368.62	$6,039.75
5	4	$ 6,039.75	6.5%	$ 392.58	$6,432.33
6	5	$ 6,432.33	6.5%	$ 418.10	$6,850.43

If we wanted to invest $7 000 instead of $5 000, and if the interest rate changes to 5% in the 5th year, all we need to do is change B2 to 7 000 and C5 to 5. The changes are automatic.

	A	B	C	D	E
1	Year	Opening Balance	Interest Rate	Interest Earned	Closing Balance
2	1	$ 7,000.00	6.5%	$455.00	$ 7,455.00
3	2	$ 7,455.00	6.5%	$484.58	$ 7,939.58
4	3	$ 7,939.58	6.5%	$516.07	$ 8,455.65
5	4	$ 8,455.65	5.0%	$422.78	$ 8,878.43
6	5	$ 8,878.43	5.0%	$443.92	$ 9,322.35

3. To buy a car, you need to take out a loan for $20 000. The bank offers you 8%. Determine how much you need to pay per year to pay off the loan in 5 years.

First, set up the spreadsheet so that your payments are subtracted from the sum of the remaining balance and the interest charged as follows:

Solution

	A	B	C	D	E	F
1	Year	Opening Balance	Interest Rate	Interest Charged	Annual Payment	Closing Balance
2	1	2000	0.08	=B2*C2		=B2+D2-E2
3	=A2+1	=F2	=C2	=B3*C3	=E2	=B3+D3-E3
4	=A3+1	=F3	=C3	=B4*C4	=E3	=B4+D4-E4
5	=A4+1	=F4	=C4	=B5*C5	=E4	=B5+D5-E5
6	=A5+1	=F5	=C5	=B6*C6	=E5	=B6+D6-E6
7	=A6+1	=F6	=C6	=B7*C7	=E6	=B7+D7-E7

In this spreadsheet, once the first two rows of calculations and entries are filled, the second row may be copied down to whatever row gives the appropriate number of years.

	A	B	C	D	E	F
1	Year	Opening Balance	Interest Rate	Interest Charged	Annual Payment	Closing Balance
2	1	$20,000.00	8%	$ 1,600.00		$21,600.00
3	2	$21,600.00	8%	$ 1,728.00	$ -	$23,328.00
4	3	$23,328.00	8%	$ 1,866.24	$ -	$25,194.24
5	4	$25,194.24	8%	$ 2,015.54	$ -	$27,209.78
6	5	$27,209.78	8%	$ 2,176.78	$ -	$29,386.56
7	6	$29,386.56	8%	$ 2,350.92	$ -	$31,737.49

Now, all the user needs to do is guess at values for the Annual Payment in cell E2 and watch the value in F7. When the final closing balance is $0.00, then the user has guessed the correct annual payment.

	A	B	C	D	E	F
1	Year	Opening Balance	Interest Rate	Interest Charged	Annual Payment	Closing Balance
2	1	$20,000.00	8%	$ 1,600.00	$ 4,326.31	$17,273.69
3	2	$17,273.69	8%	$ 1,381.90	$ 4,326.31	$14,329.28
4	3	$14,329.28	8%	$ 1,146.34	$ 4,326.31	$11,149.31
5	4	$11,149.31	8%	$ 891.94	$ 4,326.31	$ 7,714.94
6	5	$ 7,714.94	8%	$ 617.20	$ 4,326.31	$ 4,005.83
7	6	$ 4,005.83	8%	$ 320.47	$ 4,326.31	-$ 0.02

With an annual payment of $4 326.31, the loan will be paid off in 5 years (in fact we will have overpaid by 2¢).

4. Given the same initial scenario as previously detailed, assume now that the annual payment is $2 336.59. How long will it take to pay back the loan?

To solve this we set up the spreadsheet as before with the given annual payment. Complete the first 2 rows.

Solution:

	A	B	C	D	E	F
1	Year	Opening Balance	Interest Rate	Interest Charged	Annual Payment	Closing Balance
2	1	$20,000.00	8%	$ 1,600.00	$ 2,336.59	$19,263.41
3	2	$19,263.41	8%	$ 1,541.07	$ 2,336.59	$18,467.89

From here, we copy down the second row until the closing balance is as close to zero as we can make it.

	A	B	C	D	E	F
13	12	$ 7,739.10	8%	$ 619.13	$ 2,336.59	$ 6,021.64
14	13	$ 6,021.64	8%	$ 481.73	$ 2,336.59	$ 4,166.78
15	14	$ 4,166.78	8%	$ 333.34	$ 2,336.59	$ 2,163.53
16	15	$ 2,163.53	8%	$ 173.08	$ 2,336.59	$ 0.02

From this, we can read that it would take 15 years to pay off the loan in this situation.

Related Questions: 1, 2, 3, 4, 5, 6, NR1, 7

3.2 Analyze the costs and benefits of renting or buying an increasing asset, such as a house.

INCREASING ASSETS

A house is typically considered an increasing asset because the value of a house tends to increase over time.

Look at the following table that charts the value of a house from year to year.

Year	Value
0	$150 000.00
1	$162 000.00
2	$174 960.00
3	$188 956.80
4	$204 073.34

As a result of the fact that the value is steadily increasing, but not by a constant amount, we can assume that this is an example of exponential growth. Using a graphic display calculator, we may do a regression on this data to get the following equation in the form of $y = ab^x$,

$$y = 150\ 000 \times 1.08^x$$

Notice that the value of b in the equation is greater than one. The result is a model of exponential growth, as illustrated below:

Exponential Growth

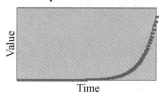

Most people require a mortgage (house loan) to buy a house. Usually these loans extend over a large period of time (amortization period) such as 10, 15, 20, and 25 years. Interest rates charged on a mortgage can fluctuate but may be locked for specified periods of time.

Copyright Protected

The longer the amortization period of a mortgage, the smaller the regular payments are, but the total amount spent on the house increases. Often people choose to rent instead of buy because although the property tax is typically included, the regular payments are smaller, and therefore more manageable for their budget. They also do not have to worry about the additional expenses related to home ownership. On the other hand, over the same period of time, although the person who chose to buy spent more overall, they are now in possession of an asset which tends to increase in value over time: the person who chose to rent did not spent the same amount, but he/she has also not purchased an asset and must continue paying rent. In other words, owners build equity in their homes, whereas renters do not.

Questions in this chapter are typically about total costs.

Example

A couple plans to buy a $180 000.00 house. They are able to make a $25 000.00 down payment, but they must finance the rest. The bank offers them the loan at 7.5%, with monthly payments of $1 237.83 for 20 years. How much do they need to borrow?

Solution

The amount they need to borrow is the value of the house less the amount they are able to provide as a down payment.

$$\text{Mortgage} = \$180\ 000 - \$25\ 000$$
$$= \$155\ 000$$

How much will they pay in total for the house?

The total amount paid for the house is equivalent to the amount of the monthly payments multiplied by the number of months it takes to repay the loan plus the amount of the down payment.

$$\text{Total} = \$1\ 237.83(12)(20) + \$25\ 000$$
$$= \$297\ 079.20 + \$25\ 000$$
$$= \$322\ 079.20$$

How much was spent on interest?

The amount spent on interest will be equivalent to the total amount spent on the house less the cost of the house.

$$\text{Interest} = \$297\ 079.20 - \$180\ 000$$
$$= \$142\ 079.20$$

Related Questions: 8, 9, 10, 11, NR2, 12, 13, 14

3.3   Analyze the costs and benefits of leasing or buying a decreasing asset, such as a vehicle or a computer.

DECREASING ASSETS

A car, like many other possessions, is an asset that decreases in value or depreciates over time.

The following table charts the change in the value of a car.

Year	Value
0	$30 000.00
1	$25 500.00
2	$21 675.00
3	$18 423.75
4	$15 660.19
5	$13 311.16

As in the previous example, the change in value is steady, but not by a constant amount.
This suggests an exponential change in the data. Using a graphic display calculator, we may once again do a regression on this data to get the following equation in the form of $y = ab^x$.

$y = 30\ 000(0.85)^x$

Notice that the value of *b* is greater than zero but less than one. The value of *b* here indicates that the vehicle is losing 15% every year.
The result is a model of exponential decay as illustrated below:

Exponential Decay

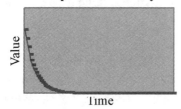

Loans for things like vehicles tend to be over a much smaller period of time as compared to a mortgage. The options people run into deal with whether a vehicle should be purchased or leased.

When a vehicle is leased, the person leasing it agrees to pay the owner on the amount that the vehicle depreciates over the lease period plus any additional taxes and charges and so forth. For instance, the GST is calculated on the amount of the vehicle and then it is divided up over the number of months of the lease.

The amount of the monthly payment on a lease is, therefore, typically lower than the amount of the monthly payment when buying a car. At the end of the lease, the car can either be traded in and a new vehicle can be leased or the original can be purchased by paying out the remaining value of the car. The questions that are asked in this outcome focus on the comparison between these methods of payment.

Example

Bill wants a new vehicle. He is looking at one priced at $24 700.00. He has saved up $2 250.00 to use as a down payment. The dealership has offered him two options:

Option 1 (Finance the full amount)	Option 2 (Lease and buy at the end)
• Monthly payment $532.40 • Number of months 48	• Monthly lease payments $435.26 • Number of months 36 • Residual value $10 019.29

a) How much will Bill pay in total in monthly payments in both options?

To buy the vehicle he will pay $532.40 × 48 = $25 555.20.

If leasing the vehicle, he will pay $435.26 × 36 = $15 669.36.

In simply monthly payments he will pay $9 885.84 more if he buys.

b) How much will Bill pay if he wants to own the vehicle in both options?

As we have seen above, the total cost to buy the vehicle is $25 555.20.

To purchase the vehicle after leasing it we need to include the balloon payment after the leasing period as follows:

$15 669.36 + $10 019.29 = $25 688.65

In this case, leasing costs $133.45 more.

c) Which option is the best option for Bill?

If Bill wants to own the vehicle it would be best to buy it right from the beginning. If Bill has trouble affording the payments per month, he should look at leasing the vehicle. This option also gives him the ability to pick a new vehicle to continue leasing after the period of the lease.

3.4 Analyze an investment portfolio, applying such concepts as interest rate, rate of return, and total return.

INVESTMENT OPTIONS

The rate of interest that a financial institution gives on an investment may vary over time. To determine the average annual rate of interest that has been earned, there are two methods that can be employed.

Because the growth of an investment is exponential, as a result of the compound interest equation, we can perform an exponential regression on the chart outlining the growth of the investment year to year.

For example; the following chart details the growth of a $2 000 dollar investment over 4 years.

Year	Investment
0	$2 000.00
1	$2 160.00
2	$2 311.20
3	$2 461.43
4	$2 633.73

By entering this data into the calculator and performing an exponential regression, we get the equation $y = 2\ 009.34(1.07)^x$

The equation is in the form of $y = ab^x$. If we compare this to the compound interest formula, $A = P(1 + i)^t$, we see that $b = 1 + i$. To find the average interest rate, we simply subtract 1 from the value of b.

This means that in our example, where $i = 0.07$, the average annual interest rate is 7%. If the value of b is less than 1 after the exponential regression is taken, then the value of the asset or investment is depreciating.

To find the rate of depreciation, we still subtract the value of b from one.

For example, if the regression equation is $y = 15\ 000(0.87)^x$, then the depreciation rate is $1 - 0.87$ or 13%.

We may also use the chart to find the interest rate that was charged yearly, and then find the mean value. To do this, we determine how much was earned each year and divide it by how much was present at the beginning of each year to get the interest rate.

Year	Interest Rate
1	$\dfrac{2\ 160 - 2\ 000}{2\ 000} = 0.08$ or 8%
2	$\dfrac{2\ 311.20 - 2\ 160.00}{2\ 160.00} = 0.07$ or 7%
3	$\dfrac{2\ 461.43 - 2\ 311.2}{2\ 311.2} = 0.065$ or 6.5%
4	$\dfrac{2\ 633.73 - 2\ 461.43}{2\ 461.43} = 0.07$ or 7%

Now, we find the average of the annual interest rates:

$$\frac{8 + 7 + 6.5 + 7}{4} = 7.125 \text{ or approximately 7%}$$

In addition to finding the average annual rate of return for an investment, we are also interested in determining the total return on the investment. The total return on the investment refers to the amount of interest that was earned. This can be determined by subtracting the initial investment from the final amount.

Copyright Protected

Not for Reproduction

In the previous example, the total return would be calculated as follows:

$2 633.73 – $2 000.00 = $633.73

Therefore, the total return was $633.73.

The previous example followed a single investment over a period of several years, but to calculate the average return when several investments are being considered requires a different approach.

Typically, the time period we are considering is one year, and to determine the average rate of return we calculate the total amount earned in interest and divide it by the total amount invested.

$$\text{Average Rate of Return} = \frac{\text{Total Earned}}{\text{Total Invested}}$$

Example

John has $5 000 to distribute between four different investments with various rates of return as listed in the chart following.

Solution

Investments	Percent Invested	Rate of Return
Chequing	10%	3%
Guaranteed Investments	40%	5%
Commodities	20%	8%
Stocks	30%	– 4%

To find the amount earned on each investment, determine the amount invested first and then multiply by the interest rate.

Chequing $= \$5\ 000(0.10)(0.03) = \$15$

Guaranteed Investment $= \$5\ 000(0.40)(0.05) = \$100$

Commodities $= \$5\ 000(0.20)(0.08) = \$80$

Stocks $= \$5\ 000(0.30)(-0.04) = -\$60$

$$\text{Average Rate of Return} = \frac{\$15 + \$100 + \$80 - \$60}{\$5\ 000}$$
$$= 0.027$$

Therefore, the average rate of return was 2.7%.

Related Questions: 15, 16, 17, 18, 19, 20, 21, 22, 23

Copyright Protected

Use the following information to answer the next two questions.

The following spreadsheet shows the beginning of an amortization table for 5 equal monthly payments to be made on a $900 loan with an interest rate of 1% per month.

	A	B	C	D	E
1	Payment Number	Payment	Interest Payment	Payment to Principal	Balance Remaining
2	1	$155.29	$9.00	$146.29	$753.71
3	2	$155.29	$7.54	$147.75	$605.96
4	3	$155.29			
5	4				
6	5				

1. How much of payment number 3 is payment to principal?

   A. $147.75

   B. $149.23

   C. $155.29

   D. $161.35

Source: January 2001

2. Which of the following formulas can be used to calculate the value of cell D4?

   A. = B4 + C4

   B. = E3 – B4

   C. = B4 – 0.1 *E3

   D. = B4 – 0.01 *E3

Source: January 2001

Not for Reproduction

Use the following information to answer the next question.

To buy a new boat, a person takes a loan of $7 400 over 60 months at 8.75% per annum, compounded monthly.

CHALLENGER QUESTION   **43.1**

3. Which of the following spreadsheets should the person use to correctly calculate the balance in cell F2?

A.

	A	B	C	D	E	F
1	Months	Loan	Interest Rate	Interest Charge	Monthly Payment	Balance
2	1	7 400	0.087 5	= (B2*C2)/12	152.72	= B2 – D2 – E2
3	2	= F2	0.087 5		152.72	

B.

	A	B	C	D	E	F
1	Months	Loan	Interest Rate	Interest Charge	Monthly Payment	Balance
2	1	7 400	0.087 5	= B2*C2	152.72	= B2 + D2 – E2
3	2	= F2	0.087 5		152.72	

C.

	A	B	C	D	E	F
1	Months	Loan	Interest Rate	Interest Charge	Monthly Payment	Balance
2	1	7 400	0.087 5	= (B2*C2)/12	152.72	= B2 + D2 – E2
3	2	= F2	0.087 5		152.72	

D.

	A	B	C	D	E	F
1	Months	Loan	Interest Rate	Interest Charge	Monthly Payment	Balance
2	1	7 400	0.087 5	= B2*C2	152.72	= B2 + D2 + E2
3	2	= F2	0.087 5		152.72	

Source: January 2001

Copyright Protected

Use the following information to answer the next question.

The following table shows the inventory statement for some of the items available at a convenience store.

	A	B	C	D	E	F	G	H
1	Inventory Statement							
2	Item	Number Purchased	Wholesale Price	Total Cost	Number Sold	Retail Price	Total Sales	Total Profit
3	Potato Chips	500	$0.45	$225.00	420	$0.85	$357.00	$132.00
4	Chocolate Bars	800	$0.52	$416.00	541	$0.75	$513.95	$97.95
5	2 L Pop	600	$1.80	$1 080.00	508	$3.25	$1 651.00	$571.00
6	Gum	1 600	$0.38	$608.00	1 275	$0.80	$1 020.00	$412.00
7	Total	3 500		$2 329.00	2 744		$3 541.95	$1 212.95

4. The formula that could have been used to determine the value in cell H4 is

   A. = B4 * C4

   B. = B4 – E4

   C. = E4 * F4

   D. = G4 – D4

Source: June 2001

Use the following information to answer the next question.

Bill takes out an $8 000 loan at 8%/a, compounded monthly, for 1 year.
The chart below shows a partial loan payment schedule.

Month	Balance	Interest	Payment	New Balance
1	$8 000.00	$53.33	$695.91	$7 357.42
2	$7 357.42	*i*	$695.91	

5. The value of *i* is

   A. $55.67

   B. $53.33

   C. $49.05

   D. $44.41

Source: June 2001

Use the following information to answer the next question.

Steve has $5 000 that he wishes to invest. After talking to an investment specialist at his bank, he decides to invest in a 2 year GIC (Guaranteed Investment Certificate) that pays 4.1% compounded annually. The following table shows the interest that Steve expects to earn over 2 years.

Year	Opening Balance	Interest Rate	Interest Earned	Closing Balance
1	$5 000.00	4.1%	$205.00	$5 205.00
2	$5 205.00	4.1%	$2 123.41	$5 418.41

6. How much interest will Steve earn on his investment over the 2 year period?

A. $231.19

B. $418.41

C. $638.66

D. $869.95

Use the following information to answer the next question.

Upon retirement, a person buys a $5 000 present value annuity. The interest rate is 18% per annum, compounded monthly. Monthly payments of $250 are made to the person. The person made the following spreadsheet.

Period	Period Balance	Monthly Interest Rate	Monthly Payment	New Balance
1	$5 000.00	1.5%	$250.00	$4 825.00
2	$4 825.00	1.5%	$250.00	$4 647.38
3	$4 647.38	1.5%	$250.00	*b*

CHALLENGER QUESTION   **44.3**

Numerical Response

1. The balance after the third monthly payment, *b*, to the nearest dollar, is $_____.

Source: June 2000

Use the following information to answer the next question.

A basketball player wishes to attend an international basketball tournament. She invests $1 600 in a savings account twice a year at 8% per annum compounded semi-annually. She uses the spreadsheet below to determine the amount of money she will have in two years.

Payment Period	Regular Payment	New Balance	Interest Per Period	Final Balance
1	$1 600	$1 600.00	$1600 × 0.04 = $64.00	$1 664.00
2	$1 600	$3 264.00	$3 264 × 0.04 = $130.56	$3 394.56
3	$1 600	$4 994.56		
4	$1 600			*b*

7. The final balance, *b*, after 2 years will be

A. $8 666.11

B. $7 066.11

C. $6 794.34

D. $5 194.24

Source: June 2000

Copyright Protected

Use the following information to answer the next question.

A couple plans to buy a house for $175 000. They will make a $30 000 down payment and take out a 25-year mortgage at 7.5% per annum, compounded semi-annually. The monthly payments on the mortgage will be $1 060.75 per month.

CHALLENGER QUESTION	26.8

8. The total amount of interest that the couple will pay for this mortgage is

A. $188 125

B. $173 225

C. $155 875

D. $143 225

Source: January 2001

CHALLENGER QUESTION	59.5

9. In most cases, a house is an increasing asset whose value, *v*, increases exponentially over time, *t*.

Which of the graphs below represents the pattern of the expected value of a house?

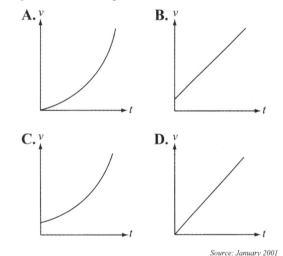

Source: January 2001

Use the following information to answer the next two questions.

John is considering whether to buy or lease a car. The price of the car he is interested in is $25 500. Regardless of the option he chooses, John will make a down payment of $3 000.

John's first option is to purchase the car. He will have to make payments of $557.25/month for 48 months.

John's second option is to lease the car. He will have to make payments of $307.50/month for 48 months, after which time he can buy the car for an additional $12 850.

10. If John wants to own the car at the end of 48 months, he should __*i*__ the car because he will save $__*ii*__.

The row that completes this statement is row

	i	*ii*
A.	lease	$862
B.	buy	$862
C.	lease	$11 988
D.	buy	$11 988

Source: June 2001

Use the following additional information to answer the next question.

It is predicted that the value of John's car will depreciate every year for the first four years according to the table below.

Year	Value
0	$25 000
1	$17 850
2	$16 065
3	$14 459
4	$13 012

Not for Reproduction

CHALLENGER QUESTION	55.3

11. If John uses an exponential regression equation to determine the value of his car in the future, then he will find that the average rate of **depreciation** is

A. 14.4% per year

B. 49.0% per year

C. 51.0% per year

D. 85.6% per year

Source: June 2001

Use the following information to answer the next question.

Geoff wants to invest some money in fixed-return investments. Matrix Q below shows the interest rate offered for three types of investments at each of three banks.

Matrix Q

Type

$$\begin{array}{c} \\ \text{Bank 1} \\ \text{Bank 2} \\ \text{Bank 3} \end{array} \begin{array}{ccc} A & B & C \\ \left[7.6\% \right. & 8.0\% & 11.8\% \\ 8.0\% & 7.3\% & 12.0\% \\ 8.3\% & 7.5\% & \left. 12.8\% \right] \end{array}$$

Matrix R shows the amount of money that Geoff is prepared to contribute to each type of investment.

Matrix R

$$\begin{array}{c} \text{Type A} \\ \text{Type B} \\ \text{Type C} \end{array} \begin{array}{c} \left[\$700 \right. \\ \$500 \\ \left. \$400 \right] \end{array}$$

Geoff intends to use only one bank for his investments.

Numerical Response

2. List the numbered banks from the one that produces the highest overall return on these types of investments to the one that produces the lowest overall return on these types of investments.

Answer:

_____, _____, _____

highest overall return   lowest overall return

Source: June 2001

Use the following information to answer the next question.

Betty wants to take out a mortgage for $115 000, amortized over 25 years. She is considering two options. One option is to make 12 monthly payments of $770.30 for 25 years. A second option is to make 52 weekly payments of $177.40 for 25 years.

12. The amount that Betty could save over the full amortization of the mortgage by making the weekly payments instead of the monthly payments is

A. $470.00

B. $592.90

C. $60.70

D. $18.80

Source: June 2001

13. A new car may be purchased for $32 500. It can be leased for 36 months with no down payment for $483/month including taxes. After the 36 months, the car has a purchase option price of $16 362, including taxes. How much can be saved by purchasing over leasing?

A. $125.00

B. $224.00

C. $483.00

D. $1 250.00

14. A couple has a mortgage of $120 000 at 8.2% per annum, amortized over 20 years. They make monthly payments of $1 011.80. How much would they save if they changed their mortgage to 15 years with monthly payments of $1 152.80

A. $705.00

B. $4 444.00

C. $33 840.00

D. $35 328.00

Use the following information to answer the next two questions.

A person has invested $20 000 with an investment firm. In the first year, her portfolio gives the following returns:

Type	Percent Invested	First-Year Profit
Guaranteed certificates	20%	4%
Blue-chip stocks	50%	9.25%
High-risk stocks	30%	−7.5%

| CHALLENGER QUESTION | 21.4 |

15. For this portfolio, the rate of return, to the nearest tenth of a percentage, is

A. 20.8%

B. 5.8%

C. 3.2%

D. 1.9%

Source: January 2001

| CHALLENGER QUESTION | 49.5 |

16. The investor's total return for the first year is

A. $317.50

B. $635.00

C. $1 066.50

D. $1 150.00

Source: January 2001

Use the following information to answer the next question.

Susan currently has $30 000 in her investment portfolio. She has $3 100 in cash equivalents, $9 600 in fixed-income investments, and $17 300 in equity investments. When Susan received a $5 000 bonus at work, her financial advisor suggested that she should reallocate her total investment portfolio as follows.

Cash Equivalents: 10%
Fixed Income: 40%
Equity Investments: 50%

Copyright Protected

CHALLENGER QUESTION   **19.9**

17. If Susan wishes to follow her financial advisor's advice, then the amount of the $5 000 bonus that she should add to her fixed-income investments so that they comprise 40% of her total investments is

   A. $1 400

   B. $2 400

   C. $3 840

   D. $4 400

Source: June 2001

Use the following information to answer the next two questions.

A 100 million dollar oil project is to begin construction some time within the next ten years. To ensure that 100 million dollars is available for starting construction in any particular year, the company's project manager examined the graphs below, which illustrate the amount of money that would need to be initially invested in 1999 at three different interest rates (*i*).

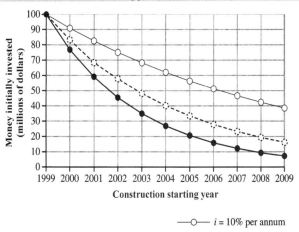

   ⊸ *i* = 10% per annum

   - -◌- -   *i* = 20% per annum

   —●—   *i* = 30% per annum

For example, if construction was to begin in the year 2004, then for an interest rate of 20% per annum (middle graph), about 40 million dollars must be invested in 1999.

18. Based on the above information, the project manager realized that for a particular

   A.   construction starting year, as the interest rate increases, the money initially invested increases

   B.   construction starting year, as the interest rate increases, the money initially invested decreases

   C.   interest rate, there is a quadratic relationship between the money initially invested and the construction starting year

   D.   interest rate, there is a linear relationship between the money initially invested and the construction starting year

Source: January 1999

19. For a construction starting year 2006, the **difference** in the amount of money that would have to be initially invested at an interest rate of 10% per annum and the amount of money that would have to be initially invested at an interest rate of 20% per annum, is approximately

   A. $23 000 000   B. $28 000 000

   C. $35 000 000   D. $51 000 000

Source: January 1999

Use the following information to answer the next question.

In order to pay for the biathlon team's Olympic expenses, a sponsor for the team deposited $1 309.32 at the beginning of every month into an annuity account that earned 12% per annum compounded monthly.

20. The number of months it will take the sponsor to save $46 000.00 is

   A.   14 months   B.   27 months

   C.   30 months   D.   35 months

Source: January 1999

Copyright Protected

Use the following information to answer the next two questions.

Hotel Macdonald, long known as one of Edmonton's most elegant hotels, was completed in 1915 by Grand Trunk Railway at a cost of $2 million. The Hotel Macdonald was designated as a Municipal Historic Resource by the City of Edmonton on January 8, 1985.

21. If $2 million was invested in 1915, at an interest rate of 3% compounded annually, the accumulated amount in 1985, to the nearest thousand, would be

   A. $2 060 000   B. $6 200 000

   C. $15 836 000   D. $21 282 000

22. What annual interest rate would be required to accumulate $32 million in 1995 from $2 million invested in 1915, if the interest is compounded semi-annually? (to the nearest tenth percent)

   A. 1.7%

   B. 3.5%

   C. 5.5%

   D. 10.9%

Use the following information to answer the next question.

Steve has $5 000 that he wishes to invest. After talking to an investment specialist at his bank, he decides to invest in a 4 year GIC (Guaranteed Investment Certificate) that pays 4.1% compounded annually. The following table shows the interest that Steve expects to earn over 4 years.

Year	Opening Balance	Interest Rate	Interest Earned	Closing Balance
1	$5 000.00	4.1%	$205.00	$5 205.00
2	$5 205.00	4.1%	$213.41	$5 418.41
3	$5 418.41	4.1%	$222.15	$5 640.56
4	$5 640.56	4.1%	$231.26	$5 871.82

23. If an additional $1 000 is invested in the GIC (at 4.1%) at the beginning of year 4, then what will Steve's closing balance be at the end of year 4?

   A. $6 912.82

   B. $6 871.82

   C. $7 168.45

   D. $6 640.56

Written Response

Use the following information to answer the next question.

The owner of a small amusement park represents the number and type of vehicles that are in his parking lot on a particular Thursday, Friday, and Saturday using the matrix below.

Type of Vehicle

Car Bus

$$\textbf{Matrix A : Day of Week} \quad \begin{matrix} T \\ F \\ S \end{matrix} \begin{bmatrix} 85 & 12 \\ 43 & 17 \\ 102 & 33 \end{bmatrix}$$

He makes a second matrix to indicate the parking cost of $8 per car and $22 per bus.

Parking Cost

$$\textbf{Matrix B : Type of Vehicle} \quad \begin{matrix} Car \\ Bus \end{matrix} \begin{bmatrix} 8 \\ 22 \end{bmatrix}$$

1. **a)** What does the value 33 in **matrix A** represent?

b) Use matrix multiplication to calculate the revenue for each of the three days. Write a statement that describes the result of this multiplication.

c) Use matrix operations to calculate an increase of 10% in the daily parking price. Show all calculations.

d) How much more money would the owner have made on Saturday as a result of a 10% price increase?

Source: January 2001

Use the following information to answer the next question.

A manufacturer has two plants: at one, acoustic guitars are made, at the other, electric guitars are made. The following table shows some information related to each plant.

	Acoustic Guitar Plant		Electric Guitar Plant	
	Model I	Model II	Model I	Model II
Material per guitar	$60	$128	$35	$93
Labour per guitar	$145	$275	$210	$290
Selling price per guitar	$500	$1 500	$510	$750
Number made and sold per month	120	75	251	109

2. **a)** Determine the total monthly revenue for each plant.

Use the following additional information to answer the next part of the question.

In addition to the cost for materials and labour, the company must cover operating costs.

The operating costs are $40 000/mo for the acoustic guitar plant and $28 000/mo for the electric guitar plant.

b) Determine the monthly profit for each plant.

c) Calculate the monthly profit
• per acoustic guitar
• per electric guitar

d) The company is experiencing financial difficulty and wishes to close one plant. Which plant should be closed? Explain your answer.

Source: June 2001

3. Complete the table below for an investment that pays 7% compounded annually.

Year	Opening Balance ($)	Interest Rate (%)	Interest Earned ($)	Closing Balance ($)
1	$5 000.00			
2				
3				
4				

Copyright Protected

UNIT TEST 3—FINANCE

Use the following information to answer the next two questions.

The following spreadsheet is a tool that can be used to follow the repayment of a loan. The user provides the specific values listed at the top of the spreadsheet. Note that the payment period is the same as the compounding period in this spreadsheet.

	A	B	C	D	E
1	Loan Repayment Schedule				
2					
3	Principal:	$ 5,000.00			
4	Interest Rate:	7%			
5	Compounding period / year:	2			
6	Payment:	$ 220.00			
7					
8	Period	Opening Balance	Interest Earned	Payment	Closing Balance
9	1	$ 5,000.00	$ 162.50	$ 220.00	$ 4,942.50
10	2	$ 4,942.50	$ 160.63	$ 220.00	$ 4,883.13
11	3	$ 4,883.13	$ 158.70	$ 220.00	$ 4,821.83
12	4	$ 4,821.83	$ 156.71	$ 220.00	$ 4,758.54
13	5	$ 4,758.54	$ 154.65	$ 220.00	$ 4,693.20

1. What formula needs to be entered in cell E9?

    A. =B9 * $B$4

    B. =B9 * B4

    C. =B9 + C9 – D9

    D. =B9 + C9 + D9

2. If the formula in cell C9 was copied down what formula would appear in cell C12?

    A. =B12 * B4

    B. =B12 * $B$4

    C. =B12 * B4 / B5

    D. =B12 * $B$4 / $B$5

Use the following information to answer the next two questions.

A couple needs to move into a larger house. If they choose to buy, they will borrow $150 000 at 5.5%, amortized over 25 years. In this case, their mortgage payments will be $750.00 per month. Their other option is to rent a house for $550.00 a month

3. How much will they pay in interest over the period of the loan if they choose to purchase the home?

    A. $75 000

    B. $15 000

    C. $12 375

    D. $8 250

4. How long could the house be rented with the total amount of money spent on buying the house?

    A. 11 years   B. 23 years

    C. 34 years   D. 36 years

Use the following information to answer the next question.

Before moving into the house you are planning to rent, you do some research to determine the amount of your regular expenses for your budget. The following chart summarizes your findings.

Rent	$875/month
Electricity	$85/month
Gas	$115/month
Water	$260/semi-annually
Insurance	$43.50/month

5. What will need to be budgeted to handle the total expenses per month to live in the house?

A. $1 182.50

B. $1 248.50

C. $1 205.17

D. $1 378.50

Use the following information to answer the next question.

The following chart represents how the value of a car changes over time.

Year	Value
0	$26 500
1	$19 760
2	$17 929
3	$16 120
4	$15 052

6. What is the average rate of depreciation?

A. 87.5%

B. 12.5%

C. 74.6%

D. 25.4%

Use the following information to answer the next question.

The following chart represents the residual value of an SUV, a minivan, a sports car and a sedan expressed as fractions percentages of the original value.

Type of Vehicle	Length of time after purchase (months)				
	12	24	36	48	60
SUV	72%	66%	62%	54%	50%
Minivan	65%	57%	52%	46%	39%
Sports car	58%	51%	43%	37%	32%
Sedan	60%	50%	42%	33%	26%

7. Using exponential regression, determine which type of vehicle maintains its value the best?

A. SUV

B. Minivan

C. Sports car

D. Sedan

Use the following information to answer the next two questions.

Jim needs a new vehicle. The vehicle he wants is valued at $28 640.00. He can afford to make a down payment of $2 500.00. After discussing his options with the people at the dealership, he has compiled the following chart outlining his expenses if he buys or leases.

Option A - Buying	Option B – Leasing with a Buyout
Amount financed - $26 140	Amount financed - $26 140
Monthly payments - $673.15	Monthly lease payments - $456.24
Period of loan - 48 months	Period of the lease - 48 months
	Final Buyout price - $12 380.05

8. How much will Jim spend in monthly payments if he chooses option A?

A. $34 811.20

B. $21 899.52

C. $32 311.20

D. $24 399.52

Not for Reproduction

9. What is the difference in overall cost between the two options if he ultimately wants to own the car?

A. $1 968.37

B. $10 411.68

C. $6 171.20

D. $4 240.48

Use the following information to answer the next two questions.

The following chart represents the progression of an investment over a period of five years.

	Time				
Investment	1 year	2 year	3 year	4 year	5 year
$5 000	$5 300	$5 538.50	$5 834.81	$5 718.11	$5 986.86

10. The average rate of return for this investment is

A. 96.6%

B. 3.4%

C. 2.8%

D. 97.2%

11. The total return on the investment after the fifth year is

A. $268.75

B. $986.86

C. $33 378.28

D. $28 378.28

Use the following information to answer the next two questions.

The following information represents the growth of several investments over the period of a year.

Investments	Amount	Rate of Return	Return
A	$1 500	4.5%	
B	$2 300	5.7%	
C	$750	−2.3%	
D	$1 250	6.1%	
E	$1 900	3.3%	
Total:			

Numerical Response

1. The total return at the end of the year was $_____.

2. For this portfolio, the total rate of return to the nearest tenth of a percent is _____%.

Copyright Protected

Use the following information to answer the next two questions.

The following information represents a partial portfolio.

Investments	Amount	Rate of Return	Return
A	$450	6%	
B	$730	4%	
C	$590	x	
D	$610	4.5%	
Total		■	

12. Given that the total value of this portfolio after one year is $2 493.15, what is the individual rate of return for investment C?

  A. 1.05%

  B. 5.0%

  C. 4.8%

  D. 19.2%

13. If the total value of this portfolio at the end of the year was $2 493.15 then what was the total return for the year?

  A. $121.54

  B. $486.16

  C. $120.50

  D. $113.15

Not for Reproduction

NOTES

CYCLIC, RECURSIVE, AND FRACTAL PATTERNS

Table of Correlations		
Topic	**Outcomes**	**Questions**
Generate and analyze cyclic, recursive, and fractal patterns.	*It is expected that students will:* 4.1 Collect sinusoidal data, graph the data using technology, and represent the data with a best-fit equation of the form; $y = a \sin(bx + c) + d$	1, 2, 3, 4, 5, 6, 7, 8
	4.2 Use best-fit sinusoidal equations and their associated graphs to make predictions by interpolation and extrapolation	9, 10, NR1
	4.3 Describe periodic events, including those represented by sinusoidal curves, using the terms amplitude, period, maximum and minimum values, and vertical and horizontal shift, and relating these terms to the parameters a, b, c, and d described in 4.1	11, NR2, NR3, 12
	4.4 Use technology to generate and graph sequences that model real-life phenomena.	13, 14, NR4, 15
	4.5 Use technology to construct a fractal pattern by repeatedly applying a procedure to a geometric figure	16, 17, 18, 19
	4.6 Use the concept of self-similarity to compare and/or predict the perimeters, areas, and volumes of fractal patterns	NR5, NR6, 20, 21, 22, NR7

Copyright Protected

Not for Reproduction

CYCLIC, RECURSIVE AND FRACTAL PATTERNS

Students will generate and analyze cyclic, recursive, and fractal patterns.

4.1   Collect sinusoidal data, graph the data using technology, and represent the data with a best-fit equation of the form:
$$y = a\sin(bx + c) + d$$

4.2   Use the best-fit sinusoidal equations, and their associated graphs, to make predictions by interpolation and extrapolation.

4.3   Describe periodic events, including those represented by sinusoidal curves, using the terms amplitude, period, maximum and minimum values, and vertical and horizontal shift, and relating these terms to the parameters a, b, c, and d described in 4.1.

SINUSOIDAL DATA

When data comes in repetitive patterns, it is called periodic. The length of the portion of the function that is regularly repeated is called the period of the function. Half the distance between the lowest and the highest value of the graph is called the amplitude. The vertical distance that the middle of the graph is from the x-axis is called the vertical displacement.

For example;

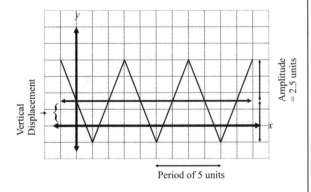

Period of 5 units

The graphs of trigonometric functions are periodic. There are two different ways in which angles can be measured, degrees and radians. For most applications, radians are used, which means that students must be careful which mode their calculators are in.

The graph of $y = 2\sin x$ is as follows:

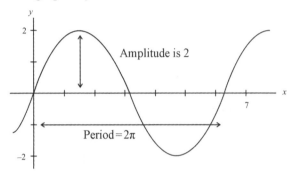

All curves with this particular shape are called *sinusoidal* because they can be modelled with the trigonometric function sine. The graph of the basic function $y = \sin x$ has an amplitude of 1 regardless of whether degrees or radians are used but the period is 2π when radians are used, as in the above diagram, and $360°$ when degrees are used. The vertical displacement, or the amount of vertical movement, is zero for this basic graph, and we can see this because the middle of the graph is along the x-axis. In addition, there has been no movement left or right. This type of movement is generally called the horizontal phase shift. The dimensions of the graph can be changed by introducing values for the variables in the following version:
$$y = a \sin(bx - c) + d.$$

The value of a is the amplitude of the graph and the value of d is the amount of vertical movement. In fact, d is the value through which the middle of the graph passes. The two values of a and d can be determined if the maximum and minimum values of the function are known.

$$d = \frac{\text{maximum value} + \text{minimum value}}{2}$$

$$a = \frac{\text{maximum value} - \text{minimum value}}{2}$$

The b value determines the period of the function. When the x-value is in radians, the period is $\frac{2\pi}{b}$, and when x is in degrees, the period is $\frac{360°}{b}$.

The value of c, in conjunction with the value of b, helps determine how much the graph has been shifted left or right. If the value of c is zero, the graph has not been horizontally shifted. More important is the direction of movement. If signs on the variables b and c are the same, the graph has been horizontally shifted left, but if the signs are different, the graph has been horizontally shifted to the right.

Most graphing calculators are able to perform a sinusoidal regression to produce an equation for the line of best fit in data in the form of $y = a \sin(bx - c) + d$, as long as the data has a repetitive pattern and there are at least 5 points given from one period. An even more accurate model can be produced from 8 or more points over two periods of the function.

If after the regression is performed and any variable is less than 10^{-4}, it is safe to assume that the value is zero and rounding should not be done until the last step of a calculation.

Example

The following is a list of average temperatures, per month, in Winnipeg, Manitoba.

Month	Temperatures (°C)
January	−18
February	−18
March	−11
April	0
May	11
June	18
July	20
August	19
September	14
October	7
November	−8
December	−17

a) What is the sinusoidal regression equation to model this data?

Solution

To answer this, students will have to become familiar with their own particular calculators.

$y = 20.61 \sin(0.52x + 2.16) + 1.21$
$a = 20.61$
$b = 0.52$
$c = 2.16$
$d = 1.21$

Graph the data and the line of best fit.

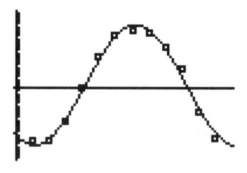

Remember to include the window settings, which can be easily obtained from the calculator:

$x : [x_{min}, x_{max}, x_{scl}] \quad x : [0, 13, 30]$
$y : [y_{min}, y_{max}, y_{scl}] \quad y : [-24.5, 26.5, 1]$

Copyright Protected

b) Identify the amplitude, the period, the vertical displacement and the direction of the horizontal phase shift.

Solution

Since $a = 20.61$, the amplitude of this function is 20.61°C, meaning that the temperatures will vary up to 20.61°C above and below the mean annual temperature, which is indicated by the d-value. The overall mean temperature is, therefore, $1.21°C = d$. To determine the period of the function, we need to use the equation:

$Period = \dfrac{2\pi}{b}$. This will work because sinusoidal models are typically in radians.

The period is $\dfrac{2\pi}{0.52}$ or 12, which is appropriate because the x-values are the months of the year. We can assume that the pattern will repeat every twelve months. Since both the values of b and c are positive, the graph has been horizontally phase-shifted to the left.

For the previous graph, the minimum value is $-19.40°C$ and the maximum value is 21.81°C.

To find d, we can use the formula:

$$d = \dfrac{max + min}{2}$$

$$d = \dfrac{21.81 + (-19.40)}{2} = 1.21$$

The value of a can be found using:

$$a = \dfrac{max - min}{2}$$

$$a = \dfrac{21.81 - (-19.40)}{2} = 20.61$$

In addition to this, we can determine the value of b, if we can compare two corresponding and consecutive points on the graph. For instance, we can compare the two consecutive low points on the graph.

They occur when $x = 1.14$ and $x = 13.27$. The period of the function is the difference between these values, therefore $P = 13.27 - 1.14 = 12.13$. To find the value of b, we simply rearrange the period formula to isolate this variable to get $b = \dfrac{2\pi}{Period}$, thus

$$b = \dfrac{2\pi}{12.13} = 0.52.$$

Once the sinusoidal function has been found, it can be used to make predictions about the data it is modelling. If the y-coordinate is known, the x-coordinate can be found by graphing the function along with the horizontal line implied by the value of y as in the following question.

c) How long is the growing season if the temperature must be above 5°C?

Solution

To determine these values, we can graph the line $y = 5$, and find the x-coordinates of the points of intersection between this line and the sinusoidal function.

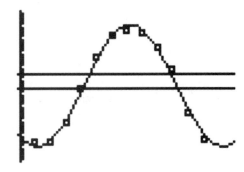

The x-coordinates are 4.53 and 9.88. This would imply a time from the middle of April to the end of September.

d) What would happen to the graph and the equation of the sinusoidal function if the average temperature of every month increased by 2°C?

Solution

Increasing the average temperature would shift the graph vertically upward 2 units. As a result, the value of *d* would increase by 2, but the shape of the graph will not change and neither will any of the other variables.

If an *x*-coordinate is known, and the corresponding *y*-coordinate is being looked for, the *x*-value can be entered into the sinusoidal function which can then be evaluated.

e) What is the average temperature on July 15?

Since July has 31 days, the 15th is approximately the middle of the 7th month. To determine the temperature, we evaluate the sinusoidal function where $x - 7.5$.

Solution

$y = 20.61\sin(0.52(7.5) + 2.16) + 1.21$
$y = -3.35°C$

Students may also be asked to interpret information given in a graph to produce the sinusoidal function without performing a regression on the calculator.

Example

A nail is in a wheel that has a diameter of 50 cm. The height of the nail has been graphed as a function of time.

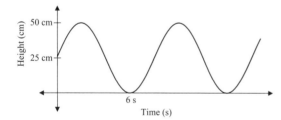

Determine the equation of the sinusoidal function given that there has been no horizontal shift left or right, i.e., the value of $c = 0$.

Solution

To determine the value of *a* and *d*, we can use the equations given previously.

$$a = \frac{\text{maximum value} - \text{minimum value}}{2}$$

$$a = \frac{50 - 0}{2} = 25$$

$$d = \frac{\text{maximum value} + \text{minimum value}}{2}$$

$$d = \frac{50 + 0}{2} = 25$$

Therefore, the amplitude is 25 and the mean value of the graph is 25.

We can determine the *b*-value from the period. Given that the graph touches the *x*-axis at 6 seconds and that this only represents three-quarters of a full period, we can determine the length of the entire period by dividing 6 by three-quarters.

$$\text{Period} = 6 \div \frac{3}{4} = 6 \times \frac{4}{3} = 8$$

A full period is eight seconds. To determine the value of *b* from the period, we use the formula:

$$\text{Period} = \frac{2\pi}{b}$$

Therefore, $b = \dfrac{2\pi}{\text{Period}} = \dfrac{2\pi}{8} = \dfrac{\pi}{4}$

Putting this together, we get the equation:

$$y = 25\sin\left(\frac{\pi}{4}x\right) + 25$$

Students may also be asked to interpret the information given to them when they are given the equation of a sinusoidal function.

Copyright Protected

Example

The given equation of a sinusoidal function is

$$y = 5\sin\left(\frac{\pi}{6}x + 3\right) - 2.$$

a) What is the amplitude, the average value of the function, the period, and the direction of horizontal shift? Since $a = 5$, the amplitude of the graph is 5 units. The average value of the graph is -2, because $d = -2$.

The period of the function is determined by calculating

$$\frac{2\pi}{b} = \frac{2\pi}{\frac{\pi}{6}} = 2\not{\pi} \times \frac{6}{\not{\pi}} = 12;$$

therefore the period is 12 units.

The graph has been horizontally shifted to the left because the signs on the variables b and c are the same, both positive.

b) What are the maximum and minimum values of the function?

Since d represents the middle of the function and a is the amplitude, the maximum value can be determined by adding a to d, and the minimum can be determined by subtracting a from d.

Maximum value $= d + a = -2 + 5 = 3$
Minimum value $= d - a = -2 - 5 = -7$

Related Questions: 1, 2, 3, 4, 5, 6, 7, 8, 9, 10, NR 1, 11, NR2, NR3, 12

4.4   *Use technology to generate and graph sequences that model real-life phenomena.*

SEQUENCES OF DATA

There are many instances in which it is helpful to be able to identify the most appropriate regression equation for a sequence of data. Being able to identify the equation of the best-fit line enables the user to more completely understand the nature of the relationship being analyzed and thus to be able to make accurate predictions.

In the Applied Mathematics 30 course, the types of relationships that are analyzed are linear, quadratic, exponential, and sinusoidal. Most graphing calculators have the ability to find regression equations from an entered sequence of data and also to calculate the correlation coefficient of the regression so that the user can decide which regression is the most appropriate. Generally, the closer the value of the correlation coefficient is to ± 1, the better the equation is at modelling the entered data.

There are times though, when a thorough understanding of the scenario being modelled is necessary to make a decision regarding the appropriate regression equation. When a sequence of data increases or decreases by a consistent amount for every evenly spaced term, the sequence is linear.

When a sequence tends to either increase or decrease to a particular value and then change direction, this indicates a quadratic sequence. On the other hand, if the sequence increases or decreases by an amount that increases or decreases for every term, the sequence is exponential. Finally, a sinusoidal sequence is one in which the values repeatedly increase and decrease through a fixed range.

Example

Identify the following sequence and the next term.

150, 133, 116, 99, 82, …

Copyright Protected

Solution

Before entering this data into a calculator, notice that the sequence decreases by a constant amount with each term, which implies that this data requires a linear regression.

A linear regression produces the equation, $y = -17x + 167$, with a regression coefficient of $r = -1$. This indicates that the regression equation fits the data perfectly and that there is a downward trend in the data. Notice that to perform the regression, we had to create a corresponding list of x-coordinates that indicate which term each value is in the sequence.

To find the sixth term in the sequence, we simply evaluate the equation where $x = 6$ and $y = -17(6) + 167 = 65$.

The sixth term is 65.

Example

The value of a car decreases as outlined in the chart below. What is the most appropriate regression model for the data?

Time since Purchase (years)	Value of the Vehicle ($)
2	14 000
3	10 000
5	5 800
6	4 200
7	2 500

Solution

This is an example of a problem where some familiarity with the nature of the scenario is important. After performing the 4 different regressions, it seems that the quadratic regression is the most accurate because the correlation coefficient of regression is closest to one.

This type of a regression implies that the trend in the data will eventually change from decreasing to increasing once it has reached a minimum value.

The reality of the situation is that this downward trend will continue, and as such the data in the chart is more accurately modelled with an exponential function in the form $y = ab^x$. The equation is $y = 27\,578.31(0.720\,7)^x$, where y is the value of the vehicle and x is the number of years that have passed since purchase.

Once we have the regression equation, we can make predictions with the data. For example, we can ask how long it will take for the vehicle to be worth $8 000. Because the data given is a value of the vehicle, it is a y-coordinate. To solve this graphically, we would graph the equation $y = 8\,000$ with our regression equation and determine the x-coordinate for the point of intersection. Based on the above information, we may enter the following equations into the calculator, with the appropriate window settings derived from the chart.

$y_1 = 27\,578.31(0.720\,7)x$
$y_2 = 8\,000$

x: [0, 8, 1]
y: [0, 16 000, 2 000]

The x-coordinate of intersection is 3.78. This means that the vehicle will be worth $8 000 in 3.78, or in just under 4 years. With this equation, we can also ask what the vehicle will be worth in 9 years. Since this is a time value, it represents an x-coordinate. To find the corresponding value, we can either enter the value in for the x-coordinate to evaluate the equation or we can use the graph of the exponential function and either the Trace feature on the calculator or the Calc menu. Students will need to familiarize themselves with these features on their individual calculators.

$y = 27\,578.13(0.720\,7)^9 = 1\,446.63$

In 9 years, the value of the vehicle will be $1 446.63.

Related Questions: 13, 14, NR4, 15

4.5   use technology to construct a fractal pattern by repeatedly applying a procedure to a geometric figure.

FRACTAL SHAPES

A *fractal* is a self-similar geometric shape created by the repeated application of a recursive calculation or procedure. In other words, a fractal is shape designed such that if someone took a piece of it and zoomed in on it, the piece would resemble the whole.
An *iteration* is the repeated calculation or procedure that is used to create the fractal. In addition, a fractal becomes increasingly more complicated with every iteration.

A) The following patterns are **not** fractal.

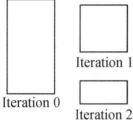

B)

The pattern in *A* is not a fractal because it is not self-similar, it is merely a repetitive alteration of the size of the original, and the shape does not get more complicated with every new iteration.
The pattern in *B* is not a fractal because the pattern is not repetitive. The first iteration places a new circle on either side of the original, but the second iteration does not repeat this same pattern.

Example

The following pattern represents the first 2 iterations of a fractal.

Iteration 0

Iteration 1

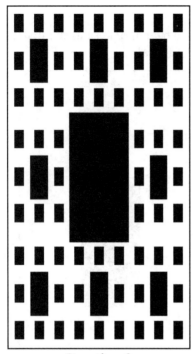

Iteration 2

The above pattern is a fractal, because a smaller portion of the shape is similar to the whole pattern, and the shape does get more complicated with every iteration.

The recursive pattern that is followed is that for every rectangle in the next step, there will be eight rectangles surrounding it that are each $\frac{1}{9}$ the size of the middle rectangle.

From here, we may be asked questions about the pattern that has been established.

For example, how many new rectangles would be introduced in the next iteration? The first iteration introduced 8 new rectangles to the pattern.

For each of these, 8 new rectangles are introduced in the next iteration, and this continues for every iteration. The pattern established is a power, and the iteration number is the exponent.

$N = 8^i$, where N is the number of new rectangles and i is the iteration number. Therefore, for the 3rd iteration, the equation is:

$N = 8^i$
$N = 8^3 = 512$

Therefore, the number of new rectangles would be 512.

This pattern could also have been found by listing the number of new rectangles next to each iteration number and performing an exponential regression. If we knew that the original rectangle had an area of $81u^2$, and each new rectangle is $\frac{1}{9}$ the size of the rectangle in the middle, then what is the area of each new rectangle in the 4th iteration?

Since the original rectangle had an area of $81u^2$, and in each iteration the length of a side is $\frac{1}{3}$ the previous length, we can assume an exponential relationship between the areas of the rectangles after any number of iterations. This can be done by building a chart to keep track of the size of each new rectangle for each iteration and perform an exponential regression.

Iteration	Length of a side (unit)	Area (unit^2)
0	9	81
1	3	9
2	1	1

Because we are looking for the area of each new rectangle, we will perform the regression on the first and third columns.

We get that $y = 81(0.\overline{11})^x$, where y is the area and x is the iteration number. To find the area of the new rectangles after the 4th iteration, we simply substitute 4 in for x and evaluate.

$y = 81(0.\overline{11})^4$
$y = 0.012u^2 = \frac{1}{81}u^2$

Related Questions: 16, 17, 18, 19

Not for Reproduction

4.6 *Use the concept of self-similarity to compare and/or predict the perimeters, areas, and volumes of fractal patterns.*

FRACTAL PERIMETERS, AREAS, AND VOLUMES

The perimeter, area, and in some cases, the volume of fractal shapes change according to regular patterns from iteration to iteration. In most cases, if the total perimeter, area and/or volume are increasing, they will not follow an exponential pattern and the data must be charted to find the appropriate pattern. The amounts added to the perimeter, area and/or volume at each iteration may follow an exponential pattern.

Example

In the following pattern, determine the total perimeter after the 4th iteration.

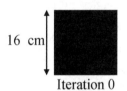

16 cm

Iteration 0

Iteration 1

Iteration 2

Solution

The pattern is that in the middle of each side of the square a new square is placed, which has a side length that is half the length of the previous square. Notice that each new square only adds the length of two sides to the overall perimeter. The outer side in each square is a piece of the perimeter of the previous square. In addition, after the first iteration, the number of new squares increases by multiples of 3 and the lengths of the sides decrease by half. This allows us to fill in the chart with the next two iterations.

Iteration	Number of new squares	Side length	Total added perimeter	Total perimeter
0	0	16	64	64
1	4	$16 \div 2$ $= 8$	$4 \times 2 \times 8$ $= 64$	$64 + 64$ $= 128$
2	$4 \times 3 = 12$	$8 \div 2 = 4$	$12 \times 2 \times 4$ $= 96$	$128 + 96$ $= 224$
3	$12 \times 3 = 36$	$4 \div 2 = 2$	$36 \times 2 \times 2$ $= 144$	$224 + 144$ $= 368$
4	$36 \times 3 = 108$	$2 \div 2 = 1$	108×2 $\times 1 = 216$	$368 + 316$ $= 584$

The 2nd, 3rd and 4th columns form exponential sequences, but the total perimeter does not, and the final result of the 4th iteration is that the total perimeter is 584 cm.

We can also set up a chart to record how the area of the shape increases with each iteration.

Iteration	Number of new squares	Side length	Total added area	Total area
0	0	16	256	256
1	4	$16 \div 2$ $= 8$	$8^2 = 64$	$256 + 4$ $\times 64 = 512$
2	$4 \times 3 = 12$	$8 \div 2 = 4$	$4^2 = 16$	$512 + 12$ $\times 16 = 704$
3	$12 \times 3 = 36$	$4 \div 2 = 2$	$2^2 = 4$	$704 + 36$ $\times 4 = 848$
4	$36 \times 3 = 108$	$2 \div 2 = 1$	$1^2 = 1$	$848 + 108$ $\times 1 = 956$

Copyright Protected

Similar to the previous chart columns, iterations 2, 3, and 4 are all exponential sequences, but the total area does not follow an exponential pattern. The total area after the 4th iteration is 956 cm^2.

There can also be fractal patterns where the area decreases but the perimeter increases.

Example

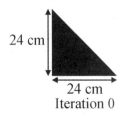

24 cm

24 cm
Iteration 0

Iteration 1

Iteration 2

Iteration 3

Each iteration in the above fractal involves removing the middle triangle from a shaded triangle. The perpendicular sides of the removed triangle are half of the length of the triangle in the previous iteration.

While filling in the following chart to find the total perimeter and total area in the 4th iteration, remember that to find the perimeter of an isosceles right triangle we multiply the length of a leg by $2\sqrt{2}$.

Iteration	Number of triangles	Side length (cm)	Total perimeter (cm)	Total area (cm^2)
0	1	24	$1\times24\times2\sqrt{2}$ ≈67.9	$\frac{1}{2}(24^2)$ $=288$
1	3	12	$3\times12\times2\sqrt{2}$ ≈101.8	$\frac{1}{2}(12^2)$ $=72$
2	9	6	$9\times6\times2\sqrt{2}$ ≈152.7	$\frac{1}{2}(6^2)=18$
3	27	3	$27\times3\times2\sqrt{2}$ ≈229.1	$\frac{1}{2}(3^2)=4.5$
4	81	1.5	$81\times1.5\times2\sqrt{2}$ ≈343.7	$\frac{1}{2}(1.5^2)$ $=1.125$

In the above situation, notice that when the area is decreasing, rows 2 through 4 all follow exponential sequences.

We may perform exponential regressions to each of these columns to get the following equations.

Number of Triangles = 3^x
Side Length = $24(0.5)^x$
Total Perimeter = $67.9(1.5)^x$
Total Area = $288(0.25)^x$

With these equations we can make predictions about the shape after ten iterations. It will have $3^{10} = 59\,049$ triangles, each side will be $24(0.5)^{10} = 0.02$ cm, the total perimeter will be $67.9(1.5)^{10} = 3\,915.5$ cm, and the total area will be $288(0.25)^{10} = 0.000\,3$ cm^2.

The interesting part of this fractal is that the perimeter increases seemingly without bound, while at the same time the area seems to be approaching zero.

Related Questions: NR5, NR6, 20, 21, 22, NR7

Use the following information to answer the next question.

The height, *h*, in metres, of a point on a ferris wheel at time, *t*, in seconds, can be represented by a sinusoidal function in the form $h = a\sin(bt + c) + d$, as shown below.

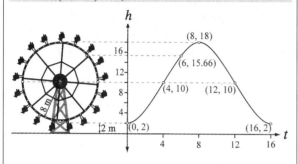

CHALLENGER QUESTION 32.3

1. The function that **best** describes the height of the point on the ferris wheel is

    A. $h = 8\sin(0.39t + 1.57) + 10$

    B. $h = 8\sin(0.39t - 1.57) + 10$

    C. $h = 8\sin(t + 4.02) + 10$

    D. $h = 8\sin(t - 4.02) + 10$

    Source: January 2001

Use the following information to answer the next question.

The path of a particular vehicle is shown below.

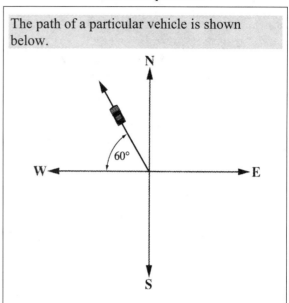

CHALLENGER QUESTION 52.5

2. The direction in which the vehicle is travelling is

    A. N30°W

    B. N60°W

    C. on a bearing of 60°

    D. on a bearing of 300°

    Source: January 2001

Use the following information to answer the next question.

The sinusoidal function that represents electrical current in Australia and the sinusoidal function that represents electrical current in Canada are graphed below.

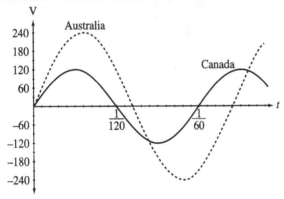

3. The sinusoidal function representing electrical current in Australia differs from the sinusoidal function representing electrical current in Canada in

A. amplitude and period

B. period and horizontal shift

C. amplitude and vertical shift

D. horizontal shift and vertical shift

Source: June 2001

Use the following information to answer the next two questions.

One of the displays at a Space and Science Centre portrays the relative positions of Jupiter's moons Europa, Ganymede, Callisto, and Io, with respect to telescopic observations of Jupiter over a period of one month.

The graphs are similar in appearance to the graph of a sine function, and each moon's path is graphed on the same scale, as shown below.

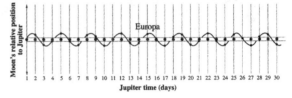

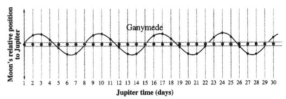

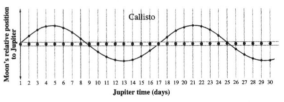

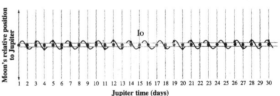

Graphs reproduced by permission
© 1996 Astronomy Magazine (November 1996).

4. The graph with the greatest amplitude is the one representing the moon

A. Io

B. Europa

C. Callisto

D. Ganymede

Source: January 1999

5. The graph with the shortest period is the one representing the moon

A. Io

B. Europa

C. Callisto

D. Ganymede

Source: January 1999

Use the following information to answer the next question.

A technologist at a plant monitors the voltage output pattern of a generator, as illustrated below.

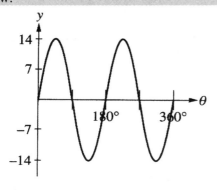

CHALLENGER QUESTION   **34.4**

6. An equation that could be used to produce the graph above is

A. $y = \sin 2\theta$

B. $y = \sin 14\theta$

C. $y = 14\sin\theta$

D. $y = 14\sin 2\theta$

Source: June 1999

Use the following information to answer the next question.

When the rotating conductor in a plant generator is rotated past two magnetic poles, the height, *h*, of a point on the tip of the rotating conductor can be modeled with respect to the rotation angle θ. The rotation produces a sine wave, as shown below.

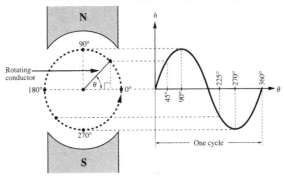

7. If a rotating conductor with a larger radius is used, then the new sine wave's

A. period will increase

B. period will decrease

C. amplitude will increase

D. amplitude will decrease

Source: June 2000

Use the following information to answer the next question.

A water pump's rotating gear has a radius of 10 cm. The displacement of this water pump's rotating gear is graphed as a sine wave, as shown below. The graph is related to the function $y = a\sin bx$.

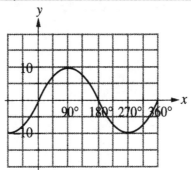

8. The amplitude of the graph is

   A. 360

   B. 90

   C. 20

   D. 10

Source: June 2000

Use the following information to answer the next question.

The height of a chair on a ferris wheel follows the equation

$$y = 5.7\sin(0.31x) + 7.9$$

where y is the height (in metres) and x is the time (in seconds).

9. A student wants to determine when the chair will be at a height of 15 m. The student could graph the given sine function and look for the

   A. x-intercepts

   B. y-intercepts

   C. points where $x = 15$

   D. points where $y = 15$

Source: January 2001

Use the following information to answer the next question.

The scatter plot below compares the incidence of cavities per 100 children and the fluoride content of water in parts per million (ppm) in a particular area.

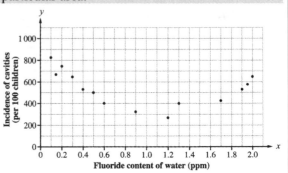

CHALLENGER QUESTION 40.4

10. Which of the following regression equations is most appropriate for the given data?

   A. Linear

   B. Quadratic

   C. Sinusoidal

   D. Exponential

Source: January 2001

Copyright Protected

*Use the following information to answer
the next question.*

In the function
$A = 23.553\sin(0.017D - 1.364) - 0.003$,
A is the angle of declination of the sun on
different days of the year, D, and D is the
number of the day in the year.

Numerical Response

1. What is the angle of declination on
day 186 (July 4) to the nearest tenth of a
degree?

*Use the following information to answer
the next question.*

The height, h, in metres, of a point on a ferris
wheel at time, t, in seconds, can be represented
by a sinusoidal function in the form
$h = a\sin(bt + c) + d$, as shown in the diagram
below.

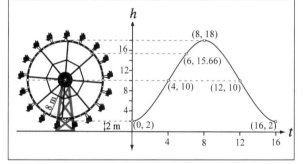

11. The amplitude of this sinusoidal function
is

A. 10 m

B. 8 m

C. 4.02 m

D. 1.57 m

Source: January 2001

*Use the following information to answer
the next question.*

The partial graph of the function
$f(\theta) = a\sin(\theta + c) + d$ is shown below.

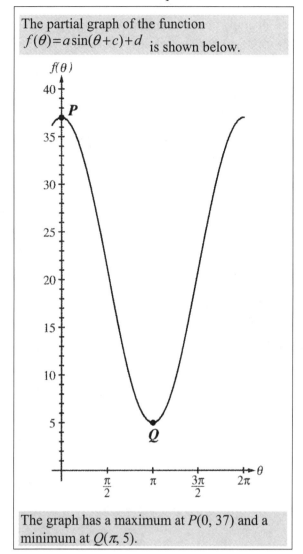

The graph has a maximum at $P(0, 37)$ and a
minimum at $Q(\pi, 5)$.

Numerical Response

2. Based on the previous graph, the value of d,
correct to the nearest whole number, is

_____ .

Source: June 1999

Copyright Protected

Use the following information to answer the next question.

A partial graph of $y = \cos bx$, $b \in N$, is shown below.

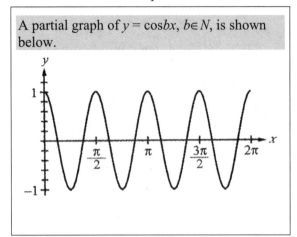

CHALLENGER QUESTION   **54.3**

Numerical Response

3. The value of b, correct to the nearest whole number, is _____.

Source: January 2000

Use the following information to answer the next question.

Four sound waves are modeled by the following graphs of trigonometric functions. The portion of each graph on the domain $0° \leq x \leq 360°$ is shown below.

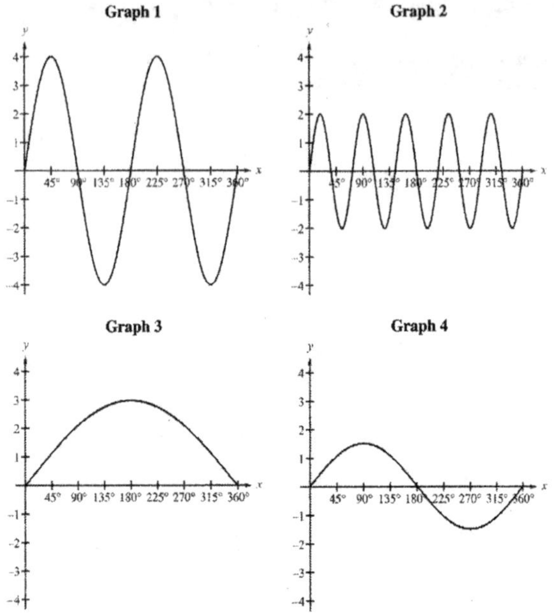

Graph 1   **Graph 2**

Graph 3   **Graph 4**

12. The louder a sound is, the greater the amplitude of its sound wave. Therefore, the graph above that corresponds to the loudest sound is

A. graph 1

B. graph 2

C. graph 3

D. graph 4

Source: June 2000

Use the following information to answer the next question.

A Set of Data

(0, 15)	(9, 18)	(25, 20)	(42, 19)
(62, 14)	(89, 10)	(104, 12)	(118, 15)

CHALLENGER QUESTION	47.6

13. This data could most appropriately be modeled by a

   A. linear regression

   B. quadratic regression

   C. sinusoidal regression

   D. exponential regression

   Source: June 2001

Use the following information to answer the next question.

The median price for houses in Calgary for each two-year period from 1988 to 1998 is given below.

Number of Years After 1988	Price ($)
0	127 526
2	127 621
4	132 868
6	134 643
8	157 353
10	176 316

These figures may be represented by an equation of the form $y = ax^2 + bx + c$.

CHALLENGER QUESTION	35.8

Numerical Response

4. The value of a in the previous equation, rounded to the nearest whole number, is

   _____.

   Source: June 2001

Use the following information to answer the next question.

The population in a particular high school was tracked over time.

School Year	Population
0	621
1	852
2	_____
3	1 250
4	1 324
5	1 348

A student used a quadratic regression equation to represent this data.

CHALLENGER QUESTION	20.2

14. The student was able to estimate that the population of the school in year 2 was

   A. 941

   B. 1 051

   C. 1 083

   D. 1 085

   Source: June 2001

Use the following information to answer the next question.

A marathon runner is in the final preparation for a race. On each successive day, she increases her water intake by 200 mL and trains $\frac{9}{10}$ of the time she did the previous day, as shown below.

Day	Water Intake (mL)	Training Time (h)
1	600	2
2	800	1.8
3	1 000	1.62
4	1 200	1.458

15. On the day she takes in 2 000 mL of water, her training time, correct to the nearest hundredth of an hour, will be

   A. 1.16 h

   B. 1.06 h

   C. 0.96 h

   D. 0.86 h

Source: January 1999

Use the following information to answer the next question.

A set of children's nesting blocks is made of plastic cubes with one open side. Each side of the largest cube is 15 cm. The sides of each subsequent cube are $\frac{2}{3}$ the size of the previous cube's sides.

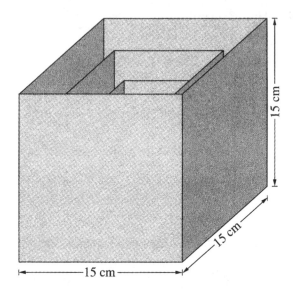

CHALLENGER QUESTION   **35.8**

16. The surface area of the smallest cube in the diagram above, correct to the nearest tenth, is

   A. 6.7 cm^2

   B. 44.4 cm^2

   C. 222.2 cm^2

   D. 1 500.0 cm^2

Source: June 2001

Copyright Protected

*Use the following diagram to answer
the next two questions.*

The following diagrams show the original
square and the first two iterations of a fractal
pattern. Each side of the square in iteration 0 is
bisected to form four new squares in iteration 1.
Iteration 2 is formed by bisecting the sides of
each small square in iteration 1, which results in
16 new smaller squares.

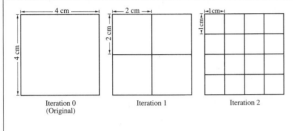

Iteration 0 (Original) Iteration 1 Iteration 2

17. If this pattern continues, the number of
smallest-sized squares in iteration 5 will
be

A. 1 024 **B.** 256

C. 64 **D.** 28

Source: June 2001

CHALLENGER QUESTION   **41.3**

18. The lengths of the sides of each new
square formed is halved after each
iteration, as shown in the diagram above.
The area of each new square formed in
iteration 4 is

A. $\dfrac{1}{2}$ cm^2

B. $\dfrac{1}{4}$ cm^2

C. $\dfrac{1}{8}$ cm^2

D. $\dfrac{1}{16}$ cm^2

Source: June 2001

---

*Use the following diagram to answer
the next question.*

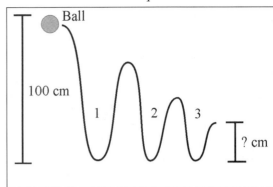

19. A golf ball was found to bounce to
60% of the height it was originally
dropped from. On each
successive bounce, it bounced to
60% of the previous bounce.
How high was the third bounce, if
the golf ball was originally
dropped from a height of 100 cm?

A. 36 cm

B. 60 cm

C. 18.6 cm

D. 21.6 cm

Use the following information to answer the next question.

A student has a 2 cm by 2 cm square piece of paper.
The student draws a diagonal of this square and shades the region of the square above this diagonal.
In the unshaded region, the student then draws a second square by using the midpoint of the diagonal as one corner.
This process produces iteration 1 shown below. The process is then continued with the smaller square, as shown in iteration 2.

Original   Iteration **1**   Iteration **2**

2 cm

2 cm

CHALLENGER QUESTION   **42.6**

Numerical Response

5. The total area of the shaded regions shown in the diagram for iteration 2, correct to the nearest tenth, is _____ cm^2.

Source: January 2001

Use the following information to answer the next two questions.

The following diagrams show the original triangle and the first two iterations in the construction of a Koch snowflake.
The original triangle is an equilateral triangle with 27 cm sides.

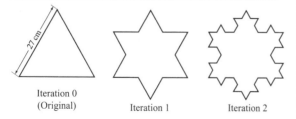

Iteration 0
(Original)   Iteration 1   Iteration 2

The following chart shows the relationship between the added perimeter and the total perimeter for the Koch snowflake.

Iteration	Added Perimeter (cm)	Total Perimeter (cm)
0	0	81
1	27	108
2	36	144
3	48	

Numerical Response

6. The total perimeter of iteration 3, to the nearest centimetre, will be _____ cm.

Source: January 2001

Use the following additional information to answer the next question.

Exponential regression can be used to relate iteration number to **total** perimeter and to determine the perimeter of a particular iteration of this Koch snowflake.

CHALLENGER QUESTION   **50.9**

20. Based on an exponential regression of the perimeters of iterations 0, 1, and 2, the perimeter, to the nearest centimetre, of iteration 10 will be

A. 1 918 cm   B. 1 081 cm

C. 1 438 cm   D. 123 cm

Source: January 2001

Use the following information to answer the next question.

The Yearbook Club decides to cut costs for the yearbook by reducing the picture size of personal photos. The original pictures have dimensions of 3.5 cm × 4.0 cm.

21. If each dimension is reduced by 15%, then the area of the reduced copy will be

A. 10.1 cm^2 B. 11.1 cm^2

C. 14.0 cm^2 D. 16.1 cm^2

Use the following diagram to answer the next question.

1   2   3   4

Numerical Response

7. The clocks above represent a sequence. How many minutes past noon, correct to the nearest whole number, would the next clock in the sequence show?

Answer: _____ Minutes.

Written Response

Use the following information to answer the next question.

The diameter of wire, in millimetres, is described by a gauge number.
The following table relates selected gauge numbers and the corresponding wire diameter.

Gauge Number	Diameter of Wire (mm)
0	8.25
5	4.62
10	2.59
15	1.45
20	0.81

1. a) Input the data above into two of your calculator lists, and graph the data with the window settings

x: [0, 30, 5]
y: [0, 9, 1]

Plot the information from your graphing calculator on the coordinate plane below.

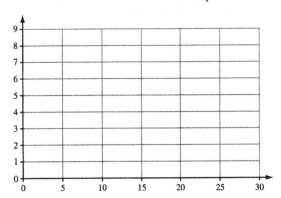

b) Perform an exponential regression on the data and sketch this regression model on the coordinate plane above.

State the exponential regression equation in the form. Round the values of a and b to the nearest hundredth.

Copyright Protected

c) What do the variables x and y represent in the context of this question?

d) Determine the diameter of a 40-gauge wire, to the nearest hundredth of a millimetre. Use the following information to answer the next part of the question.

The forces of drag on a car are measured by how much the speed drops during a 10 second interval of coasting without power.
The results of some time trials are shown below.

Speed (km/h)	Drag Force (N)
20	290
30	300
40	340
50	380
60	430

e) Use your graphing calculator to perform an exponential regression on this data. Compare the graph of this relationship with the graph relating wire gauge and diameter.

Source: January 2001

Use the following information to answer the next question.

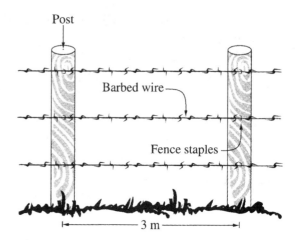

The owner of a small plot of land needs to calculate the cost of materials for completely enclosing her property with a barbed-wire fence. The plot of land measures 420 m × 420 m. The posts are pounded into the ground 3 m apart.

The owner creates the table shown below to help her determine the number of posts she will require, given the length of one side of the plot.

Side Length	Total Number of Posts
3 m	4
6 m	8
9 m	12
12 m	16
15 m	
18 m	

2. **a)** Complete the chart above.

b) Calculate the total number of posts required to completely enclose the 420 m × 420 m plot of land. Support your answer mathematically.

Not for Reproduction

The owner will require 3 rows of barbed wire for the fence. The owner needs to purchase an extra 22 m of barbed wire to build gates and braces. Barbed wire is sold in complete rolls of 440 m for $40 per roll.

Posts will cost $10.20 each. In addition to the number of posts required in part *b*, the owner needs 11 more posts for braces and gates.

The paint costs $19.50 per 4 L can. Each 4 L can of paint will cover 48 m^2. The surface area that will be painted on each post is 0.577 m^2.

a) Calculate the total cost of materials required for this project by completing the table below. Show your work.

Material Costs			
Item	**Quantity**	**Unit Cost**	**Total Cost**
Posts		$10.20	
Barbed Wire			
Fence Staples	1 box	$50.00	$50.00
Paint (4 L cans)			
		Subtotal	
		GST (6%)	
		Total Cost	

Source: June 2001

A lighting store specializes in custom-made chandeliers built in tiers. Each tier consists of a number of rectangular glass pieces arranged in a circular formation.

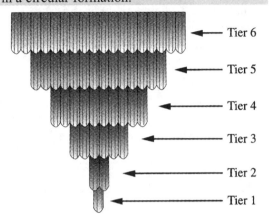

Tier 6
Tier 5
Tier 4
Tier 3
Tier 2
Tier 1

Note: The chandelier shown is not the exact one described in this written response question.

3. The numbers of pieces of glass in each successive tier of a chandelier form a geometric sequence. Every chandelier uses 1 glass piece for tier 1.
In a chandelier with 5 or more tiers, there are 81 glass pieces in tier 5.

- Complete the chart below by indicating the number of glass pieces required for tiers 2, 3, and 4, and by indicating the total number of glass pieces required for a chandelier consisting of 2, 3, 4, or 5 tiers.

Tier Number (n)	Number of glass pieces in n^{th} tier	Total number of glass pieces in a chandelier with n tiers
1	1	1
2		
3		
4		
5	81	

- The cost for each glass piece is $1.75. Determine the cost of the glass pieces required for a 7-tiered chandelier.

- The manufacturer of the glass pieces has determined that the width of each piece is normally distributed about a mean of 4.00 cm with a standard deviation of 0.05 cm. Any piece with a width less than 3.90 cm or more than 4.10 cm cannot be used for a chandelier. If 100 000 glass pieces are selected at random for chandeliers, how many pieces from this initial selection will not meet the size requirement?

Source: January 1998

Copyright Protected

UNIT TEST 4—CYCLIC, RECURSIVE AND FRACTAL PATTERNS

1. Which of the following represents a fractal pattern?

Use the following information to answer the next question.

The following data represents the length of a spring after it has been stretched and released.

Time (s)	Length (cm)
0	30.0
1	25.9
2	22.6
3	20.5
4	20.1
5	21.3
6	24.1
7	27.9
8	32.1
9	35.9
10	38.7
11	39.9
12	39.5
13	37.4
14	34.1
15	30.0

Numerical Response

1. Using technology to perform a sinusoidal regression determine the best-fit equation in the form $y = a\sin(bx + c) + d$. The value of b in this equation, rounded to the nearest hundredth is _____.

Copyright Protected

Use the following information to answer the next two questions.

The following data represents the change in the pitch of a siren over time.

Time (s)	Frequency (hertz)
0	640.0
2	706.6
4	681.1
6	598.9
8	573.4
10	640.0
12	706.6
14	681.1
16	598.8
18	573.4
20	640.0

2. Using the sinusoidal regression equation determine the frequency of the siren at 7 seconds.

   A. 586.2 Hz

   B. 573.4 Hz

   C. 598.9 Hz

   D. 579.8 Hz

3. What is the first time after 20 seconds has passed when the frequency of the siren reaches 639.96 Hz?

   A. 22.5 s   B. 27.5 s

   C. 25 s   D. 30 s

Use the following information to answer the next two questions.

The following graph represents the height of a Ferris wheel over time.

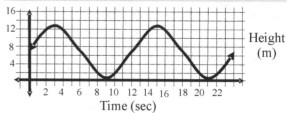

Time (sec)

4. The equation of the sinusoidal graph above can be written in the form
   $y = a\sin(bx + c) + d$ where the values of a and b respectively are

   A. 12, 0.52   B. 14, 12

   C. 6, 12   D. 6, 0.52

5. What is the vertical displacement of the graph?

   A. 2 m   B. 6 m

   C. 8 m   D. 14 m

Use the following information to answer the next two questions.

A pressure wave is modeled using a sinusoidal function written as $y = 3\sin\left(\dfrac{\pi}{3}x - 2\right) + 1$.

6. What are the maximum and minimum values respectively for the graph of this function?

   A. 1, −5   B. 3, −2

   C. 1, −1   D. 4, −2

7. What is the period of this function, and in which direction has it been shifted horizontally?

   A. 3, left   B. 6, left

   C. 3, right   D. 6, right

Use the following information to answer the next question.

Iteration 0   Iteration 1   Iteration 2

8. How many new squares will be introduced in the 5th iteration?

   A. 16   B. 32

   C. 64   D. 128

Use the following information to answer the next question.

The following data represents the average time of sunrise for each month.

Month	Time of Sunrise
January	8:42
February	7:52
March	6:48
April	6:34
May	5:33
June	5:04
July	5:23
August	6:13
September	7:07
October	8:01
November	8:00
December	8:44

9. Which of the following is the best regression for this data?

   A. Linear

   B. Quadratic

   C. Sinusoidal

   D. Exponential

Use the following information to answer the next question.

The rate of decay of a radioactive material is measured and recorded in the following chart.

Time (minutes)	Amount (grams)
0	2 000.00
1	250.00
2	—
3	3.91
4	0.49
5	0.06
6	0.01

Researchers determined that the best model of this data would be exponential.

Numerical Response

2. Using an exponential regression equation, it was found that the amount of radioactive material that was left after 2 minutes was _____ g.

Copyright Protected

Use the following information to answer the next question.

Right now the owner of a 300-seat theatre sells tickets for $20 a piece. He believes that for every dollar he increases the price of a ticket, he will lose 10 people. He has charted his research as follows:

Increase in Price ($)	Revenue ($)
0	6 000
1	6 090
2	6 160
3	6 210
4	6 240
5	6 250
6	6 240

10. Use the quadratic regression equation to determine how much the owner is charging per ticket if his revenue is $5 760.

A. 31   B. 32

C. 11   D. 12

Use the following information to answer the next question.

The following fractal is formed by successively removing the second and third fifths of the line.

11. Which expression will give the total length of the above fractal pattern after the 6th iteration?

A. $625\left(\dfrac{3}{5}\right)^{6}$ B. $625\left(\dfrac{2}{5}\right)^{6}$

C. $\dfrac{625}{3^{6}}$ D. $\dfrac{625}{2^{6}}$

Use the following information to answer the next question.

96 cm — Iteration 0 — 48 cm — Iteration 1 — Iteration 2

Each new triangle has a base length and height that is half that of the one before it.

12. What is the total new area added to the fractal in the nth iteration?

A. $2\ 304(0.5)^{n}$

B. $2\ 304(1.5)^{n}$

C. $2\ 304(0.75)^{n}$

D. $2\ 304(1.75)^{n}$

*Use the following information to answer
the next question.*

The following fractal is created by adding cones
to the diagram each of which has a base
diameter that is a third of the one previous to it.
In each case the diameter of the cone is equal to
its height.

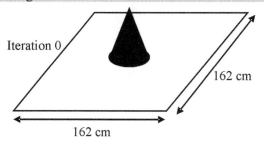

Iteration 0

162 cm

162 cm

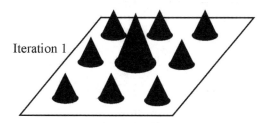

Iteration 1

The following chart follows the growth of the
fractal.

Iteration Number	Number of New Cones	Radius of the New Cones (cm)	Volume of New Cones (cm³)	Total Volume of New Cones (cm³)	Total Volume (cm³)
0	1	27	41 223.98	41 223.98	41 223.98
1	8	9	1 526.81	12 214.51	53 438.49
2	64	3	56.55		
3	512				
4	4 096				

The formula for the volume of these cones given
that the height is equal to its diameter is

$$V = \frac{2}{3}\pi r^3$$

Numerical Response

3. The total volume of the fractal after the 4th
iteration is _____.

Written Response

*Use the following information to answer
the next two questions*

The following data represents the depth of water
in a harbour over a period of a day.

Time (h)	Depth (m)
12:00 A.M.	7.0
1:00	9.5
2:00	11.3
3:00	12.0
4:00	11.3
5:00	9.5
6:00	7.0
7:00	4.5
8:00	2.7
9:00	2.0
10:00	2.7
11:00	4.5
12:00 P.M.	7.0
1:00	9.5
2:00	11.3
3:00	12.0
4:00	11.3
5:00	9.5
6:00	7.0
7:00	4.5
8:00	2.7
9:00	2.0
10:00	2.7
11:00	4.5

1. Draw a sketch of the data, provide the window settings and write the equation of the line of best fit.

x: [_____, _____, _____]

y: [_____, _____, _____]

y = _____

Use the following information to answer the next question.

The following information is a record of the fish population in a lake after it was stocked.

Year	Population
0	2 000
1	2 110
2	2 226
3	2 349
4	2 478
5	2 614

The lake has an area of 204 800 m^2, and research has been determined that each fish requires a minimum of 64 m^2 of personal space to thrive.

2. Using technology, determine the exponential regression equation for this data and sketch its graph. Use this information to determine how long it will take for the lake to reach its maximum capacity.

x: [_____, _____, _____]

y: [_____, _____, _____]

y = _____

Not for Reproduction

NOTES

VECTORS

Table of Correlations		
Topic	**Outcomes**	**Questions**

Solve problems involving polygons and vectors, including both 3-D and 2-D applications.	*It is expected that students will:*
	
	5.1 use appropriate terminology to describe:
	        vector quantities
	        scalar quantities
		1, 2, 3

	5.2 assign meaning to the multiplication of a vector by a scalar	4
	5.3 determine the magnitude and direction of a resultant vector, using triangle or parallelogram methods	5, 6, 7, 8, 9, NR1, NR2, 10, NR3, 11, 12
	5.4 model and solve problems in 2-D and simple 3-D, using vector diagrams and technology	13, 14, 15, 16, NR4

VECTORS

Students will solve problems involving polygons and vectors, including both 3-D and 2-D applications.

5.1 Use appropriate terminology to describe:

- *vector quantities*
- *scalar quantities*

TERMINOLOGY

Vectors are quantities that can only be expressed with both a magnitude and a direction. A scalar is a quantity that is expressed with a magnitude only. For example, a distance, such as 100 km, is a scalar quantity, but it becomes a vector quantity when it is combined with a direction as in 100 km east. Students also need to be familiar with speed (50 km/h) as a scalar quantity and with velocity (50 km/h North) as the corresponding vector quantity, and finally with force (12 N at an angle of 30° to the horizontal) as another vector quantity. Vectors are symbolically denoted with an arrow over the variable as follows: $\vec{a}$. To specify just the magnitude of the vector we use the absolute value signs as follows: $|\vec{a}|$.

Vectors can also be represented using arrows in which the length of the arrow is proportional to the magnitude of the vector, and the direction the arrow is pointing corresponds to the direction of the vector. It is assumed in most scenarios that the top of the page represents North unless otherwise specified. Students should have an understanding of direction and/or bearing notation in order to draw vectors accurately enough to perform operations. Direction notation starts by indicating one of the four directions on the compass. It is combined with an angle and another direction on the compass. The angle is an acute angle that indicates an amount of rotation towards the second direction indicated. All of this is usually enclosed in brackets.

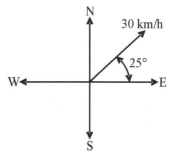

The vector represented above is 30 km/h [E 25° N]. It can also be written as 30 km/h [N 65° E]. The angles here are complementary because there are 90° between each direction on the compass.

The lengths of the vectors represent the respective magnitudes. Vector $\vec{a}$ represents a velocity that is twice as fast as vector $\vec{b}$, but in the same direction.

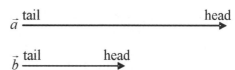

When a vector is expressed using an arrow, it is important to remember that we call the tip of the arrow the *head*, and the other end the *tail*. Naming the ends makes discussion about vector addition and subtraction easier to understand.

Another way of indicating the direction that a vector is pointing is bearing notation. The bearing of a vector is the angle, measured in degrees, that the vector has been rotated clockwise from North. As with direction notation, bearing notation is expressed in brackets. It is typically given with 3 digits regardless if the angle is acute or not.

Example

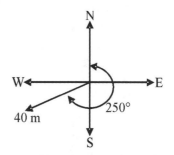

This vector can be written as 40 m [250°].

Example

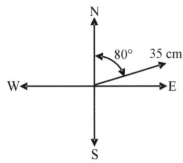

This vector would be written as 35 cm [080°].

Operations such as addition and subtraction are performed on vectors by combining the arrows into triangles and then using trigonometry to calculate the magnitude and direction of the solution, or what is called the *resultant vector*. As a result, students will need to be familiar with basic trigonometric operations, the Sine Law, and the Cosine Law. Students should also be in the habit of putting their calculators in degree mode, rounding their angles to the nearest degree, and rounding their magnitudes to the nearest tenth of a unit unless otherwise stated. The following list states trigonometric functions with the Sine and Cosine Law.

$$\sin\theta = \frac{\text{opposite side}}{\text{hypotenuse}}$$

$$\cos\theta = \frac{\text{adjacent side}}{\text{hypotenuse}}$$

$$\tan\theta = \frac{\text{opposite side}}{\text{adjacent side}}$$

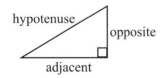

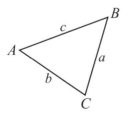

Sine Law $\dfrac{a}{\sin A} = \dfrac{b}{\sin B} = \dfrac{c}{\sin C}$

Cosine Law $c^2 = a^2 + b^2 - 2ab\cos C$

In addition to being familiar with trigonometric functions, students should also be familiar with the properties of parallel lines and transversals.

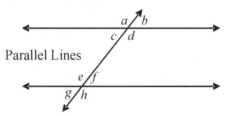

Parallel Lines

Corresponding Angles are equal. The pairs of corresponding angles are: $\angle a = \angle e$, $\angle b = \angle f$, $\angle c = \angle g$, $\angle d = \angle h$.

Alternate Interior Angles are equal. The pairs of alternate interior angles are: $\angle c = \angle f$, $\angle d = \angle e$.

Same Side Interior Angles are supplementary. For example: $\angle d + \angle f = 180°$, $\angle c + \angle e = 180°$.

Vertically Opposite Angles are equal. The vertically opposite pairs are: $\angle a = \angle d$, $\angle b = \angle c$, $\angle e = \angle h$, $\angle g = \angle f$.

Finally, students should be aware of the properties of parallelograms, as they will be used to combine vectors.

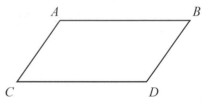

Sides $\overline{AB}$ and $\overline{CD}$ are parallel and sides $\overline{AC}$ and $\overline{BD}$ are parallel. In addition, opposite angles are equal: $\angle CAB = \angle BDC$, and $\angle ACD = \angle ABD$.

Related Questions: 1, 2, 3

Copyright Protected

Not for Reproduction

5.2 Assign meaning to the multiplication of a vector by a scalar.

SCALAR MULTIPLICATION

A scalar value multiplied by a vector can do two things. In most cases, the value of a scalar changes the magnitude of the vector, but in some cases it can, to a certain degree, change the direction of the vector.

If $\vec{a}$, is a vector then $2\vec{a}$ represents a vector that points in the same direction as $\vec{a}$, but has a magnitude that is twice as large.

The vector $\dfrac{1}{2}\vec{a}$ represents a vector that is half the magnitude of $\vec{a}$, but pointing in the same direction.

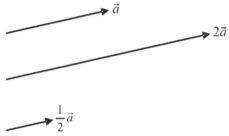

If the value of the scalar is negative, the result is a vector whose magnitude has not been proportionally changed by the absolute value of the scalar, but it is pointing in the exact opposite direction. The following diagram represents vector $\vec{a}$, and vector $-2\vec{a}$.

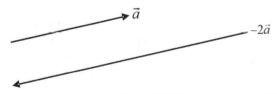

If vector $\vec{a}$ is 50 km/h [E 30°N], then vector $3\vec{a}$ represents a vector that is 150 km/h [E 30°N].

The vector written as $\dfrac{1}{5}\vec{a}$ is 10 km/h [E 30°N].

If the scalar multiple is negative, it changes the direction of the vector so that it is in the exact opposite direction.

When the direction of a vector is written in direction notation, such as [E 30°N], to find the exact opposite direction we need to make two changes. The first direction given must be changed to its exact opposite direction, as does the second direction given. Therefore [E 30°N] becomes [W 30°S]. So, east and west are interchanged, as are north and south. For example, if vector $\vec{z}$ is 20 km [S 60°E], then $-\vec{z}$ would be 20 km [N 60°W]. This works because of the properties of vertically opposite angles.

If the direction is given in bearing notation, then to find the opposite direction we need to first take note of the value of the angle. If the angle is less than 180°, then to calculate the opposite we add 180° to the bearing. On the other hand, if the angle is greater than 180°, then to calculate the opposite we subtract 180° from the bearing.

For example, if vector $\vec{b}$ is 20 N [072°] then the vector $-4\vec{b}$. is 80 N [252°]. Notice that the original direction was less than 180°, so, that to find the opposite direction, we added 180°. On the other hand, if vector $\vec{c}$ is 35 N [330°], then vector $-\vec{c}$ is 35 N [150°]. In this case, the original bearing was greater than 180°, so, to find the opposite direction we subtract 180°.

Related Question: 4

5.3 Determine the magnitude and direction of a resultant vector, using triangle or parallelogram methods.

VECTOR ADDITION AND SUBTRACTION

There are two methods for adding and subtracting vectors. The first method of adding vectors is the triangle method. It is most commonly used to add velocity and displacement vectors. The parallelogram method for adding vectors is used specifically for adding force vectors. These force vectors should be drawn such that the tail is in the body on which the force is acting and the head points in the direction in which the force is acting. Both of these methods are graphical but require skill with geometry and trigonometry to make sense of the results.

The triangle method requires that vectors be added head to tail. We simply draw the first vector with its tail at the origin of the plane, and then we move the second vector so that its tail meets the head of the first vector. Bear in mind that equal vectors have the same magnitude and the same direction, even though they may not be in the same position. This allows us to move a vector around the plane without changing it. Finally, the solution, or *resultant vector*, is the vector that connects the tail of the first vector to the head of the second vector. It is then necessary to calculate the length of the vector and the direction it is pointing using the laws of geometry and trigonometry.

Example

Add and then subtract the following two vectors.

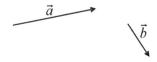

Solution

The following represents $\vec{a}+\vec{b}$, where $\vec{r}$ is the resultant vector. Vector addition is commutative, as can be shown by adding $\vec{b}+\vec{a}$.

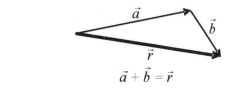

$$\vec{a}+\vec{b}=\vec{r}$$

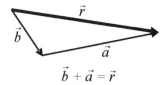

$$\vec{b}+\vec{a}=\vec{r}$$

In both these cases, the resultant vectors are the same since they have the same length and point in the same direction.

Vector subtraction can also be performed using this method. It is necessary to understand that subtraction is the same as adding a vector that has been multiplied by a negative scalar; therefore $\vec{a}-\vec{b}=\vec{r}$ is the same as $\vec{a}+(\vec{b})=\vec{r}$.

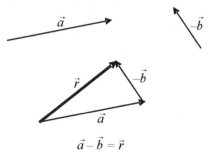

$$\vec{a}-\vec{b}=\vec{r}$$

The parallelogram method is one in which we connect vectors tail to tail and create a parallelogram with the vectors as the sides of the parallelogram. The resultant is the diagonal that connects the two tails to the two heads in the parallelogram.

Example

Add the following two vectors.

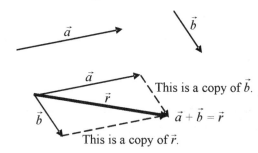

Subtraction with the parallelogram method is very similar to how it is done with the triangle method. The first vector is added to the second one after multiplying it by a negative scalar.

Solution

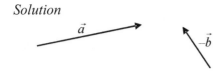

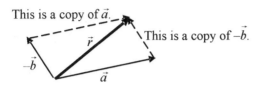

This represents $\vec{a}+(-\vec{b})=\vec{r}$, which is the same as $\vec{a}-\vec{b}=\vec{r}$.

When the vectors are specified such that their magnitudes and directions are specified, the resultant must also have its magnitude and direction specified. In these scenarios, we must utilize both the rules of geometry and trigonometry.

We use the triangle method specifically for vector problems involving displacement and velocity. The first step is to create a drawing. The first vector is drawn on the compass such that its tail is at the origin. The tail of the second vector is connected to the head of the first vector. To do this, it is often helpful to redraw the compass at the head of the first vector. This not only helps in drawing the second vector, but it aids in determining the direction of the resultant vector. For most questions, we will use the Cosine Law to determine the magnitude of the resultant and the sine law to determine the angle at which it is oriented.

Example

A ship leaves a harbour and travels 300 km [S 50° E]
The ship then travels 250 km [N 20° E]. What displacement vector, $\vec{r}$, represents the ship's final position with respect to the harbour?

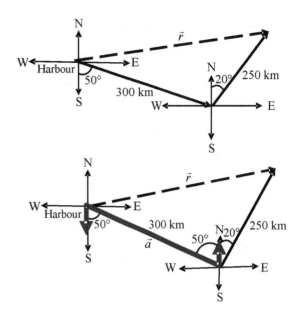

Solution

In most cases, once the vectors are added in this form, we can make use of the properties of parallel lines and transversals. The vertical axes of the two compass diagrams are parallel, and thus the first vector acts as a transversal. The properties of alternate interior angles are used to find the missing part of the total angle between the given vectors.

The total angle between the displacement vectors is 50° + 20° = 70°. Now, with the lengths of the two sides and the angle between them we can calculate the length of the resultant vector that is known, opposite the given angle using the Cosine Law.

$$\left|\vec{r}\right|^2=\left|\vec{a}\right|^2+\left|\vec{b}\right|^2-2\left|\vec{a}\right|\left|\vec{b}\right|\cos\theta$$
$$\left|\vec{r}\right|^2=300^2+250^2-2(300)(250)\cos(70°)$$
$$\left|\vec{r}\right|=\sqrt{300^2+250^2-2(300)(250)\cos(70°)}$$
$$\left|\vec{r}\right|=318.11\,\text{km}$$

Copyright Protected

Once the magnitude of the resultant is known, we need to determine the angle at which the resultant is oriented. With the laws of trigonometry, we cannot determine directly the angle that the resultant makes with the vertical or the horizontal. However, we can determine the angle within the triangle between the tails of the first vector and the resultant using the Sine Law.

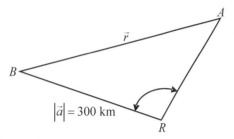

$$\frac{|\vec{r}|}{\sin R}=\frac{|\vec{b}|}{\sin B}$$

$$\frac{318.11}{\sin 70°}=\frac{250}{\sin B}$$

$$\sin B=\frac{250\sin 70°}{318.11}$$

$$B=\sin^{-1}\left(\frac{250\sin 70°}{318.11}\right)=47.60°$$

We know that there are 90° in each quadrant. Since the first vector is 50° away from due South, it is therefore also 40° down from due East. Because the angle in the triangle with a vertex at B is 47.60°, we can conclude that the resultant vector must be pointing 7.60° above due East. Our final conclusion is that the resultant displacement vector is 318.11 km [E 7.60° N].

Example

A farmer wishes to move a large boulder that is in his field. He attaches two teams of horses to the boulder. One team pulls with a force of 3 500 N and the other team pulls with a force of 5 000 N in the directions specified by the diagram. What is the resultant force that the boulder experiences and in what direction is this force?

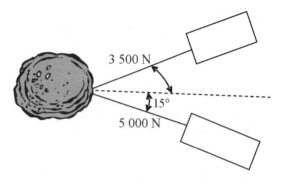

Solution

Since this is a force question and both forces are acting on the same spot, we will use the parallelogram method. This involves copying the vectors and using them to create a parallelogram. This can be done because the opposite vectors in the parallelogram are still considered equal as long as they are the same length and are pointing in the same direction. The resultant vector is the vector that connects the point where the two tails of the vectors meet to the place where the two heads of the vectors meet. The dotted lines have been introduced to facilitate the calculation of the angles where the head of the vector meets the tail of the copied vector. Once this angle is measured, the magnitude of the resultant can once again be calculated using the Cosine Law.

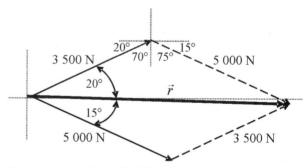

By the rules of parallel lines and transversals, and the properties of complementary angles, we can calculate the angles required. At this point, we can calculate that the total angle between the 3 500 N vector and the copied 5 000 N vector is 145°. Now the magnitude of the resultant can be calculated as follows.

$$|\vec{r}|=\sqrt{3\,500^{2}+5\,000^{2}-2(3\,500)(5\,000)\cos(145°)}$$

$$|\vec{r}|=8\,119.13\,N$$

Therefore, the boulder experiences a net pull of 8 119.13 N. Now we need to determine the angle at which the force is being exerted. Because the initial angles are given with respect to a line that points directly ahead of the boulder, the final angle should also be found with respect to this line.

To do this, we first find the angle between the resultant and one of the initial matrices. In this case, let's choose the 3 500 N matrix. Bear in mind that the 20° shown is not the angle of the resultant. To find this angle, we use the Sine Law as follows:

$$\frac{8\,119.13}{\sin 145°} = \frac{5\,000}{\sin \theta}$$

$$\sin \theta = \frac{5\,000 \sin 145°}{8\,119.13}$$

$$\theta = \sin^{-1}\left(\frac{5\,000 \sin 145°}{8\,119.13}\right) = 20.7°$$

Now, to find the angle that the resultant makes with the straight line we can simply subtract the angle we calculated from the angle that the 3 500 N vector makes with the straight line.

$$20° - 20.7° = -0.7°$$

The negative here indicates that the angle is below the straight line. Therefore, the resultant is 8 119.13 N 0.7° of the straight line and in the direction of the 5 000 N vector.

Related Questions: 5, 6, 7, 8, 9, NR1, NR2, 10, NR 3, 11, 12

5.4   Model and solve problems in 2-D and simple 3-D, using vector diagrams and technology.

2-D AND 3-D PROBLEMS

Some vector problems can be solved by using a two-dimensional model, whereas others require a three-dimensional model. In many cases, three-dimensional models can be broken down into two-dimensional right triangles that are situated in three dimensions. The question is then broken into several steps, which can all be solved using basic trigonometric functions.

Two-dimensional problems require an understanding of the geometry of triangles and some trigonometry. In some scenarios, only basic right triangle trigonometry will be required, whereas other questions may require the use oblique triangles.

Example

The pilot of a plane notices that her altitude is increasing at a rate of 20 m/s.
In addition to this, ground control notes that the plane's velocity relative to the ground is 250 km/h north. At what velocity is the plane moving through the air?

Solution

Before beginning this problem, it is important to convert the 20 m/s into km/h to be consistent. The conversion factor is 3.6; therefore, the plane's altitude is increasing at a rate of 72 km/h. Because these motions are at right angles to each other, we can use a right angle triangle as the model.

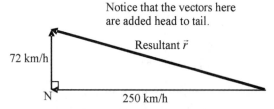

Notice that the vectors here are added head to tail.

Resultant $\vec{r}$

72 km/h

N

250 km/h

We can use the Pythagorean Theorem to determine the magnitude of the resultant.

$$|\vec{r}| = \sqrt{72^2 + 250^2}$$

$$|\vec{r}| = 260.2 \text{ km/h}$$

Now, we can use basic trigonometry to determine the angle at which the plane is flying with respect to the ground. Since we are given the lengths of the opposite side and the adjacent side, we will use the tangent ratio.

$$\tan \theta = \frac{72}{250}$$

$$\theta = \tan^{-1}\left(\frac{72}{250}\right) = 16.1°$$

Therefore, the plane is flying north at 260.2 km/h at an angle of inclination of 16.1°.

Example

If a plane has an air velocity of 300 km/h [055°] and the wind is blowing from the west at a speed of 60 km/h, what is the velocity of the plane with respect to the ground?

Solution

First, it helps to draw the vector diagram.

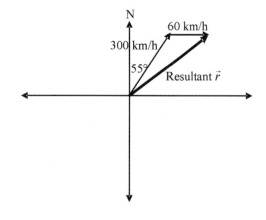

N

60 km/h

300 km/h

55°

Resultant $\vec{r}$

Notice again that the vectors are added head to tail and the resultant then connects the tail to the head of the system.

In this case, we cannot use basic trigonometric functions because the triangle is oblique. We therefore need to make use of the geometry of parallel lines and oblique triangles.

First, we need to find the angle between the two given vectors.

By drawing a dotted lines where the two vectors meet, we can more easily determine the angle between them.

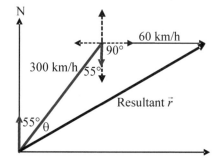

N

60 km/h

90°

300 km/h 55°

Resultant $\vec{r}$

55° θ

From the above diagram, we can see that the angle between the vectors is 55° + 90° = 145°.

Now, using the Cosine Law, we can determine the magnitude of the resultant vector.

$$|\vec{r}| = \sqrt{300^2 + 60^2 - 2(300)(60)\cos 145°}$$

$$|\vec{r}| = 350.8 \text{ km/h}$$

To determine the angle at which the resultant is oriented, we need to find the angle within the triangle at the origin. We use the Sine Law to find this angle:

$$\frac{350.8}{\sin 145°} = \frac{60}{\sin \theta}$$

$$\sin \theta = \frac{60 \sin 145°}{350.8}$$

$$\theta = \sin^{-1}\left(\frac{60 \sin 145°}{350.8}\right) \approx 60°$$

This means that the total angle between the resultant and due North is 55° + 6° = 61°. Therefore, the resultant is 350.8 km/h [061°].

Many three-dimensional problems can be broken down into multiple two-dimensional problems. An easy way to model this is to use the faces of a rectangular prism.

Example

A submarine at a port travels 3 km due South and dives to a depth of 1 500 m. From there, the submarine turns East and travels an additional 5 km. What is the final displacement vector of the submarine with respect to the port?

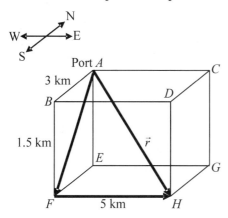

Solution

The first step in finding the resultant vector from point A to point H, is to add the vector connecting points A to B, to the vector from B to F. This would yield the displacement vector for the first part of the submarine's trip. We will then add the vector connecting F to H.

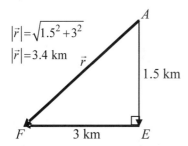

With this side, another right triangle can be formed that contains the resultant.

The magnitude of the resultant can be found as follows:

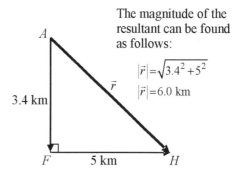

$$|\vec{r}|=\sqrt{3.4^2+5^2}$$
$$|\vec{r}|=6.0 \text{ km}$$

Because this is a three-dimensional problem, to specify the direction of the displacement requires two angles. The first will describe the horizontal direction that the submarine travelled, and the second will describe how the submarine has traversed vertically.

To determine the horizontal direction of movement, we need only compare the points A and D in the plane because D corresponds vertically to the final position of the submarine.

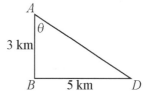

Then angle θ can be determined as follows:

$$\tan\theta=\frac{5}{3}$$

$$\theta=\tan^{-1}\left(\frac{5}{3}\right)=59°$$

Comparing this to the compass settings, the submarine has moved [N 59° E].

Now, to determine how the submarine has been displaced vertically, we need to look at the vertical triangle containing the resultant.

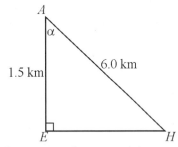

To find the angle of depression at which the submarine dived, we need to use some basic trigonometric functions as follows:

$$\cos\alpha = \frac{1.5}{6.0}$$

$$\alpha = \cos^{-1}\left(\frac{1.5}{6.0}\right) \approx 76°$$

Therefore, the final displacement vector for the submarine is 6.0 km at a heading of [N 59° E] at an angle of depression of 76°.

Related Questions: 13, 14, 15, 16, NR4

Faculty of

SCIENCE

University of Alberta

Your science career begins at the U of A Faculty of Science

With close to 60 degrees in over 40 subject areas, the Faculty of Science at the U of A offers some of the best undergraduate Science programs in North America. Our Faculty is internationally recognized for its teaching and research excellence – **Explore what we have to offer!**

CW 223 Biological Sciences Building

University of Alberta

Edmonton, Alberta T6G 2E9

Tel: (780) 492-4758

E-mail: dean.science@ualberta.ca

www.science.ualberta.ca

www.science.ualberta.ca

UNIVERSITY OF
ALBERTA

... inspire generations

University of Alberta EDUCATION
The largest, the first and the most diverse education faculty in the country

Undergraduate Degrees
- Elementary Education (K-6)
- Secondary Education (7-12)
- Combined Degrees (5 years) in Native Studies, Physical Education and Recreation, Science, Music, and Science in Human Ecology
- After Degree (2 years)

Admissions Information
- Application deadline is March 1
- No direct admission from high school
- Students complete a minimum of 8 half-courses before applying to the Faculty of Education

FACULTY OF
EDUCATION
UNIVERSITY OF ALBERT

Education. Rethough

Undergraduate Student Services   1-107 Education North Building
Phone: (780) 492-3659   www.education.ualberta.ca/uss/

Our pre-service teachers thrive in a research environment related to current teaching practi

FACULTY OF ARTS

UNIVERSITY OF ALBERTA

QUAECUMQUE VERA

Choosing a university is one of the most important choices you will ever make. Why not choose one with a 100-year history in academic and teaching excellence? We offer programs in the fine arts, humanities, social sciences and interdisciplinary studies. With more than 20 departments and programs, passionate professors who are leaders in their fields, study abroad opportunities, work experiences, and a satellite campus in Italy, the opportunities here are endless!

Visit www.arts.ualberta.ca

DEPARTMENTS AND PROGRAMS

- Anthropology
- Art & Design
- Community Service-Learning
- Comparative Literature
- Creative Writing
- Criminology
- Drama
- East Asian Studies
- Economics
- English & Film Studies
- History & Classics
- International Relations
- Linguistics
- Middle Eastern & African Studies
- Modern Languages & Cultural Studies
- Music
- Peace & Post-Conflict Studies
- Philosophy
- Political Science
- Psychology
- Religious Studies
- Science, Technology & Society
- Sociology
- Women's Studies

100 YEARS 1908-2008

* Chi-Chi, BA 2007

Faculty of Arts 6-7 Humanities Centre University of Alberta Edmonton, AB T6G 2E5 Tel: (780) 492-4295 www.arts.ualberta.ca

20 Years of Success!

Scholarship Opportunities Available!

"Academy of Learning gives you the career training that gets you hired!"

- Business Administration
- Medical Office Assistant / Unit Clerk Specialty *
- Government of Alberta Health Care Aide *
- Dental Administrative Assistant *
- Computerized Payroll Accounting
- Network Security Specialist *
- Retail Pharmacy Technician *
- Office Administration
- Web Designer
- Network Administrator
- Payroll Administrator
- Computerized Accounting
- PC Support Specialist
- Web and Applications Developer *
- Insurance Advisor *
- and more!

Call Today, START TRAINING Right Away!

Consumers' Choice Award 2002 - 2007 For Business Excellence

* May not be available at all locations.

www.academyoflearning.ab.ca

Academy OF LEARNING
Career and Business College

Simply a BETTER Way to Learn!

Financial assistance may be available to qualified applicants.

Airdrie .... (403) 912-3430	
Calgary Central .... (403) 282-3166	West Edmonton Mall .... (780) 496-9428
Calgary Northeast .... (403) 569-8973	High River .... (403) 652-2116
Calgary South .... (403) 252-8973	Lethbridge .... (403) 329-3244
Edmonton Downtown .... (780) 424-1144	Medicine Hat .... (403) 526-5833
Edmonton South .... (780) 433-7284	Red Deer .... (403) 347-6676

Your Career in AutoCAD

Scholarship Opportunities Available!

What is AutoCAD?

A structure doesn't create itself. It takes design. And the design must be communicated in a way that everyone who needs to use it can understand. Drafters prepare technical drawings and plans used by production and construction workers to build everything from manufactured products such as spacecraft or industrial machinery to structures such as office buildings or gas pipelines. Their drawings provide visual guidelines showing the technical details of the products and structures, specifying dimensions, materials to be used, procedures and processes.

Computer Aided Drafting is the link between creative design concepts and reality, and it can be your link to a rewarding and interesting career. In architecture, interior design, the trades, or the world's largest oil sand development, AutoCAD is there! AutoCAD is the world's leading design software for architecture, manufacturing and resource management. Learn with us at Digital School and become part of the Alberta Advantage!

Career Programs in:

- Architectural CAD Technician
- Engineering CAD Technician
- Engineering CAD Technician with Process Piping Specialization
- Computer Aided Drafter and more!

DIGITAL School
computer aided drafting & design training

#304, 10205-101 Street, Edmonton, Alberta T5J 4H5   Call (780) 414-0200   www.digitalschool.ca

make an enlightened choice

St. Mary's University College in Calgary is a Catholic liberal arts and sciences post-secondary institution open to people of all faiths and traditions. Get a **Bachelor of Arts degree** or take **university courses in 27 different academic subjects.**

At St. Mary's University College, you'll experience:

■ A liberal arts core curriculum that explores a wide range of subjects in the humanities, social sciences, mathematical sciences and natural sciences

■ Small class sizes and personalized attention

■ Generous scholarships and bursaries

StMARY'S
UNIVERSITY COLLEGE

14500 Bannister Road SE, Calgary, AB ph. 403.531.9130 **www.stmu.ab.ca**

I want a great university experience.

Concordia provides the kind of education you need to achieve your goals and make a difference in the world.

One of the top smaller universities in Canada (Globe and Mail University Report Card, 2006 and 2007), we are committed to providing you with an interactive classroom experience with outstanding profs and recognized excellence in teaching and research.

Join a vibrant and caring university community that will help you realize your dreams.

University degree programs...
- Bachelor of Arts
- Bachelor of Education (After Degree)
- Bachelor of Environmental Health (After Degree)
- Bachelor of Management
- Bachelor of Science
- Master of Information Systems Security Management
- Church Work Programs

CONCORDIA
University College of Alberta

You can do that here.

7128 Ada Boulevard, Edmonton, Alberta, T5B 4E4
Telephone: (780) 479.9220 Toll Free: 1.866.479.5200
Email: ses@concordia.ab.ca

youcandothathere.com

brain fuel

People who eat breakfast perform better [at] school and at work. This is just one of the many ways good nutrition contributes to [a] healthy lifestyle.

Aim to meet your nutritional needs as recommended in *Eating Well with Canad[a's] Food Guide.*

Teens 14–18 years old need the followin[g] number of servings each day from the 4 food groups:

	females	males
vegetables and fruit	7	8
grain products	6	7
milk and alternatives	3–4	3–4
meat and alternatives	2	4

Find a complete food guide on line at:
www.healthcanada.gc.ca/foodguide

To learn more about healthy eating, visi[t] **www.saveonfoods.com** and send you[r] nutrition questions to our dietitians, register for an in-store Nutrition Tour [or] find healthy recipes and eating advice.

more

food and health solutions

save on foods

SO MUCH *more* IN STORE

THE BEAR CHILDREN'S FUND

Think of it as 'Tough Love'

Since 1992, The Bear has been giving back to Edmonton's kids through The Bear Children's Fund. In the years since the Fund's inception, over $1,500,000 has been directed back into the greater Edmonton community and its charities. To make the Fund work requires the dedication of both management and staff, who have volunteered thousands of hours of their time to this worthwhile cause. As a rock station, The Bear may be loud, but it's proud too. Proud to be a part of a community as generous as Edmonton.

Edmonton's Best Rock 100.3 fm

The BEAR

To apply for grants from the Bear Children's Fund please visit **www.thebearrocks.com**

Alberta Committee for Citizens with Disabilities | Alberta Rose Chapter | Alberta Special Olympics | Arbutus Volunteer Foundation Belmont Elementary School | Ben Calf Robe Native Elementary & Junior High Catholic School | Bent Arrow Traditional Healing Society | Boyle Street Co-op Playground | Boys & Girls Club of Edmonton | Canadian Progress Club | Century Services Inc. Stollery Children's Hospital Foundation | Children's Heart Society City Centre Education Project | CNIB | Cross Cancer Institute Early Head Start Program | Edmonton City Police D.A.R.E. Program | Edmonton Food Bank | Edmonton Garrison Base Fund Edmonton Jaycees | Edmonton School Lunch Program | Edmonton Spring Board & Platform Diving Club | Employabilities | EMS Social Club | Firefighter's Burn Unit | Fort Saskatchewan Boys & Girls Club | Friends of Rosecrest | Garden Valley Pony Club | Glenrose Rehabilitation Hospital | Griesbach School Council | Inner City Youth Development Association | Head First Foundation | Hug-A-Bear Express | Kid's Kottage | Kinsmen Club of St. Albert | Mansion Youth Drop-In Centre for Teens | McCauley Community After School Care Association | Morinville Panthers | New York City Police & Fire Widows' & Children's Benefit | Northern Alberta Brain Injury Society | Norwood Community Centre | Nottingham Playground Association | Parents Empowering Parents | P.A.R.T.Y. Program Project Literacy | Queen Mary Park School | Rainbow Society Ronald McDonald House | Royal Alexandra Hospital | Southwest Area Council of Community Leagues | St. Michael's School | St. Patrick's School (Edmonton) Parents Society | Terra Association | Uncles At Large | Various Trust Funds & Confidential Donations | Westview Regional Health Authority Youth Health Centre | Wetaskiwin Head Start Society | Yellowhead Youth Centre | Youth Emergency Shelter Society | Skills Woodcroft Respite Home | Royal Alexandra Hospital NICU Family Room (Bear Den) | Brightview Elementary School

You're curious about the world
UNIVERSITY OF CALGARY FACULTY OF SCIENCE
You want to use the latest technology to advance your career. At the University of Calgary, you will learn from world-class researchers who generate the latest knowledge in petroleum geology, information security, astrophysics and forward looking fields like quantum computing. From biochemistry and statistics to water quality and resource management, you will acquire the problem-solving skills that will help you succeed in the oil and gas, agricultural, pharmaceutical, environmental science and financial industries.
www.science.ucalgary.ca
World-class research + hands-on learning
+ international opportunities + work experience
= Knowledge that will advance your career
UofC
THIS IS NOW

We're everywhere.

Information technology is more than computers and programming. IT is a driving force for progress in industries such as oil and gas, health care, and global communications. IT is even helping biologists predict the spread of disease among trees.

Where will you make your mark? Invent information security technologies that will ensure people's privacy. Visualize oil reserves so they can be discovered and managed for future generations. Or build a database that could be instrumental in treating and finding cures for cancer.

Join us to embark on a meaningful IT career. **Your future starts here:** www.cpsc.ucalgary.ca

UOFC
THIS IS NOW

FACULTY OF | UNIVERSITY OF
SCIENCE | **CALGARY**
COMPUTER SCIENCE

teacher.
entrepreneur.
problem solver.
designer.
leader.

The Schulich Engineer.

At the Schulich School of Engineering, we inspire students to be more than highly skilled engineers.

Visit www.schulich.ucalgary.ca to find out more.

SCHULICH
School of Engineering

UNIVERSITY OF
CALGARY

UOFC
THIS IS NOW

CHALLENGER QUESTION   43.9

1. Which of the following statements about vectors is **false**?

 A. A vector diagram consists of directed line segments.

 B. The vector sum of two vectors is called the resultant.

 C. Two vectors are equal if they have the same magnitude and opposite directions.

 D. The scalar multiplication of a vector by n, $n > 0$, keeps the direction of the vector the same but alters its magnitude by a factor of n.

 Source: January 2001

2. Which of the following is a vector quantity?

 A. Displacement

 B. Time

 C. Mass

 D. Length

3. Which of the following is a scalar quantity?

 A. Velocity

 B. Gravity

 C. Temperature

 D. Position

4. The vector $\vec{z}$ represents a velocity of 70 km/h N 40° W. Then $-3\vec{z}$ represents;

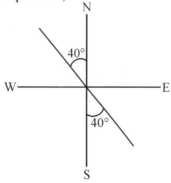

 A. 67 km/h   N 40° W

 B. 210 km/h   N 40° W

 C. 67 km/h   S 40° E

 D. 210 km/h   S 40° E

Use the following information to answer the next question.

Three forces are simultaneously acting on an object. The first force is 1 200 N upward, the second force is 700 N to the east, and the third force is 500 N to the west.

5. As a result of these three forces, the object will

 A. move up and to the east

 B. move up and to the west

 C. move straight up

 D. not move

 Source: January 2001

Copyright Protected

Use the following information to answer the next question.

Two tugboats are pulling a ship, as shown below. Each tugboat exerts a force of 420 MN.

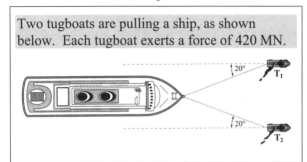

CHALLENGER QUESTION   **25.8**

6. If R represents the resultant force, then which of the following diagrams is an appropriate vector diagram for this situation?

   A.

         420 MN   420 MN   20° R

   B.

         420 MN   420 MN   40° R

   C.

         420 MN   40° R 420 MN

   D.

         420 MN   20° R 420 MN

Source: January 2001

CHALLENGER QUESTION   **38.7**

7. The angle, θ, by which the aircraft is flying off-course is, to the nearest degree,

   A. 7°

   B. 22°

   C. 61°

   D. 68°

Source: January 2001

Use the following information to answer the next question.

Two people are trying to raise an object from a hole using two ropes, as shown in the diagram below.
Person 1 exerts a force of 355 N, and Person 2 exerts a force of 425 N.

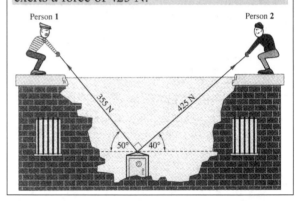

CHALLENGER QUESTION   **56.0**

8. The total amount of resultant force applied by the two people is

   A. 273 N   **B.** 336 N

   C. 554 N   **D.** 780 N

Source: January 2001

Use the following information to answer the next question.

An object located at the origin of a coordinate grid is acted upon by two forces. One force is 20 N along the positive x-axis, and the other force is 30 N along the negative y-axis.
The diagram below shows a coordinate plane with the quadrants labelled.

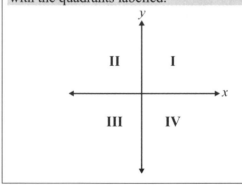

9. The resultant vector of the two forces will be directed into quadrant

   A. I

   B. II

   C. III

   D. IV

Source: June 2001

Use the following information to answer the next question.

A person in a motor boat that has a forward velocity of 25 km/h is trying to travel directly north across a river. A current of 8 km/h affects the course of the boat, as shown below.

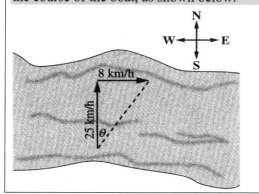

CHALLENGER QUESTION   **25.3**

Numerical Response

1. Relative to the direct path, the angle of the boat's course, θ, to the nearest tenth of a degree, is _____°.

Source: June 2001

Use the following information to answer the next question.

A small plane is flying 180 km/h on a bearing of 120°. It is affected by a 45 km/h wind blowing toward a bearing of 300°.

CHALLENGER QUESTION   **35.5**

Numerical Response

2. The actual speed of the plane is _____ km/h.

Source: June 2001

Use the following information to answer the next question.

Two dogs are pulling a wagon. Each dog exerts a force of 150 N. Each dog is pulling in a direction that is 30° away from the direction of travel, as shown below.

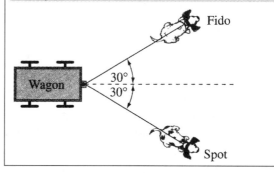

CHALLENGER QUESTION   **48.4**

10. The resultant force in the direction of travel, to the nearest newton, is

   A. 75 N

   B. 150 N

   C. 260 N

   D. 290 N

Source: June 2001

Copyright Protected

Use the following diagram to answer the next question.

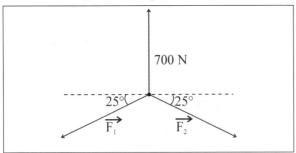

Numerical Response

3. A motor boat traveling at a constant velocity pulls two water skiers behind it. Each rope makes an angle of 25.0° with respect to the back of the boat. If the boat exerts a force of 700 N, the tension in each rope is _____ N. (Record your answer to three significant digits.)

Use the following diagram to answer the next two questions.

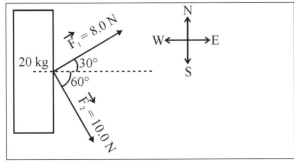

11. Two forces are acting on a 20 kg mass. Force 1 is 8.0 N, 30° north of east. Force 2 is 10 N, 60° south of east. What is the magnitude of the net force on the mass?

A. 2.0 N

B. 13 N

C. 18 N

D. 164 N

12. What is the direction of the net force in the previous question?

A. 8.7° south of east

B. 39° north of east

C. 21° south of east

D. 51° north of east

Use the following information to answer the next question.

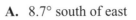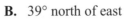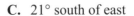

A 737 aircraft is flying on a bearing of 310° with an air speed of 700 km/h.
It is being affected by a 100 km/h wind blowing from the east, as shown in the diagram below.

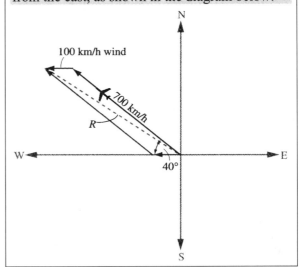

CHALLENGER QUESTION	30.9

13. The distance, *R*, relative to the ground, that the plane has traveled after 1 hour is, to the nearest kilometre,

A. 627 km

B. 640 km

C. 707 km

D. 779 km

Source: January 2001

Not for Reproduction

Use the following information to answer the next question.

A small aircraft leaves Calgary on a heading of E 30° S, travelling 200 km/h. It is affected by a 40 km/h wind blowing toward S 60° W.

CHALLENGER QUESTION	30.0

14. After one hour, the plane's position relative to Calgary will be

   A. 183 km E 41° S

   B. 183 km S 30° W

   C. 204 km E 41° S

   D. 204 km S 30° W

Source: June 2001

Use the following information to answer the next question.

A particular plane takes 45 min to fly 300 km due north from Calgary to Edmonton when there is no wind.

CHALLENGER QUESTION	40.3

15. If the plane were to experience a 70 km/h wind blowing directly from the west, what would be the magnitude of the resultant velocity?

   A. 470 km/h

   B. 406 km/h

   C. 400 km/h

   D. 394 km/h

Source: June 2001

16. A small aircraft sets a course of S 25° W at a speed of 250 km/h. A wind blowing at 25 km/h directly from the west acts on the aircraft. What is the plane's resultant speed?

   A. 225 km/h

   B. 240 km/h

   C. 262 km/h

   D. 275 km/h

Use the following information to answer the next question.

A small airplane climbs at an angle of 15° and travels due north. There is a wind from the west at 35 km/h. The velocity of the plane is 120 km/h north, 15° above the horizontal.

Numerical Response

4. To travel north while climbing, the pilot is compensating for the wind by actually aiming the plane _____ ° W of N.
(Record your answer to the nearest tenth of a degree.)

UNIT TEST 5—VECTORS

1. Which of the following is a vector quantity?

   A. 100 km

   B. [S 30° W]

   C. 75 km/h for 3 hours

   D. 3 cm [N 45° W]

2. A scalar quantity is

   A. a magnitude with a direction

   B. a magnitude

   C. a direction

   D. the result of multiplying two matrices

*Use the following information to answer
the next two questions.*

A team of mechanics are working to improve the
rate at which their racing car covers the straight
away on a race track. Their car can average
220 km/h on the small stretch of track that runs
directly east. Thus far, they have been able to
improve the speed of their car by 6%.

3. Which aspect of the above scenario is a
   vector quantity?

   A. 220 km/h   B. 220 km/h [east]

   C. 7%   D. east

Numerical Response

1. In the above scenario, for the mechanics to
determine the new velocity of their car on
the straightaway, they will need to multiply
the old velocity vector by _____.

*Use the following information to answer
the next question.*

A plane is traveling 200 km/h [N 30° E].

4. If we multiply this vector by –1, we get

   A. –200 km/h [N 30° E]

   B. –200 km/h [S 30° W]

   C. 200 km/h [N –30° W]

   D. 200 km/h [S 30° W]

*Use the following information to answer
the next question.*

A ship in distress has a displacement vector of
200 km [080°]. A rescue vessel heads straight
for it and soon is in a position that represents $\frac{3}{4}$
of the original displacement vector.

5. The magnitude of the final displacement
   vector of the ship in distress from the rescue
   ship is

   A. 150 km   B. 200 km

   C. 50 km   D. 25 km

Numerical Response

2. When vector $\vec{a}$ = 50 m [130°] is added to
vector $\vec{b}$ = 80 m [220°] then the bearing at
which the resultant points is [_____°].

6. When using the triangle method to add 75 m
   [045°] and 130 m [165°] together, the angle
   between the given vectors is

   A. 75°

   B. 120°

   C. 30°

   D. 60°

Copyright Protected

*Use the following information to answer
the next question.*

Two kids are pulling on ropes connected to a
broken go-cart that they wish to take home to
fix. One pulls with a force of 30 N, and the
other pulls with a force of 50 N as shown in the
diagram.

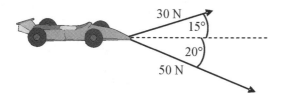

7. The resultant force vector, where the
magnitude is rounded to the nearest tenth
and the angle is rounded to the nearest
degree, is

   A. 30.7 N at 69° below the horizontal line

   B. 30.7 N at 34° below the horizontal line

   C. 76.5 N at 7° below the horizontal line

   D. 76.5 N at 13° below the horizontal line

*Use the following information to answer
the next question.*

Two vectors are acting on an object as shown in
the following diagram.

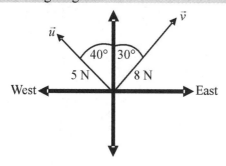

8. Given the information about the vectors $\vec{u}$
and $\vec{v}$ in the above diagram, the magnitude
and bearing of the resultant vector when we
evaluate $\vec{u} - \vec{v}$ is

   A. 7.85 N [247°]   B. 10.79 N [004°]

   C. 10.79 N [184°]   D. 7.85 N [067°]

*Use the following information to answer
the next question.*

A canoeist is attempting to cross a river that
flows at a speed of 4 km/h directly east. In still
water, he paddles at a rate of 6 km/h.

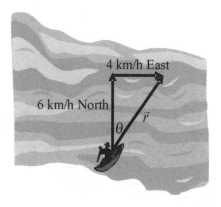

9. What is his actual speed, rounded to the
nearest tenth of a km/h, and direction as he
travels across the river?

   A. 7.2 km/h [N 56° E]

   B. 7.2 km/h [N 34° E]

   C. 4.5 km/h [N 56° E]

   D. 4.5 km/h [N 34° E]

*Use the following information to answer
the next question.*

A plane is flying on a bearing of [050°] at
275 km/hr. The wind is blowing on a bearing of
[140°] at 20 km/hr.

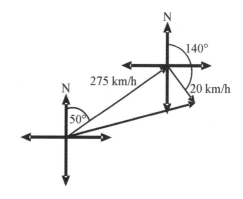

10. The magnitude, to the nearest tenth, and bearing of the resultant are

   A. 275.7 km/h [004°]

   B. 275.7 km/h [086°]

   C. 275.7 km/h [054°]

   D. 275.7 km/h [226°]

Use the following information to answer the next question.

The pilot of a submarine sets a course to move with a ground speed of 90 km/h due west while submerging at an angle of 13° to the horizontal. From the time of departure, the submarine is affected by a horizontal 20 km/h current flowing from the south, as shown in the diagram below.

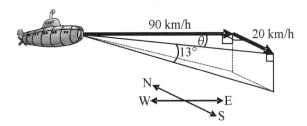

11. The magnitude of the final velocity vector, to the nearest tenth, of the submarine and the value of θ, to the nearest degree, in the above diagram are

   A. 94.6 km/h, $\theta = 13°$

   B. 94.6 km/h, $\theta = 77°$

   C. 92.2 km/h, $\theta = 13°$

   D. 92.2 km/h, $\theta = 77°$

Use the following information to answer the next question.

Vector $\vec{A}$ is defined to be 3 m [E 10° S], and vector $\vec{B}$ is defined to be 5 m [W 50° S].

12. Which of the following diagrams represents $\vec{A} - \vec{B}$?

   A.

   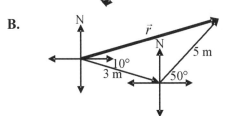

   B.

   C.

   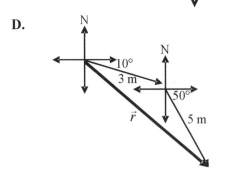

   D.

Written Response

Use the following information to answer
the next question.

Two horses are being used to pull a fallen tree off of a path. The tree will require 1 200 N of force to move it. Each one pulls with a force of about 800 N as represented in the diagram below.

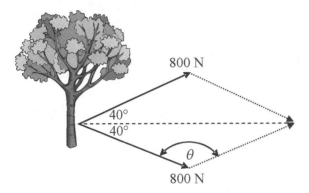

1. Using the parallelogram method of vector addition, determine the value of θ, the magnitude of the resultant, and determine whether or not the horses are able to move the tree from off the path.

Use the following information to answer
the next question.

A helicopter is attempting to fly at 150 km/h on a bearing of [040°], but a wind, blowing at 35 km/h [090°], is blowing it off course.

2. Determine the final velocity vector of the helicopter flying in the wind.

Use the following information to answer
the next question.

A hiker has driven to a mountain to do some climbing. From the parking lot, point A, he hikes 2 km due east. From that point he turns north and begins to climb. As he climbs, he moves 3 km north, while at the same time traveling 4 km vertically. Finally he arrives at point B.

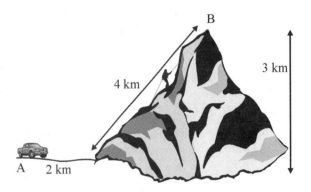

3. Determine the magnitude of the displacement vector connecting points A and B, and determine the angle this vector makes with the horizontal.

Copyright Protected

DESIGN

Table of Correlations		
Topic	**Outcomes**	**Questions**
Analyze objects, shapes and processes to solve cost and design problems.	*It is expected that students will:* 6.1 use dimensions and unit prices to solve problems involving perimeter, area, and volume	NR1, 1, 2, 3, 4, 5, NR2, 6, 7, 8
	6.2 solve problems involving estimation and cost for objects, shapes, or processes when a design is given	9, 10, 11, 12, NR3, 13, 14, 15
	6.3 use appropriate variables to design an object, shape, layout, or process within a specified budget	
	6.4 use mathematical models to estimate the solutions to complex measurement problems	16, 17, 18

DESIGN

Students will analyze objects, shapes and processes to solve cost and design problems.

6.1   Use dimensions and unit prices to solve problems involving perimeter, area, and volume.

PERIMETER, AREA, AND VOLUME

In order to answer problems related to the properties of shapes, students must first be familiar with the basic equations for the perimeter of two-dimensional objects, the area of two-dimensional objects, and the volume of three-dimensional objects. In addition to this, students must be aware of how to perform operations utilizing trigonometry, the Pythagorean theorem, and the properties of similar shapes. Students should also be comfortable with unit conversions.

When asked for the total value of a product given a unit price and its dimensions, we must first determine the total amount of whatever product the unit price is given for respect to. This may mean we may need to find a total area, or a total volume. Once the total value has been calculated, to determine the total value we simply multiply it by the unit price.
These questions may or may not provide a diagram.

Example

a farmer wants to build a corral as indicated in the following diagram. If it costs $45/m to put up the type of fencing that the farmer wants, how much will this fence cost him?

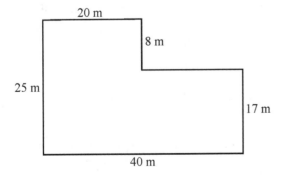

Because we are being asked for the total amount it will cost to build the fence, we need to find out first what will be the total amount of fencing required will be. This is a perimeter question. The total perimeter is found by adding up the lengths of all the sides of the object.

20 m + 8 m + 20 m + 17 m + 40 m + 25 m
= 130 m

Now, to determine the total amount this will cost, we multiply the total length by the unit price.

130 m × $45/m = $5 850

Therefore, it will cost the farmer $5 850 to build a fence around this corral.

One other consideration in a problem like this could be a gate. If the farmer needs to put a gate in the fence that is 2.5 m long and costs $250, how does this change the overall price of the corral?

The first thing we need to do is remove 2.5 m from the length of the fence, because the gate will now replace it. This means that the total length of fencing required is
130 m – 2.5 m = 127.5 m. Now, we continue to calculate the cost of the fence using the unit price, but we include the cost of the gate.

127.5 m × $45/m + $250 = $5 987.50

So, the fence with the gate will cost $5 987.50.

The problems are not always specifically related to the price of a project, but the approach we take will be similar.

Example

As bricks are being produced they are placed in a storage room to await their sale.
The storage room is 3 m wide, 2 m deep, and 3 m high. Each brick is 43 cm long, 22 cm wide, and 18 cm high. What is the maximum number of bricks that the storage room can hold if the bricks are arranged lengthwise along the length of the storage room?

Solution

First, convert the dimensions of the brick to metres to match the units for the storage room.

43 cm = 0.43 m
22 cm = 0.22 m
18 cm = 0.18 m

Now, determine how many bricks can fit along the length of the storage room, the width of the storage room and height of the room.

3 m ÷ 0.43 m = 6.98
2 m ÷ 0.22 m = 9.09
3 m ÷ 0.18 m = 16.67

Notice that we could only fit 6 bricks across the length of the storage room, 9 bricks across the width of the room, and 16 stacked on top of each other. In each case we need to round the value down because there isn't enough room to fit another brick. The total number of bricks will be equivalent to the multiple of the number of bricks across the length, width and depth of the storage room.

$6 \times 9 \times 16 = 864$

Therefore, the total number of bricks that the storage room can handle is 864.

Students must also be careful to round appropriately when it comes to purchasing materials to complete a project. When materials cannot be purchased in fractional amounts, students must be sure to round up so as not to come up short.

Example

A couple wants to create a "feature" wall in their house by painting it a different colour. Each can of paint they want costs $47.50, with tax, and covers 3.6 m^2. Using the diagram provided, and knowing that they will want to put on two coats of paint, how much will this couple need to spend on paint?

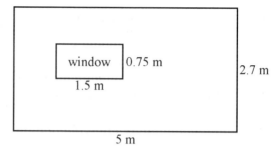

Solution

First, we need to determine the total area of the wall to be painted, which means finding the total area of the complete wall (including the window) and then subtracting the area of the window.

complete area: $2.7 \text{ m} \times 5 \text{ m} = 13.5 \text{ m}^2$

window area: $1.5 \text{ m} \times 0.75 \text{ m} = 1.125 \text{ m}^2$

total area to be painted: $13.5 \text{ m}^2 - 1.125 \text{ m}^2$
$= 12.375 \text{ m}^2$

Now, because we know that the couple wants to put on two coats of paint the total area to be painted will actually be double this amount.

$12.375 \text{ m}^2 \times 2 = 24.75 \text{ m}^2$

To determine the number of cans that will be needed, we divide the total area by the area that a single can of paint is able to cover and whatever the decimal value is, we will round the final answer up so as not to leave any part of the wall out.

$$\frac{24.75 \text{ m}^2}{3.6 \text{ m}^2} = 6.875 \approx 7$$

Because we cannot purchase fractional cans, we round this up to 7 cans of paint. The total cost will, therefore, be found as follows:

$7 \times \$47.50 = \$332.50.$

Therefore, the total cost to paint this wall is $332.50.

Related Questions: NR1, 1, 2, 3, 4, 5, NR2, 6, 7, 8

Not for Reproduction

6.2 Solve problems involving estimation and cost for objects, shapes, or processes when a design is given.

ESTIMATION

In many industries, people are required to make judgments based on their calculations.
There can be a times when quick calculations, or the need for just a general idea, calls for estimating the results.

Example

The company you work for is producing a new energy drink that will come in a small can with a height of 13.2 cm and a diameter of 5.2 cm.

Because the lid must have a tab in it, it will be made in a different department.
Your department is responsible for putting together the bottom and sides of the can.

You have been given 2 sheets of tin. From one, you will punch out the bottoms and from the other, you will punch out the sides. These sheets are 2.4 m by 3.6 m. Your boss is in a hurry to report to a board of directors about this new product. He wants to know how many cans you can make with this much tin.

Solution

Before answering this question, one must realize that it is not appropriate to simply find the area of the tin sheet and divide it by the area of the circular bottom. This assumes that these pieces can be punched out without any waste. We need to take into consideration that punching out circular shapes is going to create waste as illustrated in the following diagram.

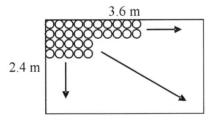

To determine how many we can punch out lengthwise, we take the total length in cm and divide it by the diameter of the circular base.

$$\frac{360\,cm}{5.2\ cm}=69.32\approx 69$$

Therefore, we can punch out 69 along the length of the sheet.

Next, we need to determine how many we can punch out along the width of the sheet. To do this, we simply divide the width of the sheet by the diameter as we did previously.

$$\frac{240\ cm}{5.2\ cm}=46.15\approx 46$$

So, now we can punch out 69 lengthwise and 46 along the width. To determine the total number we multiply these together as if we were calculating an area.

$$69 \times 46 = 3\ 174$$

This gives us a total of 3 174 bottom pieces.

Now, we need to determine how many sidepieces we punch out of a similar sheet.
The sides of the can will simply be a rectangular piece that is rolled up. We already know that the rectangle will be 13.2 cm wide. The length must be equivalent to the circumference of the bottom piece if it is to wrap around it. Therefore, we need to find the circumference of the circular bottom.

$C = \pi d$
$C = \pi(5.1\ cm)$
$C = 16.0\ cm$

Therefore, the pieces will be 16.0 cm by 13.2 cm. Now, we need to compare these dimensions to the sheet of tin that you are provided. Lay out the length of the rectangular side against the length of the sheet.
To determine how many there can be, we divide the length of the sheet by the length of the side. We will also do this with the width of the side, and then calculate how many pieces we can cut out as we did with the round pieces.

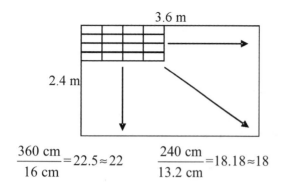

$$\frac{360 \text{ cm}}{16 \text{ cm}} = 22.5 \approx 22 \qquad \frac{240 \text{ cm}}{13.2 \text{ cm}} = 18.18 \approx 18$$

Notice that we round down with these because it is impossible to lay out another complete rectangular piece. Now we multiply these values together to find the total number of side pieces.

$22 \times 18 = 396$

The limiting number here is 396, and so we would probably communicate to our boss that with just the two pieces of tin we could make 396 cans. This is just an estimate because with careful planning it would be possible to create more. We would simply punch out less bottom pieces and use some of that tin to create more sidepieces.

Now, by extension, if the boss told us that each sheet of tin cost $3.45, and that we require 2 seals at 0.7¢ each, to combine the bottom to the side, how much would it cost to produce all the cans, and how much would it cost per can?

The two pieces of tin cost a combined total of $3.45 + $3.45 = $6.90. In addition to this, we need to consider the cost of the seals, to find this, we need to multiply the number of cans produced by 2, because there are two seals for every can.

$396 \times 2 = 792$

We will need 792 seals at 0.7¢ which will cost a total of $792 \times \$0.007 = \$5.544$. Therefore, the total cost of the 396 cans is $6.90 + $5.54 = $12.44.

The cost per can is calculated by taking the total cost and dividing by the number of cans produced:

$$\frac{\$12.44}{396} \approx \$0.03$$

Therefore, each can costs about three cents to produce.

Related to problems similar to the one above, is the ability to draw scale diagrams of objects when a description is provided. This involves using a scale factor and the properties of proportions to calculate the lengths that you use in your diagram. Recall that the scale factor is a ratio between the length of a line segment in the diagram, compared to the actual length that it represents.

Example

Suppose you want to build a planter in the shape of the letter "T". You want to create several scale diagrams first to help you build the actual planter. You want the length along the top of the "T" shape to be 1.75 m long, and you want the width of this piece to be 50 cm . The lower portion of the "T" should come out of the middle of the top piece, but you want it to be 1.5 m long and 40 cm wide. The entire planter should be 60 cm deep. If the scale factor you have decided upon is 5 cm: 1 m, then draw the top view, the front view and a three-dimensional shape.

Solution

First, calculate the lengths required in the diagram.

$$\frac{5 \text{ cm}}{1 \text{ m}} = \frac{x}{1.75 \text{ m}}$$

$x = 8.75$ cm   It will be 8.75 cm long along the top.

$$\frac{5 \text{ cm}}{1 \text{ m}} = \frac{y}{0.5 \text{ m}}$$

$y = 2.5$ cm   The top part is 2.5 cm wide.

$$\frac{5 \text{ cm}}{1 \text{ m}} = \frac{z}{1.5 \text{ m}}$$

$z = 7.5$ cm   The bottom part is 7.5 cm long.

$$\frac{5 \text{ cm}}{1 \text{ m}} = \frac{w}{0.4 \text{ m}}$$

$w = 2$ cm   The bottom part is 2 cm wide.

$$\frac{5 \text{ cm}}{1 \text{ m}} = \frac{v}{0.6 \text{ m}}$$

$v = 3$ cm   The diagram is 3 cm high.

Not for Reproduction

Top View

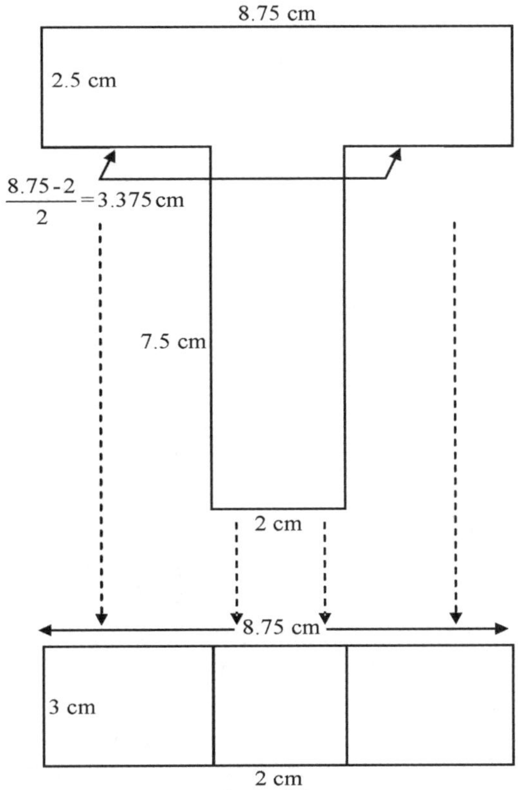
8.75 cm
2.5 cm
$\frac{8.75-2}{2}=3.375$ cm
7.5 cm
2 cm
8.75 cm
3 cm
2 cm

Front View

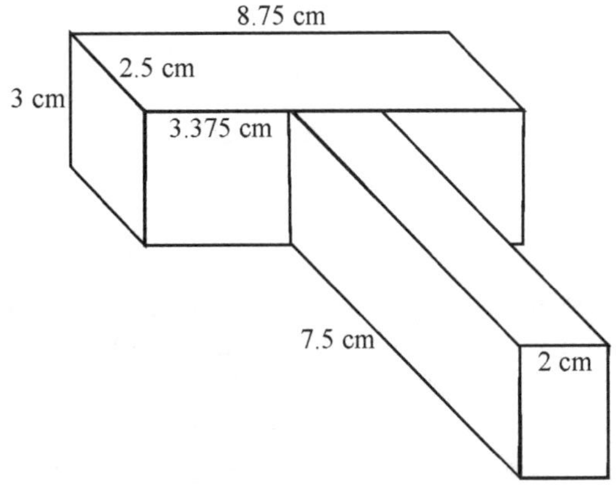
8.75 cm
2.5 cm
3 cm
3.375 cm
7.5 cm
2 cm

The key to drawing the front view is to connect it to the top view with dotted arrows. Using this method it is quite easy to see where the lines should go.

The key to drawing the three-dimensional diagram is that it is similar to the top view except that the vertical lines are now drawn at an angle of 45°, and at the corners, lines are drawn down representing the height of the planter.

Related Questions: 9, 10, 11, 12, NR3, 13, 14, 15

6.3 Use appropriate variables to design an object, shape, layout, or process within a specified budget.

DESIGN AND BUDGETING

When answering questions from this outcome, students are required to consider that their resources are limited by the amount of money at their disposal. This means that certain options will be ignored because they are cost-prohibitive. On the other hand, students will also have to make decisions about what is important in a project to the end that they will have to determine what they are willing to forego and what they are not.

Example

The Willcox family wants to renovate their backyard, and they have budgeted $800.00 for the project. The following is a diagram of the plans they have for the yard. They want a small patio made from paving stones near the house and sod on most of the yard. They are planning on surrounding the grass with a small fence and they want to surround the yard with rose bushes on the other side of the fence.

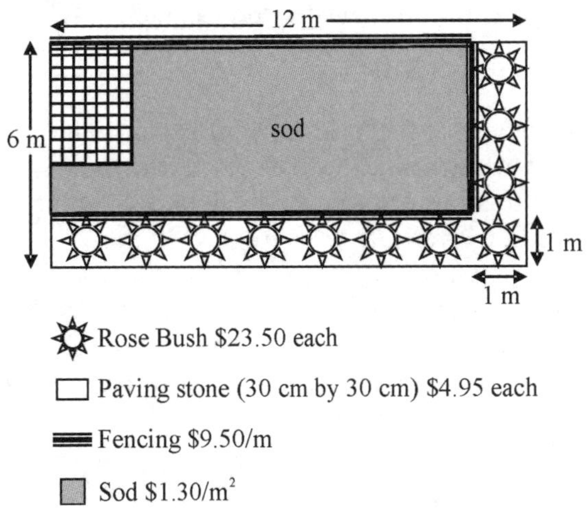
12 m
6 m
sod
1 m
1 m
Rose Bush $23.50 each
Paving stone (30 cm by 30 cm) $4.95 each
Fencing $9.50/m
Sod $1.30/m²

How much will it cost the Willcox family to landscape their backyard?

Solution

To answer this question, we need to break the problem up into smaller pieces.

First, we should determine how much the rose bushes would cost.

There are 11 bushes at $23.50 each, so, to determine the total cost, we multiply.

$11 \times \$23.50 = \$258.50$

The roses will cost them $258.50.

Next, consider the paving stones. There are 10 rows of 7 paving stones each yielding a total of 70 paving stones. Each stone costs $4.95, so to determine the total cost we would multiply.

$70 \times \$4.95 = \$346.50$

The paving stones will cost a total of $346.50.

After that, we should consider the fencing. The short fence will run the length of the yard, less one metre, and the width of the yard less one metre. This means that fence will require 2 sections of 11 m and one section of 5 m. This makes a total of 27 m when we add them up. Since the fence is $9.50/m, we only need to multiply to determine the total amount.

$27 \times \$9.50 = \$104.50$

So, the fence will cost $104.50. Finally, we need to determine the total cost of the sod. This requires determining the total area of the part of the yard we want covered in grass. The easiest way to do this would be to find the area of the 5 m by 11 m section that will contain the paving stones and grass, and then subtract the area of the patio. This means the area of the grass and patio together will be $5 \text{ m} \times 11 \text{ m} = 55 \text{ m}^2$.

Each paving stone is 30 cm on a side, or 0.3 m. Since there are 7 of them along a row, the patio will be $7 \times 0.3 \text{ m} = 2.1 \text{ m}$ long. There are 10 paving stones along the length of the patio making the patio $10 \times 0.3 \text{ m} = 3 \text{ m}$ long. When we multiply these together we find that the area of the patio will be $2.1 \text{ m} \times 3.0 \text{ m} = 6.3 \text{ m}^2$. Now, we subtract the two areas to determine that we need $55 \text{ m}^2 - 6.3 \text{ m}^2 = 48.7 \text{ m}^2$ of sod.

Since we purchase sod by the square metre, and we cannot buy a fraction of a piece we must buy at least 49 m^2. Common sense says that it would be wiser to purchase a little extra in case we need to cut pieces, so we buy 50 m^2. To determine the total cost, we simply multiply and find that sod will cost $50 \text{ m}^2 \times \$1.30/\text{m}^2 = \$65.00$.

Now, we add up all of the costs of the individual projects to determine that the total cost is $\$258.50 + \$346.50 + \$104.50 + \$65.00 = \$774.50$. Since they are doing all the work, they do not need to pay for landscapers, but they must still consider the GST. This brings the total price to $\$774.50 \times 1.06 = \$820.97$.

The Willcox family cannot afford to do what they want with the yard. They are $20.97 over budget. To save on costs, they may want to buy less rose bushes and space them out more. They may want to have a smaller patio as paving stones cost more than sod does. They may choose a different style of fencing. In any case, they will need to make decisions because they cannot have their yard exactly as they planned it.

A variation to this style of problem gives students a specific budget and requires that they determine how much can be done within their budget.

Example

Suppose that a coach is looking for an award for his star soccer player, but he only has a budget of $30.00 to buy it with. He would like to purchase a trophy for $26.00. The engraving will cost $0.10 a letter or number, and he would like to have "Most Valuable Player 2005" engraved on it, with the name "Albert Pascal" underneath it, and the name of their team, the "Edmonton Eulers" at the bottom. How many letters can he actually afford? Do not consider GST.

Solution

In this situation, there is $4.00 left for the engraving. Each letter costs $0.10 so we simply need to divide to determine the total number of allowable letters.

Not for Reproduction

$$\frac{\$4.00}{\$0.10} = 40$$

Therefore, he can afford to have 40 letters engraved. Can he engrave everything he wants? No, because the writing he wants has 48 letters. He may want to leave off the name of the team, or perhaps use one of his player's initials instead of the whole name.

6.4   Use mathematical models to estimate the solutions to complex measurement problems.

MATHEMATICAL MODELS

There are times when we may build mathematical models to help us make decisions and solve more complicated problems. These models may come in the form of equations relating different aspects of a problem, graphs that model relationships between two variables or even spreadsheets that create lists of data to model a process. The important thing when working with mathematical models is to remember what they represent. Once a problem has been represented mathematically and the problem is solved, it is often difficult to interpret the results. To aid in this process, it is imperative that students make a note of what all the variables that they use represent.

Example

Suppose you want to build a gift-box from a piece of cardboard with dimensions 40 cm by 60 cm. The box will not need a top as you plan on using decorative paper to cover your gift. To build the box you will cut equal sized squares out of the corners of the piece of cardboard and then you will fold up the remaining flaps to form the sides. Before you do this though, you want to make sure that you are making the best use of the cardboard. In other words, you want to make the biggest box possible.

Solution

The problem is that you do not know how large to make the squares that you cut out. The size of the squares you remove will determine the size of the box. At this point, you can represent the dimensions of the squares with an *x* as follows.

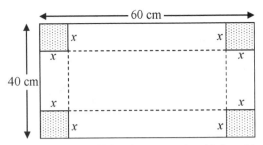

The squares must all be the same size if the sides of the box are to meet up appropriately. Now to determine the volume of the resulting box, we need to find out the box's length, width and height.

The multiple of these three dimensions will give the volume of the box, because the volume of a rectangular prism is $V = lwh$.

The width of the piece of cardboard is 40 cm, and if we cut out squares with sides that are *x* by *x* on either end, then the width of the box will be $w = (40 - 2x)$ cm, once the sides have been folded up.

In the same way we can determine the length of the resulting box. The length of the cardboard is 60 cm, but once the squares have been cut out and the sides are folded up, we will lose *x* cm on both sides of the cardboard.

This means that the length of the box will be $l = (60 - 2x)$ cm. Finally, because the flap was created by cutting out the squares from the corners, when they are folded up, the height of the box will be *x* cm.

These expressions can now be used to determine an equation for the volume of the box.

$V = (40 - 2x)(60 - x)x$

Here is a model for the volume of a box. Notice that there are limits to how large *x* can be. Because we are cutting the squares out of the corners of the cardboard, the square cannot be larger than half the width of the cardboard.

This means that the largest square that can be cut out of the corner of the piece of cardboard is 20 cm by 20 cm. At this point, the squares that are being cut out end up cutting the cardboard in half.

Now, we can use this information to produce a graphical model of how the volume of a box changes as the size of the x changes. We graph the equation using technology (such as a calculator). It should be clear that the horizontal window settings should be x: [0, 20, 2] seeing as the minimum size that the square side length can be is zero and the maximum value must be twenty.

To determine the vertical window settings, the minimum value must also be zero because the smallest possible volume is zero, but it may require a bit of experimentation to determine the maximum value.

Soon it will be clear that the vertical window settings should be y:[0, 10 000, 500].

Together, these give the graph:

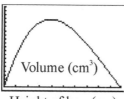

Height of box (cm)

Now, we can use the technology that graphed this function to find the maximum volume of the box, and the size of the square that created it.

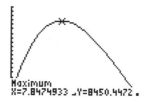

The maximum volume is 8 450.4 cm³, when the length of the cut out square is 7.8 cm. If the value of x is 7.8 cm, then
$l = 60 - 2(7.8) = 44.4$ cm, and
$w = 40 - 2(7.8) = 24.4$ cm.

In addition to finding out the maximum volume, we can also determine an equation for the surface area of the box by finding the area of each side of the box.

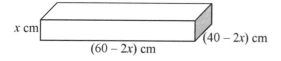

First, we need to find the expressions for the areas of the front piece and the side piece.

$A_{front} = lw$ $A_{side} = lw$
$A_{front} = (60 - 2x)x$ $A_{side} = (40 - 2x)x$

In addition to this, we need to determine the area of the base of the box.

$A_{base} = lw$
$A_{base} = (60 - 2x)(40 - 2x)$

Now, to put together all of these pieces of information students must realize that the total surface area will include two pieces identical to the front, two side pieces, and the bottom piece.

$SA = 2x(60 - 2x) + 2x(40 - 2x)$
$\quad\quad + (60 - 2x)(40 - 2x)$

With an equation for the surface area we can create a graph to help us determine the maximum volume with the minimum surface area.

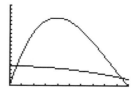

From this, we can see that the surface area does not hit a minimum value along the domain that we graphed for the volume, but the two graphs intersect where the values of x, the side of the square, are 1.1 cm and 18.8 cm.

Since the maximum volume occurs for a value of x between these two, a value between 1.1 cm and 18.8 cm should produce a box with an acceptable relationship between surface area and volume. When the values of x are less than 1.1 cm, or greater than 18.8 cm, the volume of the resulting box will be too small.

Related Questions: 16, 17, 18

Not for Reproduction

*Use the following information to answer
the next question.*

A rectangular plot of land is 200 m by 400 m.
The owner wishes to develop a campground
where each campsite must be at least 5 m by
10 m. The county allows the owner to develop
70% of the property as campsites.

Numerical Response

1. The greatest number of campsites that the
owner can develop on this property is

_____.

Source: January 2001

*Use the following information to answer
the next question.*

A home-based business produces cans of maple
syrup. To produce the maple syrup, it costs the
owner $0.02/mL, and he knows that 1 mL is
equivalent to 1 cm³.

CHALLENGER QUESTION	48.7

1. If the maple syrup is packaged in
cylindrical cans that have a radius of
5 cm and a height of 13 cm, then the cost to
produce 1 can is

A. $4.08

B. $6.81

C. $11.31

D. $20.42

Source: June 2001

*Use the following information to answer
the next question.*

The usable space in a farm storage shed has the
dimensions 20 m × 10 m × 5 m. The straw bales
to be stored in the shed each measure
1.4 m × 0.6 m × 0.6 m. The bales are to be
stacked in such a way that the long side of the
bale runs parallel to the long side of the shed, as
shown in the diagram. Bales must not be
broken.

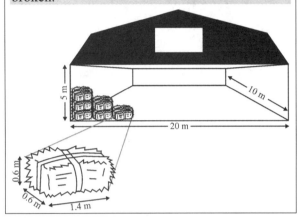

CHALLENGER QUESTION	23.4

2. The maximum number of bales that can
be stored in this shed is

A. 1 120 **B.** 1 792

C. 1 982 **D.** 1 984

Source: June 2001

3. A glass has a diameter
of 10 cm at the brim
and is 18 cm high. If
the glass has the shape
shown below, what is
its volume?

A. 1 885 cm³

B. 1 414 cm³

C. 600 cm³

D. 471 cm³

Copyright Protected

4. Another 18 cm high glass has the shape shown below where the cone and the stem are each half the height of the glass. How much liquid can the glass hold?

   A. 942 cm³

   B. 707 cm³

   C. 236 cm³

   D. 150 cm³

5. A military tent has a base of 4 m by 4 m, and the walls are 3 m high. The pyramid-shaped roof has a height of 3 m. What is the total volume of the tent?

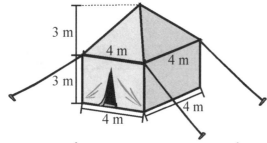

   A. 12 m³   **B.** 48 m³

   C. 60 m³   **D.** 64 m³

Use the following information to answer the next question.

The Alaskan Pipeline extends 1 270 km, carrying up to 2 million barrels of oil per day.

Numerical Response

2. If the diameter of the pipe is 1.5 m, the length of pipe that will have a volume of 106 m³ is _____ m. (Record your answer to one decimal place)

6. A 355 mL soft drink container is made of aluminum that costs $0.000 5/cm². What is the cost to the nearest cent of producing one soft drink container with radius 3 cm?

   A. 5¢

   B. 10¢

   C. 15¢

   D. 20¢

7. A 25 m × 6 m portion of highway needs to be resurfaced. The depth of material required on the highway is 0.15 m. The material cost is $900/m³. The approximate cost of material needed to resurface this section of highway is

   A. $810

   B. $3 375

   C. $20 250

   D. $135 000

8. What is the total cost of the steel needed to build a 5 000 L steel storage tank that has a height of 15 m, given that the steel to be used costs $30/m²?

   A. $49 119.90

   B. $4 911.99

   C. $19 997.40

   D. $29 122.50

Use the following information to answer the next question.

In a parkade, cylindrical concrete pillars that will be 0.8 m high and have a radius of 0.3 m are to be built. Each pillar will house a rectangular electrical box that measures 0.2 m × 0.2 m × 0.1 m. The pillars will be solid concrete except for this electrical box.

CHALLENGER QUESTION   **35.**

9. If concrete costs $134/m^3, then the cost of concrete for each pillar will be

   A. $29.77

   B. $30.85

   C. $31.60

   D. $32.70

   Source: January 2001

10. A plumber installs a drainage line that uses 2 elbow pieces that cost $5.15 each, 1 trap that costs $8.40, and 4.95 m of straight pipe that costs $4.05/m. The total cost of the components in this drainage line is

    A. $47.15

    B. $38.75

    C. $33.60

    D. $17.60

    Source: January 2001

Use the following information to answer the next question.

A family has moved into a new home. A room with the dimensions shown below requires carpeting. The portion of the floor under the fireplace requires no carpet and is not included in the cost. The cost of the carpet they want is $2.48/ft^2.

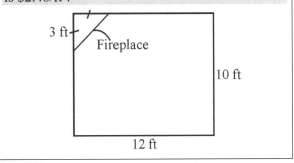

11. The cost of carpet for the room will be

    A. $156.24   **B.** $275.28

    C. $286.44   **D.** $297.60

    Source: January 2001

Use the following information to answer the next question.

The family would like to repaint the room and buy some new furniture and wall hangings for it. Their budget for this project is $2 500.
The items that they would like to buy are listed below along with their prices (including taxes).

sofa	$799	television	$527
loveseat	$504	VCR	$238
chair	$280	wall hangings	$478
lamps	$177	paint	$31/gallon
			(need 3 gallons)

12. To remain within their budget, the family could choose to not buy

    A. any wall hangings

    B. the chair and lamps

    C. the loveseat and paint

    D. wall hangings and paint

    Source: January 2001

Copyright Protected

Use the following information to answer the next question.

A student has been given a budget of $120 to make a banner acknowledging the victory of the school's wrestling team in the district playoffs.
The combined cost of the material and the dowel is $86.59, and the cost of the logo is $20.00.

Numerical Response

3. If lettering, priced at $0.23 per letter, is also to be placed on the banner, then the maximum number of letters that the student can buy is _____ letters.

Source: January 2001

Use the following information to answer the next question.

Frank wants to produce and market "Infinity Marbles" in packages of 100. Frank expects material costs of 1.2¢ per marble, production costs of 1.5¢ per marble, and packaging costs of 30¢ per package. To make this business worthwhile, Frank requires a 200% profit on sales.

13. To cover his costs and make a 200% profit, Frank should sell each package of marbles for

A. $9.00

B. $6.00

C. $3.60

D. $3.00

Source: June 2001

Use the following information to answer the next question.

The glass for a large picture frame must be 2 cm smaller than the outer dimensions of the frame, as shown below. Glass can be purchased for $41.82/m².

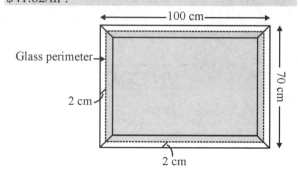

14. The cost of the glass will be

A. $29.27   B. $27.87

C. $27.30   D. $26.50

Source: June 2001

Use the following information to answer the next question.

A cylindrical storage tank that measures 6 m tall and has a radius of 2 m is going to be covered with sheet metal.

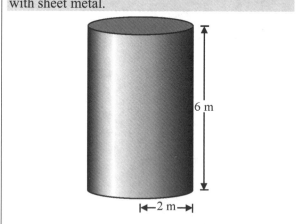

Not for Reproduction

15. If sheet metal costs $2.08/m^2$, then the cost to cover the entire cylinder, including the top and bottom, will be

A. $75.40

B. $156.83

C. $182.97

D. $209.10

Source: June 2001

Use the following information to answer the next question.

A piece of cardboard that measures 20 cm by 15 cm is used to construct a rectangular box. Equal-sized squares are removed from each corner and then the ends are folded up.

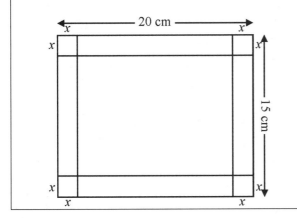

16. An equation that could be used to calculate the volume of the box is

A. $v = x(20 - 2x)(15 - 2x)$

B. $v = x(20 - x)(15 - x)$

C. $v = 2x(20 - x)(15 - 2x)$

D. $v = 2x(20 - x)(15 - x)$

ource: June 2001

Use the following information to answer the next question.

A 12×16 rectangular piece of cardboard is to be cut as shown, below

x cm

16 cm

x cm

x cm

12 cm   **Removed**

x cm

17. Given that the area of the cardboard that is removed is to be equal to the area of the remaining piece, the value of x is

A. 1 cm

B. 2 cm

C. 4 cm

D. 12 cm

18. While looking out the windows in the boarding area of an air terminal, you notice a cargo plane being loaded. The total volume of storage space available on the cargo plane is 1.488×10^3 m^3. How many crates with a volume of 1.24×10^1 m^3 each can fit in this storage space?

A. 1.20×10^4 crates

B. 1.20×10^3 crates

C. 1.20×10^2 crates

D. 1.20×10^2 crates

Use the following information to answer the next question.

A family is planning to cover their 20 ft × 25 ft living room/dining room with carpet and hardwood. Their budget for this project is $5 000. The cost of the carpet is $7.25/ft^2, and the cost of the hardwood is $12.50/ft^2.
The family would like to cover the entire area with hardwood, but they know that it would cost more than the budgeted amount. In order to determine the maximum area of hardwood that they can afford, they calculated the total cost of the flooring each time a 1 ft wide section of hardwood was added to the room, as shown below.

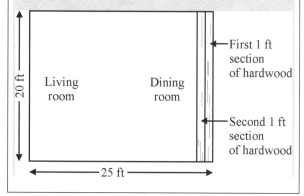

The family used the following spreadsheet to calculate costs and to determine the maximum area of hardwood that they could afford.

	A	B	C	D	E
1	Area of floor w/ hardwood (ft^2)	Area of floor w/ carpet (ft^2)	Cost of hardwood at $12.50/ft^2	Cost of carpet at $7.25/ft^2	Total cost of flooring
2	500	0	$6 250	$0	$6 250
3	480	20	$6 000	$145	$6 145
4	460	40	$5 750	$290	$6 040
5	440	60	$5 500	$435	$5 935
6	420	80	$5 250	$580	$5 830
7	400	100	$5 000	$725	$5 725
8	380	120	$4 750	$870	$5 620
9	360	140	$4 500	$1 015	$5 515
10	340	160	$4 250	$1 160	$5 410
11	320	180	$4 000	$1 305	$5 305
12	300	200	$3 750	$1 450	$5 200
13	280	220	$3 500	$1 595	$5 095
14	260	240	$3 250	$1 740	$4 990
15	240	260	$3 000	$1 885	$4 885
16	220	280	$2 750	$2 030	$4 780
17	200	300	$2 500	$2 175	$4 675
18	180	320	$2 250	$2 320	$4 570
19	160	340	$2 000	$2 465	$4 465
20	140	360	$1 750	$2 610	$4 360
21	120	380	$1 500	$2 755	$4 255
22	100	400	$1 250	$2 900	$4 150
23	80	420	$1 000	$3 045	$4 045
24	60	440	$750	$3 190	$3 940
25	40	460	$500	$3 335	$3 835
26	20	480	$250	$3 480	$3 730
27	0	500	$0	$3 625	$3 625

Copyright Protected

Not for Reproduction

Written Response

1. **a)** Explain the relationship between the values in columns A and B.

b) Show, by writing a statement or a formula, how the value in cell E9 ($5 515) was calculated.
Make reference to other cells in row 9.

c) If the family is to remain within their budget, what is the maximum area of hardwood that they can place into this living room/dining room area?

Use the following additional information to answer the next part of the question.

The family decided that they would finish one-half of the floor in carpet and one-half in hardwood.

d) What is the total cost for this plan?
Will the family remain within their budget? Explain.

Source: January 2001

Copyright Protected

UNIT TEST 6—DESIGN

Use the following information to answer the next two questions.

Matt bought an acreage the shape of which can be approximated using a rectangle, a right triangle and a square. The following diagram illustrates the dimensions and shape of his acreage.

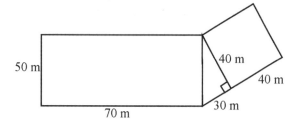

1. If Matt wants to put a special type of polymer fencing all around his property that costs $6.50/m regardless if it is used on the fence or the gate, then how much will he pay total for the fencing material?

   A. $2 210.00

   B. $2 795.00

   C. $2 470.00

   D. $1 495.00

2. For tax purposes, Matt needs to know the area of his property. He is informed that he will pay $0.45/m² for monthly tax. His total monthly tax is

   A. $2 835.00

   B. $2 970.00

   C. $2 565.00

   D. $2 295.00

Use the following information to answer the next question.

A manufacturer can produce ice cream at a price of $0.002/cm³. They are in the process of changing the design of their container. They are proposing a hemispherical container with a radius of 12 cm.

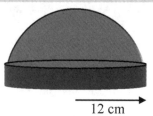

3. How much will it cost them to fill the container with ice cream?

   A. $14.48

   B. $7.24

   C. $1.81

   D. $0.90

Use the following information to answer the next question.

For a specific piece of jewellery, a company has designed a cylindrical container with a diameter of 6 cm and a height of 4 cm. Felt costs $0.03/cm².

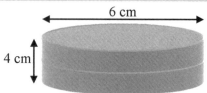

4. To cover the box with felt will cost

   A. $7.92

   B. $3.11

   C. $11.31

   D. $3.96

Use the following information to answer the next question.

To make a banner to honour the school's championship like the one drawn below, the students need to purchase the cloth for the banner at $1.30/m^2. It will cost $0.80 for each letter that will be embroidered onto the banner. The students wish to have the words "PROVINCIAL CHAMPIONS" put on the banner.

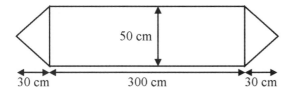

50 cm

30 cm   300 cm   30 cm

5. How much will it cost them to make the banner?

    A. $2.15   **B.** $15.20

    C. $17.25   **D.** $17.35

Use the following information to answer the next two questions.

To make a tin can one needs to punch the material out of sheets of tin that are 2 m by 3 m. The top of the can requires special treatment elsewhere in the factory to put in the tab and so it won't be considered here.   The first thing that needs to be done in making the tin cans is to punch out the bottom and the sides of the can. The can is to be 5 cm in diameter and 13 cm tall. To make the process of making the cans faster, all of the tops are punched out of the same piece of tin and all of the sidepieces are punched out of another piece of tin.

Numerical Response

1. The total number of cans that can be made from these two sheets of tin is _____.

2. If each piece of tin costs $7.00, then each individual can costs $_____.

Use the following information to answer the next question.

A wall is 9 ft by 20 ft with a window in it that is 2.5 ft by 4 ft. A door in the wall is 7 ft by 2.5 ft. A can of paint can cover 36 ft^2 and costs $12.00/can.

6. How much will it cost to cover the wall with two coats of paint?

    A. $101.67   **B.** $60.00

    C. $108.00   **D.** $120.00

Use the following information to answer the next question.

A couple has budgeted $2 000.00 to renovate their bathroom. They wish to buy a new bathtub, a new toilet, a new pedestal sink and tiles to go around the tub. The tub will cost $900.00, the toilet will cost $220.00 and the sink will cost $320.00 total. The tub is 32" wide, 60" long and the height that the tiles extend above the tub is another 60".

Numerical Response

3. If each tile is 6" by 6", then they can afford to spend $_____ on each tile to stay within their budget.

Use the following information to answer the next question.

A farmer wants to build a silo for storing grain. He has $270 to spend on the material. The metal costs $3.00/m^2, and the silo he needs must have a diameter of 4 m but it does not require a bottom.

7. Assuming that the silo must be cylindrical, the maximum height that his silo can be is

    A. 1.6 m

    B. 6.2 m

    C. 3.6 m

    D. 5.2 m

Copyright Protected

Written Response

Use the following information to answer the next question.

A box is to be made from a piece of tin. The box is to have a lid that can be folded over it. The sheet of tin measures 150 cm by 50 cm.

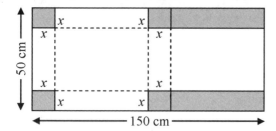

The volume of the resulting box can be calculated using the formula

$$V = x(50-2x)\left(\frac{150-2x}{2}\right).$$

1. **a)** How do the different factors of the volume equation relate to the dimensions of the box?

b) Using a graphing calculator, determine the maximum volume of the box and its dimensions (answers to the nearest hundredth).

c) Find an expression for the surface area of the box, as a function of the value of x.

ANSWERS AND SOLUTIONS
UNIT REVIEW—MATRICES AND PATHWAYS

1. C	6. B	11. B	16. A
2. C	NR2. 120	12. C	17. C
3. B	7. B	13. D	NR4. 126
4. C	8. B	14. B	WR1. See Solution
5. A	9. C	NR3. 8149	
NR1. 60	10. A	15. C	

1. C

We can find the total number of different paths that a marble may take if we display the number of paths from each junction. Using Pascal's Triangle, we get.

$$
\begin{array}{ccccccc}
1 & 5 & 10 & 10 & 5 & 1 & \quad 32 \\
 & 1 & 4 & 6 & 4 & 1 & \\
 & & 1 & 3 & 3 & 1 & \\
 & & & 1 & 2 & 1 & \\
 & & & & 1 & 1 & \\
 & & & & & 1 & \\
\end{array}
$$

2. C

The numbers of routes that John can take follow a pattern.

For one block, John has two paths to the opposite corner.

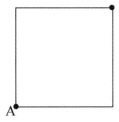

Organize the number of choices by recording them at each node or intersection. We obtain the number of choices for each node by adding the number of routes to it.

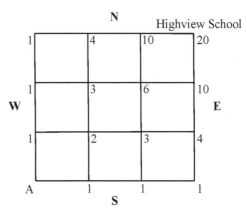

At the final block, we have a total of 20 different paths.

3. B

Mary's number of unique paths follows a specific pattern. At each intersection, there's a node. Here, we add the number of routes to this point and write the sum of each corner.

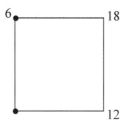

Example: For one block in her route, she has 6 ways around one side, and 12 ways around the other. The total number of paths to the next node is $12 + 6 = 18$.

The following diagram shows the number of routes to arrive at each node.

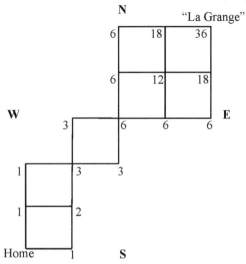

"La Grange"

From the diagram, we can see that there are 36 routes for Mary to travel from home to work.

4. C

The pattern for each "word" must follow the pattern consonant – vowel – consonant and each letter can be repeated.

Using the Fundamental Counting Principle, we can write out our possibilities.

C – V– C
$7 \times 5 \times 7 = 245$

5. A

This problem can be solved using the Fundamental Counting Principle. We have a line of five places with no repetitions.

$5 \times 4 \times 3 \times 2 \times 1 = 120$

Method 1
The total number of 3-digit numbers less than 400 are from 100 to 399, i.e. 300.

The last digit can be any of the 10 digits 0–9. Hence, the proportion of numbers with last digit either a 4 or a 5

$$=\frac{2}{10}=\frac{1}{5}$$

Therefore, the number of 3-digit numbers less than 400

$$=300 \times \frac{1}{5}=60$$

Method 2
Using the Fundamental Counting Principle:

First digit – 3 possible (1, 2 or 3)
Second digit –10 possible (any digit 0 to 9)
Third digit – 2 possible (4 or 5)

$\underline{3} \times \underline{10} \times \underline{2} = 60$

6. B

Given that the letter y is a consonant, there are 5 vowels and 21 consonants in the alphabet.

Therefore, the number of two-letter combinations that start with a consonant and end with a vowel
= the number of ways of choosing a consonant × the number of ways of choosing a vowel

$= 21 \times 5 = 105$

NR2. 120

A flight attendant has to wear a pair of slacks, a shirt, a tie, and a blazer. Attendants can choose from 3 different pairs of slacks, 5 different shirts, 4 different ties, and 2 different blazers.
The maximum number of different outfits can be calculated using the Fundamental Counting Principle.

$3 \times 5 \times 4 \times 2 = 120$ outfits

7. B

Five different tents are to be arranged vertically in a flyer. Three of the tents are shown in blue (B) and the other two tents in non-blue (N) colours. As no two blue illustrations should be together, and as there are more Bs than Ns, they should be displayed as shown below.

B   N   B   N   B
$3 \times 2 \times 2 \times 1 \times 1 = 12$

8. B

Two matrices can be multiplied if the number of columns in the first equals the number of rows in the second. Since Deanna's first matrix is 3×4, the second must be 4×1.

9. C

To determine which shop has the lowest cost for the entire order, Deanna should perform a matrix multiplication.

10. A

In order to multiply matrices, the number of columns in the first matrix must equal the number of rows in the second; therefore the answer is A.

11. B

In order for matrices to be added, they must have the same number of rows and columns. Then to add or subtract, we do so with corresponding entries.

Example:
row 1 column 1: $1 + 6 = 7$
row 1 column 2: $5 + 1 = 6$

Therefore,
row 2 column 1: $-1 + x = -2$
$x = -1$

12. C

In order to multiply matrices, the dimensions must match as follows:
$$[A]_{m \times n} \times [B]_{n \times r} \, [C]_{m \times r}$$

In this case,
$$[A]_{2 \times 3} \, [B]_{3 \times 1} \, [C]_{2 \times 1}$$

If the dimensions allow multiplication, we multiply each entry in a column with each entry in a row.

$$[A]_{\text{row 1}} \times [B]_{\text{column 1}} = [C]_{\text{row 1 column 1}}$$
$$[(1)(1) + (2)(-1) + (4)(7)] = [1 - 2 + 28] = 27$$

Following this pattern, we assemble the solution matrix,

$$\begin{bmatrix} 27 \\ -4 \end{bmatrix}_{2 \times 1}$$

13. D

In order to be able to perform operations of addition or subtraction on matrices, the dimensions must be the same. Once this requirement has been met, we perform the operation on matching entries. Also, when a matrix is multiplied by a number, each entry is multiplied by that number.

With this in mind, we can solve for c.

$$c - 2(6) = 0$$
$$c - 12 = 0$$
$$c = 12$$

14. B

For addition or subtraction of matrices, the dimension of each matrix must be the same. Here, the requirement has been met, so we can perform the intended operations.

$$3 + 4x = 11$$
$$4x = 8$$
$$x = 2$$

NR3. 8 1 4 9

Using matrices in our calculator, we enter values for matrix A and B.

Matrix A (4×3)   Matrix B (3×1)

$$\begin{bmatrix} 2 & 0 & 3 \\ 5 & 0 & -2 \\ 3 & -1 & -2 \\ 1 & 0 & 4 \end{bmatrix} \times \begin{bmatrix} 1 \\ -5 \\ 2 \end{bmatrix} = \begin{bmatrix} 8 \\ 1 \\ 4 \\ 9 \end{bmatrix}$$

15. C

The matrix is organized as follows.

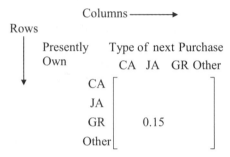

The entry in row 3, column 2 shows that 15% of people who presently own German-produced cars would purchase a Japanese-produced car for their next car.

16. A

Warehouse letters fill the rows and item types fill the columns. Each cell displays the number of items of each type in a particular warehouse. The sum of any row is equal to the number of items in a particular warehouse.

17. C

Norma's first movement when she enters the building is to head east. Since she is facing north when she enters, she must immediately go to her right. Look at the choices to find the proper directions. Choices **A**, **C** and **D** all have Norma's first movement to the right as we look at the page. For those diagrams to be correct, that direction must be east. Since she was facing north when she entered the building, north must be into the page and up, therefore, must be toward the top of the page.

Choice **B** has Norma's first movement towards the top of the page. If that is east, and she entered facing north, then north must be to the right of the page and up must be into the page. (That is, we are looking at the building from the bottom.)

Copyright Protected

Not for Reproduction

We are told that Norma's next movement is up. We can now eliminate **A** and **B** (both show her next movement to the north). Both **C** and **D** have her going up.

Next, she goes north to her office. North for both **C** and **D** is into the page. **D** shows her going west (left of the page) and is, therefore, not correct. **C** shows her going into the page, that is, north.

Norma's path is best depicted through model **C**.

NR 4. 126

We can think of the pattern as a 5×4 grid. The number of paths of an $x \times y$ grid is given by

$$\frac{(x+y)!}{x!y!} = \frac{(4+5)!}{4!5!} = \frac{362\,880}{(24)(120)} = 126$$

Or, using Pascal's Triangle, we can make the following grid.

1	6	21	56	126
1	5	15	35	70
1	4	10	20	35
1	3	6	10	15
1	2	3	4	5
	1	1	1	1

A

Written Response

1. **a)** In order to set up this network matrix, we label each column and row. Then, if we find a route between destination, denote it with a "1". If not, write "0".

This is our solution matrix.

$$\begin{array}{c} R \\ E \\ W \end{array} \begin{bmatrix} 0 & 1 & 1 \\ 1 & 0 & 0 \\ 1 & 0 & 0 \end{bmatrix}$$

b) The multiplication of matrices involves the following pattern.

$$\begin{array}{c} \\ R \\ E \\ W \end{array} \begin{array}{ccc} R & E & W \\ \begin{bmatrix} 0 & 1 & 1 \\ 1 & 0 & 0 \\ 1 & 0 & 0 \end{bmatrix} \end{array} \times \begin{array}{c} \\ R \\ E \\ W \end{array} \begin{array}{ccc} R & E & W \\ \begin{bmatrix} 0 & 1 & 1 \\ 1 & 0 & 0 \\ 1 & 0 & 0 \end{bmatrix} \end{array}$$

Each row of matrix 1 and each column of matrix 2 are multiplied as follows

Row 1 × Column 1
$[(0)(0) + (1)(1) + (1)(1)] = 2$

Row 1 × Column 2
$[(0)(1) + (1)(0) + (1)(0)] = 0$

Row 1 × Column 3
$[(0)(1) + (1)(0) + (1)(0)] = 0$

This gives us the first row of the solution matrix. Continue in the same way with rows 2 and 3 to complete the solution matrix.

The solution matrix is

$$\begin{bmatrix} 2 & 0 & 0 \\ 0 & 1 & 1 \\ 0 & 1 & 1 \end{bmatrix}$$

Copyright Protected

ANSWERS AND SOLUTIONS
UNIT TEST 1—MATRICES AND PATHWAYS

1. B	4. D	NR3. 220	NR4. 15 210 000
NR1. –6	5. B	7. A	WR1. See Solution
2. A	NR2. 62.8, 37.3	8. B	WR2. See Solution
3. C	6. A	9. D	WR3. See Solution

1. B

$$(A+B)-C = \left(\begin{bmatrix} 2 & -4 \\ 5 & 1 \end{bmatrix} + \begin{bmatrix} 0 & 2 \\ -3 & 8 \end{bmatrix} \right) - \begin{bmatrix} 6 & 1 \\ 1 & -3 \end{bmatrix}$$

$$= \left(\begin{bmatrix} 2+0 & -4+2 \\ 5+-3 & 1+8 \end{bmatrix} \right) - \begin{bmatrix} 6 & 1 \\ 1 & -3 \end{bmatrix}$$

$$= \begin{bmatrix} 2 & -2 \\ 2 & 9 \end{bmatrix} - \begin{bmatrix} 6 & 1 \\ 1 & -3 \end{bmatrix}$$

$$= \begin{bmatrix} 2-6 & -2-1 \\ 2-1 & 9--3 \end{bmatrix}$$

$$= \begin{bmatrix} -4 & -3 \\ 1 & 12 \end{bmatrix}$$

NR1. –6

$$B = kA$$

$$= 2 \begin{bmatrix} 7 & -11 & 5 \\ 8 & 4 & -3 \\ 1 & 1 & 9 \end{bmatrix}$$

$$= \begin{bmatrix} 14 & -22 & 10 \\ 16 & 8 & -6 \\ 2 & 2 & 18 \end{bmatrix}$$

$\therefore$ element $b_{23} = -6$

2. A

First we have to look at the dimensions of each matrix.

$A_{32}, B_{23}, C_{22}, D_{31}$

To multiply matrices, the number of columns of the first factor must equal the number of the second factor.
This is true for the following pairs: AB, BA, CB, AC, BD

The only pair represented in the question is AB.

3. C

When $C = AB$ then, by the rules for matrix multiplication the rows of A are being multiplied by the columns of B.
The element denoted C_{12} refers to the element of matrix C that was calculated from multiplying row 1 of matrix A by column 2 of matrix B. This is as follows:

$$c_{12} = af + bi$$

4. D

To determine the total amount of revenue from the sales of the wrenches, screwdrivers and hammers, we need to multiply the number of each sold by their respective prices and add the results.
This pattern of multiplying and dividing is part of matrix multiplication. To get the result requested, we need to multiply a row matrix by a column matrix. The data must therefore be organized as:

$$\begin{bmatrix} 5 & 4 & 8 \end{bmatrix}\begin{bmatrix} 550 \\ 700 \\ 430 \end{bmatrix} \text{ or } \begin{bmatrix} 550 & 700 & 430 \end{bmatrix}\begin{bmatrix} 5 \\ 4 \\ 8 \end{bmatrix}.$$

5. B

Since every price is increasing by the same amount, we can consider this scalar multiplication. To get an increase of 10% in every price, we multiply each one by 1.1. This represents 100% of the original (1) plus an additional 10% (0.1) on top of that.

$$1.1\begin{bmatrix} 5 \\ 4 \\ 8 \end{bmatrix}$$

NR2. 62.8, 37.3

Our initial probability matrix should be as follows:

$$\begin{matrix} & G & CF \end{matrix}$$
$$P_0 = \begin{bmatrix} .65 & .35 \end{bmatrix}$$

Next we need to build the transition matrix as follows:

$$\begin{matrix} & & To \\ & & G & CF \end{matrix}$$
$$T = \text{From} \begin{matrix} G \\ CF \end{matrix}\begin{bmatrix} 0.75 & 0.25 \\ 0.40 & 0.60 \end{bmatrix}$$

(Remember that the rows of a transition matrix must add to one.)

Next, we multiply the two matrices to determine the new percentages after one transition period.

$$P_0 \times T = \begin{bmatrix} .65 & .35 \end{bmatrix}\begin{bmatrix} 0.75 & 0.25 \\ 0.40 & 0.60 \end{bmatrix} = \begin{bmatrix} 0.6275 & 0.3725 \end{bmatrix}$$

From this we see that after one month, 62.8% of the customers are eating glazed donuts and 37.3% are eating cream filled.

6. **A**

To answer this question, we simply need to cube the transition matrix to get the distribution of customers after three months. These values are then multiplied by 2 000 to find the actual number of customers.

$$P_0 \times T^3 = \begin{bmatrix} 0.65 & 0.35 \end{bmatrix} \begin{bmatrix} 0.75 & 0.25 \\ 0.40 & 0.60 \end{bmatrix}^3$$

$$= \begin{bmatrix} 0.616\,868\,75 & 0.383\,131\,25 \end{bmatrix}$$

To find the number of cream filled eaters we multiply
2 000 × 0.383 131 25 = 766.262 5.

Rounded to the nearest customer, this is 766.

NR3. **220**

To solve this we need to apply the pattern derived from Pascal's Triangle. We simply add the number of pathways that lead to the nodes above and to the left of any given node.

A	1	1	1
1	2	3	4
	2	5	
	2	7	11
	2	9	20

		20	20	
20		20	40	
20		40	80	
20		60	140	
20		80	220	
			B	

7. **A**

To solve this we need to apply the pattern derived from Pascal's Triangle. We look at each city and the cities that lead to it.
We add up the number of pathways that can be taken to each of the cities that lead to the given city. Follow this pattern to Montreal.

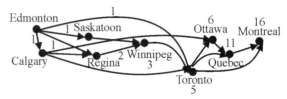

8. **B**

There are 8 choices for the first letter, 7 for the second, 6 for the third and so on until the last one is used. Multiply these choices all together to determine the total number of choices.

$$8 \times 7 \times 6 \times 5 \times 4 \times 3 \times 2 \times 1 = 40\,320$$

9. **D**

To answer this question, simply multiply all the choices together.

$$4 \times 3 \times 3 \times 5 = 180$$

NR4. **15 210 000**

To answer this question, we simply multiply all the choices together. There are 25 choices for the first letter and 26 for the other two. There are 9 choices for the first number and 10 choices for the other two.

$$25 \times 26 \times 26 \times 9 \times 10 \times 10 = 15\,210\,000$$

Written Response

1. When multiplying matrices, the result has the same number of rows as the first factor and the same number of columns as the second factor. In word problems, the rows of the first factor and the columns have the same meaning as the columns of the second factor.

The chart that is provided can be written as the matrix:

$$\text{Stores} \begin{bmatrix} 350 & 570 & 1100 \\ 1\,200 & 200 & 610 \\ 800 & 975 & 420 \end{bmatrix}$$

Because we are looking for the money generated for each store, we want to keep the meaning of the rows of this matrix, therefore it is the first factor. We now need a second matrix with money for its columns. For the columns of the first matrix to then match with the rows of the second we need this matrix:

$$\text{Items} \begin{matrix} \text{Money} \\ \begin{bmatrix} 5 \\ 4 \\ 8 \end{bmatrix} \end{matrix}$$

Now when we multiply them, we get:

$$\begin{bmatrix} 350 & 570 & 1100 \\ 1\,200 & 200 & 610 \\ 800 & 975 & 420 \end{bmatrix} \begin{bmatrix} 5 \\ 4 \\ 8 \end{bmatrix} = \text{Stores} \begin{matrix} \text{Money} \\ \begin{bmatrix} 12\,830 \\ 11\,680 \\ 11\,260 \end{bmatrix} \end{matrix}$$

Therefore, store A brought in $12 830, store B brought in $11 680 and store C brought in $11 260.

2. To set up the network matrix, we first need to list the variables in the same order along the rows as along the columns, but this order can be determined by the student. Entries in the matrix will be either 1 or 0. The 1 signifies a direct link between people and the 0 signifies that no direct link exists between the two people.

$$N = \text{From:} \begin{matrix} & & \text{To} \\ & \begin{matrix} T & M & C & B & S \end{matrix} \\ \begin{matrix} T \\ M \\ C \\ B \\ S \end{matrix} & \begin{bmatrix} 0 & 1 & 1 & 0 & 1 \\ 1 & 0 & 0 & 1 & 1 \\ 1 & 0 & 0 & 0 & 1 \\ 0 & 1 & 0 & 0 & 1 \\ 1 & 1 & 1 & 1 & 0 \end{bmatrix} \end{matrix}$$

3. When a network matrix is squared, the result represents the number of connections between items with 1 intermediate step. When the matrix is cubed, it represents the number of connections with 2 intermediate steps, and so on. To find the number of connections that can be described as friends, or friends of friends we need to take the initial matrix and add it to the square of itself. The resulting matrix will represent the number of connections between people that are either direct or with one intermediate.

$$N + N^2 = \begin{bmatrix} 0 & 1 & 1 & 0 & 1 \\ 1 & 0 & 0 & 1 & 1 \\ 1 & 0 & 0 & 0 & 1 \\ 0 & 1 & 0 & 0 & 1 \\ 1 & 1 & 1 & 1 & 0 \end{bmatrix} + \begin{bmatrix} 0 & 1 & 1 & 0 & 1 \\ 1 & 0 & 0 & 1 & 1 \\ 1 & 0 & 0 & 0 & 1 \\ 0 & 1 & 0 & 0 & 1 \\ 1 & 1 & 1 & 1 & 0 \end{bmatrix}^2$$

$$= \begin{bmatrix} 3 & 2 & 2 & 2 & 3 \\ 2 & 3 & 2 & 2 & 3 \\ 2 & 2 & 2 & 1 & 2 \\ 2 & 2 & 1 & 2 & 2 \\ 3 & 3 & 2 & 2 & 4 \end{bmatrix}$$

Once we have this matrix, we need only add up all the entries to determine the total number of connections.

$\therefore$ the total number of connections = 56

ANSWERS AND SOLUTIONS
UNIT REVIEW—STATISTICS AND PROBABILITY

1. C	NR2. 63	15. D	22. B
2. A	8. A	16. C	NR4. 0.67
3. B	9. C	17. A	23. A
NR1. 3, 1, 4, 2	10. D	18. C	NR5. 0.46
4. B	11. B	19. B	24. D
5. A	12. D	20. D	WR1. See Solution
6. B	13. D	NR3. 40	WR2. See Solution
7. C	14. D	21. A	

1.　C

The mean and standard deviation of a box of 10 cues can be calculated using your calculator. Enter the information in a list, then calculate 1– variable statistics on that list. We find that
$\mu = 17.07 \approx 17.1$, $\sigma = 0.232 \approx 0.2$.

2.　A

Standard deviation is a measure of how tightly grouped data is around an average. A low standard deviation means the data closely resembles the mean or average. Because Henry's scores for the first season had a lower standard deviation than for his second season, his scores were more consistent for the first season.

3.　B

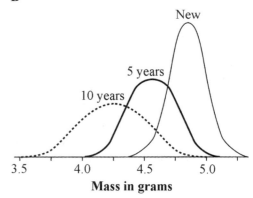

Mass in grams

The graphs of three normal curves using the same scale are shown in the above figure. The curve with the smallest standard deviation are the curve where the mass of the dimes is the most closely clustered around its mean—in the above diagram it is the curve for new coins. As time passes, the mass of the dimes is becoming more dispersed—i.e., the standard deviation is increasing.

NR1. **3, 1, 4, 2**

The graphs of four normal distributions are shown below. The graphs are drawn using the same scale.

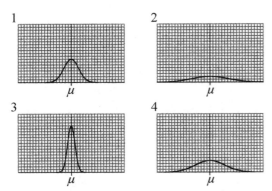

Standard deviations tell us about the dispersion or spread of data. The greater the spread of values, the larger the standard deviation.

The graphs in the diagram are drawn using the same scale.

Therefore, graph 3 has the smallest standard deviation, followed by graph 1, 4, and 2.

These standard deviations arranged in increasing order are: 3, 1, 4, and 2.

4. **B**

$$z_{score} = \frac{x - \mu}{\sigma}$$
$$= \frac{180 - 185}{15}$$
$$= -\frac{5}{15}$$
$$= -0.333$$

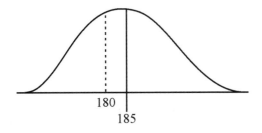

From the data tables, we can see that a z-score of -0.333 translates to a probability of $0.369\ 567$

$\approx 37\%$

Or, after calculating the z-score, use your calculator as follows:

shadenorm(lower boundary, z-score) for area left of 180

shadenorm(-5, -0.333)
Area $= 0.370\ 3$

Or

normalcdf(-5, -0.333)
Area $= 0.369\ 566$

The total area under a normal distribution curve is 1 or 100%. The area under the curve from any point x is less than 1. We use the z-score formula and the z-score tables to find the area under the curve left of 180.

5. **A**

A confidence interval gives upper and lower boundaries for a range of acceptable values. All values within this range will occur with 95% certainty.

Copyright Protected

6. B

The cue data follows a normal distribution curve. To find the probability of randomly selecting a cue weighing 16.8 or less, we use z-scores.

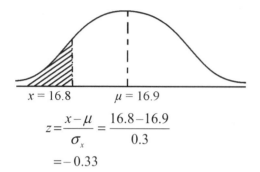

$$z = \frac{x - \mu}{\sigma_x} = \frac{16.8 - 16.9}{0.3}$$
$$= -0.33$$

We then can use data tables provided to translate the z-score to a probability. Alternatively, we can use our calculator;

shadenorm(–5, –0.33)

∴ area under the curve = 0.370 7

Therefore, probability = 0.370 7

Or, normalcdf(–5, –0.33)
= 0.369 566 14
∴ probability = 0.37

7. C

Using probability tables, we calculate the area between the upper and lower boundaries.

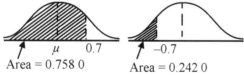

Area = 0.758 0   Area = 0.242 0

Subtracting the area defined by the lower boundary from the upper boundary, leaves the area between.

Area between = 0.758 0 – 0.242 0
= 0.516

Using our calculator, we could also type

shadenorm(–0.7, 0.7)
= 0.516 073

Using window settings
$x_{min} = -4.7$
$x_{max} = 4.7$
$x_{scl} = 1$
$y_{min} = -0.15$
$y_{max} = 0.5$
$y_{scl} = 0.1$
$x_{res} = 1$

Or

normalcdf(–0.7, 0.7)
= 0.516 072 843 7

NR2. 63

We are given that the marks on a final examination in Biology 20 are normally distributed with a standard deviation of 4%. Susan's marks of 68% corresponds to a z-score of 1.25. To find the mean of the marks on this examination, we use the formula for z-scores, $z = \frac{x - \mu}{\sigma}$, and substitute the values z = 1.25, x = 68% and $\sigma = 4$.

$$1.25 = \frac{68 - \mu}{4}$$
$$(1.25)4 = 68 - \mu$$
$$5 = 68 - \mu$$
and $\mu = 68 - 5 = 63\%$.

8. A

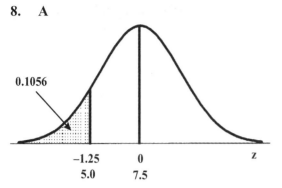

0.1056

−1.25 0
5.0 7.5 z

The data on how soon mowers require their first repair is normally distributed with a mean of 7.5 years and a standard deviation of 2 years.

To find out what proportion of mowers require repairs in the first 5 years after sale, we first calculate the z-score corresponding to 5 years and then find the area under the standard normal curve to the left of that z-score. The z-score corresponding to 5 years is

$$z=\frac{x-\mu}{\sigma}=\frac{5-7.5}{2}=\frac{-2.5}{2}=-1.25$$

The area under the curve to the left of $z = -1.25$ is

$=0.105\ 6$

Alternatively,

Shadenorm(−5, −1.25)
Area = 0.105 6

Or

Normalcdf(−5, −1.25)
Area = 0.105 649 551 9

That is, of the 35 000 mowers sold in one year, 10.56% of them will require repairs in the first 5 years.

$35\ 000 \times 0.105\ 6 = 3\ 696$

9. C

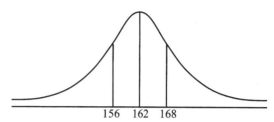

156 162 168

We are given the following information about the heights of men and women between ages 18 and 24:

women: mean = 162 cm
standard deviation = 6 cm

men: mean = 175 cm
standard deviation = 6 cm

If the two graphs are drawn on the same axes, the graph corresponding to men has the same shape as that for women shown above, since the standard deviation for both distributions is the same, but since the mean for the men is greater, that graph would be shifted to the right.

10. D

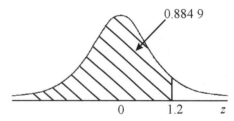

0.884 9

0 1.2 z

The raw scores for an examination are normally distributed with a mean of 67.4% and a standard deviation of 10.5%. The z-score for a mark of 80% can be calculated by using the formula:

$$z=\frac{x-\mu}{\sigma}=\frac{80-67.4}{10.5}=1.2$$

Method One
The probability that a student gets less than 80% on the examination is the area under the standard normal curve to the left of $z = 1.2$.

The area for values of $z : 0 \leq z \leq 1.2 = 0.384\ 9$, and the area for $z : z \leq 0 = 0.5$.

Therefore, the probability that a student gets less than 80%

= area for $z \leq 1.2 = 0.884\ 9$

Method Two
Shadenorm(−5, −12)
Area = 0.884 9

Method Three
Normalcdf(−5, −12)
Area = 0.884 9

11. B

A symmetric 95% confidence interval is a particular area of the normal distribution curve spanning two standard deviations above and below the mean.

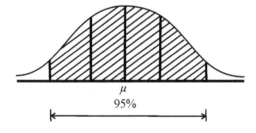

To find the upper and lower boundaries of this, we use the following equations.

$$\text{Probability of success} = p = \frac{21\ 500}{50\ 000}$$

$$= 0.43$$
$$\sigma = \sqrt{np(1-p)}$$
$$= \sqrt{100 \times 0.43(1-0.43)}$$
$$= 4.95$$
$$\mu = np$$
$$\mu = 100 \times 0.43$$
$$\mu = 43$$

From the formula sheet, for 95% confidence interval $\mu \pm 1.96\sigma$

Lower boundary = $43 - 1.96 \times 4.95 = 33$
Upper boundary = $43 + 1.96 \times 4.95 = 53$

12. D

There are 3 different styles for the car Mark wants, and there are 4 different colours for each car type. This can be illustrated through a tree diagram.

Car Type — Style 1, Style 2, Style 3 → R, B, B, W

This can also be shown as
Sample space = (3)(4) = 12

13. D

A sample space, in statistics, is a list of all possible outcomes of an experiment. Because the green die only has values up to, and including, 3, we cannot have a value of 4 on this die.

Copyright Protected

14. D

This is from statistics and uses the idea of Dependent and Independent Events. Dependent Events are such that the occurrence of the first event affects the probability of the occurrence of the second event. By removing the green marble out of the jar without first replacing the red marble, the number of possible outcomes changes.

15. D

Two cards are drawn without replacement from a deck of 52 cards.

The probability the first card drawn is the 5 of hearts or the 2 of hearts = $\dfrac{2}{52}$.

Given that one of those two cards is drawn on the first draw, the *probability* that the other card is drawn second out of the remaining 51 = $\dfrac{1}{51}$.

Therefore, the probability that the 5 of hearts and the 2 of hearts are chosen in either order = $\dfrac{2}{52} \times \dfrac{1}{51} = \dfrac{1}{1\,326}$.

16. C

In roulette, a ball can land on only **one** colour after a spin. That is, the outcomes are mutually exclusive—one outcome excludes the possibility of other outcomes.

17. A

The probability that the three cards drawn are all aces is

P(Ace and Ace and Ace)

$= \dfrac{4}{52} \times \dfrac{3}{51} \times \dfrac{2}{50}$

$\approx 0.000\,181$

18. C

In backgammon, when two dice are rolled there are 36 possible outcomes:

Outcome (1, 2) is the same as (2, 1), and (1, 3) is the same as (3, 1), and so on.

Therefore, referring to the diagram below of the 36 possible outcomes, the distinct outcomes are the terms on the diagonal and to the right of (the shaded outcomes below). There are a total of 21 distinct outcomes.

(1,1)	(1,2)	(1,3)	(1,4)	(1,5)	(1,6)
(2,1)	(2,2)	(2,3)	(2,4)	(2,5)	(2,6)
(3,1)	(3,2)	(3,3)	(3,4)	(3,5)	(3,6)
(4,1)	(4,2)	(4,3)	(4,4)	(4,5)	(4,6)
(5,1)	(5,2)	(5,3)	(5,4)	(5,5)	(5,6)
(6,1)	(6,2)	(6,3)	(6,4)	(6,5)	(6,6)

Of course, it is also correct to consider the distinct outcomes to be the terms on the diagonal and to the left of the diagonal, again a total of 21 (the shaded outcome below).

(1,1)	(1,2)	(1,3)	(1,4)	(1,5)	(1,6)
(2,1)	(2,2)	(2,3)	(2,4)	(2,5)	(2,6)
(3,1)	(3,2)	(3,3)	(3,4)	(3,5)	(3,6)
(4,1)	(4,2)	(4,3)	(4,4)	(4,5)	(4,6)
(5,1)	(5,2)	(5,3)	(5,4)	(5,5)	(5,6)
(6,1)	(6,2)	(6,3)	(6,4)	(6,5)	(6,6)

19. B

Using a graphing calculator, binompdf$(7, 0.5) \rightarrow L_2$.

L_1	L_2
0	0.007 81
1	0.054 69
2	0.164 06
3	0.273 44
4	0.273 44
5	0.164 06
6	0.054 69
7	0.007 81

The probability of 4 boys and 3 girls is 0.273 44.

20. D

One marble is drawn from each bag. Probability of getting one white and one green = P(of getting one white from bag A and one green from bag B) + P(of getting one white from bag B and one green from bag A).

(i) P(of one white from bag A and one green from bag B)

$$= \frac{2}{4} \times \frac{4}{12} = \frac{1}{6}$$

(ii) P(of one white from B and one green from A)

$$= \frac{3}{12} \times \frac{2}{4} = \frac{1}{8}$$

Therefore, P(of one white and one green) = (i) + (ii)

$$= \frac{1}{6} + \frac{1}{8} = \frac{4}{24} + \frac{3}{24} = \frac{7}{24}$$

NR3. 40

The probability of an event that is certain is 1. The probability of an event occurring that is **not certain** is less than 1, but greater than zero (i.e., $0 < p < 1$). Here, we are given the probability of a sunny day to be 0.89. Then, the probability of weather **other** than sunny is $1 - 0.89 = 0.11$. The number of days of this type of weather is $365(0.11) = 40.11$, which, to the nearest **whole** number, is 40 days.

21. A

$$z_{score} = \frac{x - \mu}{\sigma}$$
$$= \frac{720 - 700}{14.49}$$
$$= 1.38$$

Method One
$p = 0.916\ 2$ from the table of areas to the left of the curve.

$p = 1 - 0.916\ 2$ for area to the right of the curve.
$= 0.083\ 8$.

Method Two
shadenorm$(1.38, 5)$
Area = 0.083 793

Method Three
normalcdf$(1.38, 5)$
Area = 0.083 793 090 9

22. B

The probability that a current owner of a Canadian-produced car **will** buy a Japanese-produced or German-produced car is $0.32 + 0.12 = 0.44$.

The probability that this person will **not** buy either of these cars is then
$= 1 - 0.44 = 0.56$

Copyright Protected

NR4. 0.67

The probability of an event happening for certain is 1. To find the probability of an event **not** happening, we can first calculate the probability that it **will** happen. We then subtract this from 1.

Probability of rolling a 4 or 6 =

$$\frac{\text{favourable outcomes}}{\text{total possible outcomes}} = \frac{1+1}{6} = \frac{2}{6} = \frac{1}{3}$$

Probability of **not** rolling a 4 or 6

$$= 1 - \frac{1}{3} = \frac{2}{3} \text{ or } 0.67.$$

23. A

To find the probability that a randomly chosen element in matrix C is even, we must find the number of even numbers in matrix C. We enter matrix A and matrix B in our calculator and multiply.

$$\begin{array}{ccc}\text{Matrix } A & \text{Matrix } B & \text{Matrix } C \\ (3 \times 3) & (3 \times 4) & (3 \times 4)\end{array}$$

$$\begin{bmatrix} 8 & 7 & 4 \\ 3 & 1 & 2 \\ 5 & 6 & 9 \end{bmatrix} \times \begin{bmatrix} 2 & 1 & 0 & 4 \\ 1 & 2 & 3 & 2 \\ 4 & 2 & 1 & 5 \end{bmatrix} = \begin{bmatrix} 39 & 30 & 25 & 66 \\ 15 & 9 & 5 & 24 \\ 52 & 35 & 27 & 77 \end{bmatrix}$$

$$\text{Prob} = \frac{\text{number of favourable outcomes}}{\text{total number of outcomes}}$$

$$= \frac{4}{12} = \frac{1}{3} \text{ or } 0.33.$$

NR5. 0.46

The probability of picking red and red is

$$P(\text{red and red}) = \frac{6}{13} \times \frac{5}{12} = 0.192\,3$$

The probability of picking black and black is

$$P(\text{black and black}) = \frac{7}{13} \times \frac{6}{12} = 0.269\,2$$

Thus, the probability that both are red balls or both are black balls is
$0.192\,3 + 0.269\,2 = 0.46.$

24. D

The probability of picking any one letter is $\frac{1}{7}$.

There are two **T**s and three **O**s in the seven letters. Therefore, the probability that the one letter chosen is a **T** or an **O** is

$$\frac{2}{7} + \frac{3}{7} = \frac{5}{7}$$

Written Response

1. a) Complete the Punnet square below to show the sample-space for the offspring of two parents who both carry one dominant (E) gene for the free earlobe.

Solution:

		Mother	
		E	e
Father	E	EE	Ee
	e	Ee	ee

b) *What is the probability that one offspring from these parents will have detached earlobes?*

Solution:
The probability that one offspring from these parents has detached earlobes is $\frac{3}{4}$ or 0.75

c) *Calculate the mean and standard deviation for the number of people in a sample of 8 748 that will have attached earlobes. Round your answers to the nearest hundredth.*

Solution:

$$n=8\ 748 \quad \mu=np \quad \sigma=\sqrt{np(1-p)}$$
$$p=0.39 \quad \mu=8\ 748(0.39)$$
$$\sigma=\sqrt{8\ 478(0.39)(0.61)}$$
$$q=0.61 \quad \mu=3\ 411.72 \ \sigma=45.62$$

The mean is 3 411.72 and the standard deviation is 45.62.

d) Calculate the 95% confidence interval for the number of people in this sample that will have attached earlobes.

Solution
95% confidence int. $= \mu \pm 1.96\sigma$
$$= 3\ 411.72 \pm 1.96(45.62)$$
$$= 3\ 411.72 \pm 89.415\ 2$$
$$= 3\ 322.304\ 8,\ 3\ 501.352$$

It can be predicted, with 95% confidence, that between 3 322 and 3 502 people in this sample will have attached earlobes.

2. a) The given distribution is a binomial distribution with probability of success (voting yes) is: $p = 0.7$ and probability of failure is: $1 - p = 1 - 0.7 = 0.3$.

If the sample size is n, a binomial distribution can be approximated by a normal distribution when both $np \geq 5$ and $n(1 - p) \geq 5$. In this example, $n = 400$.

Hence, $np = 400 \times 0.7 = 280$ and $n(1 - p) = 400 \times 0.3 = 120$ and the binomial distribution can be approximated by a normal distribution.

The expected mean and standard deviation of a binomial distribution are:
$$\mu = np = 400 \times 0.7 = 280 \text{ and}$$
$$\sigma = \sqrt{np(1-p)}$$
$$= \sqrt{400 \times 0.7 \times 0.3}$$
$$= \sqrt{84} = 9.17$$

b)

$$\mu = 280, \sigma = 9.17$$

To construct a symmetric 95% confidence interval, we use the z-scores (from the table) of $z_1 = -1.96$ and $z_2 = 1.96$. Hence, using the formula $z = \dfrac{x - \mu}{\sigma}$ we have

$$z_1 = -1.96 = \frac{x_1 - 280}{9.17},$$
$$x_1 = (-1.96)9.17 + 280 = 262.03, \text{ and}$$
$$z_2 = 1.96 = \frac{x_2 - 280}{9.17},$$
$$x_2 = (1.96)(9.17) + 280 = 297.97.$$

Therefore, the 95% confidence interval for the expected number of "yes" voters is 262.03 to 297.97.

The confidence interval for the expected percentage of "yes" voters is

$$\frac{262.03}{400} \text{ to } \frac{297.97}{400} \text{ or } 65.5\% \text{ to } 74.5\%.$$

Copyright Protected

c)

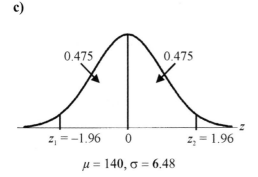

$\mu = 140,\ \sigma = 6.48$

If the sample size is 200 instead of 400, then the 95% confidence interval for the expected percentage of "yes" voters can be calculated as follows:

$$\mu - np = 200 \times 0.7 = 140$$

$$\sigma = \sqrt{np(1-p)} = \sqrt{200 \times 0.7 \times 0.3} = \sqrt{42} = 6.48$$

$$z_1 = -1.96 = \frac{x_1 - \mu}{\sigma} = \frac{x_1 - 140}{6.48}, \text{and}$$

$$x_1 = 140 - (1.96 \times 6.48) = 127.3$$

$$z_2 = 1.96 = \frac{x_2 - \mu}{\sigma} = \frac{x_2 - 140}{6.48}, \text{and}$$

$$x_2 = 140 + (1.96 \times 6.48) = 152.7$$

The 95% confidence interval for the expected percentage of "yes" voters is

$$\frac{127.3}{200} \text{ to } \frac{152.7}{200} \text{ or 63.7\% to 76.4\%}$$

We can note that this 95% confidence interval, 63.7% to 76.4% , for a sample size of 200 is **larger** than the 95% confidence interval of 65.5% to 74.5% for a sample size of 400.

That is, as the sample size **decreases**, the confidence interval **increases**— sample sizes and confidence intervals are **inversely** related.

Copyright Protected

ANSWERS AND SOLUTIONS
UNIT TEST 2—STATISTICS AND PROBABILITY

NR1. 3.67	NR2. 1.8 years	9. A	13. B
1. B	5. C	10. D	14. D
2. A	6. A	11. A	WR1. See Solution
3. D	7. B	NR3. 0.83	WR2. See Solution
4. C	8. B	NR4. 0.61	WR3. See Solution

NR1. 3.67

Enter the values into the lists in the calculator and use the single variable statistics feature to calculate the standard deviation.

1. B

Standard deviation is a measure of the spread of the data. The higher the standard deviation is the greater the spread in the data. The smaller the standard deviation is, the smaller the spread in the data.
If class B has a smaller standard deviation there is less spread in the data, and therefore they scored more consistently.

2. A

To determine the number of crates that have 90 or more apples we simply multiply the number of crates by the percentage of crates that have 90 or more apples.
To determine this percentage, we need to use normalcdf feature of the graphing calculator as follows
$N = 650 * normalcdf(90, 10 \wedge 99, 77, 9)$

$N = 48$

3. D

To determine the probability that the number of defective valves produced is less than 18, we simply need to use the normalcdf function on the graphing calculator as follows
$P = normalcdf(-10 \wedge 99, 18, 20, 4)$

$P = 0.308\,5$

4. C

To determine the minimum speed that a car needs to drive to be in the fastest 15% of the traffic, we use the invNorm feature on the graphing calculator as shown below. Remember that the area given must be to the left of the data value we are looking for. This means that instead of 0.15, we need to enter $1 - 0.15$ as the area.
$S = invNorm(1 - 0.15, 115.5, 9.3)$

$S = 125.1$

NR2. 1.8 years

To determine the number of years the warranty should be for, we use the invNorm function on the calculator. In this case, the area to the left of the data value we are looking for is given as 0.10. We only need to enter the information into the function as follows:
$W = invNorm(0.10, 4, 1.75)$

$W = 1.8$

5. C

To determine the mean and standard deviation of the data provided in this scenario, we simply make use of the formulas used for a normal approximation to a binomial distribution.

$\mu = np$

$\mu = (850\ 000)(0.098)$

$\mu = 83\ 300$

$\sigma = \sqrt{np(1-p)}$

$\sigma = \sqrt{850\ 000(0.098)(1-0.098)}$

$\sigma \approx 274.11$

6. A

To determine the maximum and minimum values of the 95% confidence interval, we simply need to substitute the values evaluated above into the appropriate expression. Remember that the lower bound should be rounded down, while the upper bound should be rounded up.

$\mu - 1.96\ \sigma$ to $\mu + 1.96\ \sigma$

$83300 - 1.96(274.11)$ to $83\ 300 + 1.96\ (274.11)$

82 762.74 to 83 837.26

82 762 people to 83 838 people

7. B

To determine the size of the sample space, simply create the sample space and count the entries.

A1	B1	C1	D1	E1	F1
A2	B2	C2	D2	E2	F2
A3	B3	C3	D3	E3	F3

There are 18, or 6×3 entries.

8. B

The sample space for the choice of the second card is altered because the first card was not replaced in the deck. Because the first selection changed the sample space for the second, these are considered dependent events.

9. A

Since the sample space for every choice is the same, the event of choosing a student for October is independent of the decision that was made in September.

10. D

Since these two events are dependent, we only need to multiply their probabilities after taking into account how the first choice will alter the sample space for the second choice.

$$P(1^{st}\text{ an apple, }2^{nd}\text{ an orange}) = \frac{4}{11} \times \frac{7}{10}$$
$$= \frac{28}{110}$$
$$= \frac{14}{55}$$

11. A

Since these events are independent, we only need to multiply the probabilities that it will rain on each day. Since each probability is identical we need only to cube the probability given. This is the same as cubing the numerator and cubing the denominator.

$$\left(\frac{5}{7}\right)^3 = \frac{5^3}{7^3}$$
$$= \frac{25}{343}$$

NR3. 0.83

Since the events are independent, they must follow the formula
$P(A \text{ and } B) = P(A) \times P(B)$.
To isolate the probability of event B, $P(B)$, in this equation we simply need to divide both sides by the probability of event A, $P(A)$. The result is the following equation for the probability of B:

$$P(B) = \frac{P(A \text{ and } B)}{P(A)}$$

Now if we substitute the values that we are given in the scenario, we get the following:

$$P(B) = \frac{\left(\dfrac{15}{24}\right)}{\left(\dfrac{3}{4}\right)} = \left(\frac{15}{24}\right)\left(\frac{4}{3}\right) = 0.83$$

12. C

The definition of complementary events is that their probabilities add up to one.

NR4. 0.61

Since Darlene can only grab boys or girls, the probabilities of these events are complementary. When added together the sum is one. To determine the probability that she grabs a girl, we simply subtract the probability of grabbing a boy from one.

$1 - 0.39 = 0.61$

13. B

If we look at the diagram, we can see that the events of being coloured black and being a circle are mutually exclusive.
In this case, to determine the probability of being coloured black or being a circle we need only add the individual probabilities.
The probability of being black is $P(\text{black}) = \dfrac{1}{3}$, and the probability of being a circle is $P(\text{circle}) = \dfrac{4}{9}$. If we add them together we get

$$P(\text{black or a circle}) = \frac{1}{3} + \frac{4}{9} = \frac{3}{9} + \frac{4}{9} = \frac{7}{9}$$

14. D

Notice that the two sets given are mutually exclusive. If there are twenty chips in the bag, then the probability of drawing a prime is

$$P(\text{prime}) = \frac{8}{20}$$

and the probability of drawing a perfect square is $P(\text{perfect square}) = \dfrac{4}{20}$.

Now, applying the formula for the probabilities of mutually exclusive events we get

$$P(\text{prime or perfect square}) = \frac{8}{20} + \frac{4}{20} = \frac{12}{20} = \frac{3}{5}$$

Copyright Protected

Written Response

1. To determine the 95% confidence interval we need to find the μ and the σ for the described scenario. Because a bag can be either accepted or rejected, and the probability is the same for every bag, we can assume this is a binomial experiment.

To find the μ and the σ, we need to know the number of items, 3 000, and the probability of success, success being a bag that has the inappropriate mass. In this case, we are not given the probability of success directly, but it can be calculated from the data given. The probability of getting a bag that has the wrong mass is

$$\frac{21}{3\ 000} = 0.007 \text{ or } 0.7\%.$$

Now we can determine the μ and the σ.

$$\mu = np$$
$$\mu = (3\ 000)(0.007)$$
$$\mu = 21$$

$$\sigma = \sqrt{np(1-p)}$$
$$\sigma = \sqrt{3\ 000(0.007)(1-0.007)}$$
$$\sigma = 4.57$$

Now we substitute these values into the expression we use to build the 95% confidence interval as follows:

$$\mu - 1.96\sigma \text{ to } \mu + 1.96\sigma$$
$$21 - (1.96)(4.57) \text{ to } 21 + (1.96)(4.57)$$
$$12.05 \text{ bags to } 29.95 \text{ bags}$$

We conclude that quality control can be 95% confident that between 12 and 30 bags will need to be rejected every hour.

2. The sample space for the described game is easily listed using a chart as follows:

Card Numbers	1	2	3	4	5
1	1,1	1,2	1,3	1,4	1,5
2	2,1	2,2	2,3	2,4	2,5
3	3,1	3,2	3,3	3,4	3,5
4	4,1	4,2	4,3	4,4	4,5
5	5,1	5,2	5,3	5,4	5,5

3. To determine the probability of getting either an odd or an even sum, let's first rewrite the chart, replacing each entry with the sum.

Card Numbers	1	2	3	4	5
1	2	3	4	5	6
2	3	4	5	6	7
3	4	5	6	7	8
4	5	6	7	8	9
5	6	7	8	9	10

First, notice that there are 25 entries in the sample space. Now by simply counting, we can see that there are 13 even sums and 12 odd sums. Therefore, the probability of getting an even sum is

$$P(\text{even sum}) = \frac{13}{25},$$

and the probability of getting an odd sum is

$$P(\text{odd sum}) = \frac{12}{25}.$$

Because the probability of getting an even sum is slightly better than that of the odd sum it would be wiser to guess that the sum will be even.

Copyright Protected

ANSWERS AND SOLUTIONS
UNIT REVIEW—FINANCE

1. B	NR1. $4 467	NR2. 3, 2, 1	17. D	23. C
2. D	7. B	12. A	18. B	WR1. See Solution
3. C	8. B	13. D	19. A	WR2. See Solution
4. D	9. C	14. D	20. C	WR3. See Solution
5. C	10. B	15. C	21. C	
6. B	11. A	16. B	22. B	

1. B

The amount of the payment applied to the principal is the total payment – interest charged.

Interest is 1% of the previous month's balance, $605.96 (column E), i.e.,
$605.96 ×0.01 = $6.06
$155.29 – $6.06 = $149.23

2. D

The formula used to calculate cell D4 is B4 – C4. However, C4 = 0.01 * E3

Therefore, D4 = B4 – 0.01 * E3

3. C

In order to calculate a new balance on the spreadsheet (column F), we must take the previous balance (column B), add the interest charge (column D), and subtract the payment (column E). Only **B** and **C** have the correct operations in column F, so we can eliminate **A** and **D** as possible answers.

Since we are calculating for each month, but the interest rate is an annual rate, the interest charge (column D) must be divided by 12.

4. D

Total profit is given by Sales – Cost.

In this spreadsheet, H4 = G4 – D4.

5. C

To find the monthly interest charge, we divide the yearly rate by 12.

$$\text{Monthly rate} = \frac{8\%/a}{12\,m/a} = 0.667\%/month$$

$$i = \frac{0.667}{100} \times \$7\,357.42$$
$$= \$49.05$$

6. B

Steve's opening balance was $5 000.00
Steve's closing balance was $5 418.41

The interest earned can be calculated by subtracting the principal ($5 000) from the closing balance ($5 418.41) because the difference in the two amounts results from the interest earned.

Interest Earned =
Closing Balance – Opening Balance
= $5 418.41 – $5 000.00 = $418.41

NR1. $4 467

For period 3, the previous balance is $4 647.38. Monthly interest at a rate 1.5% is $69.710 7 and the monthly payment is $250. Therefore, the new balance is:

$4 647.38 + $69.71 – $250 = $4 467.

7. B

Payment Period	Regular Payment	New Balance	Interest Per Period	Final Balance
1	$1 600	$1 600.00	$1 600 × 0.04 = $64.00	$1 664.00
2	$1 600	$3 264.00	$3 264 × 0.04 = $130.56	$3 394.56
3	$1 600	$4 994.56		
4	$1 600	$		b

From the information given in the above chart, we can calculate the following:

interest in period 3
= $4 994.56 × 0.04 = $199.78

final balance in period 3
= $4 994.56 + $199.78 = $5 194.34

new balance in period 4
= $1 600 + $5 194.34 = $6 794.34

interest in period 4
= $6 794.34 × 0.04 = $271.77

final balance in period 4
= 6 794.34 + 271.77 = $7 066.11

Therefore, the final balance b is $7 066.11.

8. B

The amount of interest this couple pays is the total amount they pay – the initial cost of the home.
(Total Amount = Monthly Payment × Number of Payments + Down Payment)

Total Cost =
($1 060.75/month)(12 months/year)
(25 years) + ($30 000)
= $348 225.00

Amount of Interest
= $348 225.00 – $175 000
= $173 225.00

9. C

An exponential graph follows the basic equation $y = a \times b^x$ where a is the original value when $x = 0$, (this is because $b^0 = 1$.)

So, the answer is **C**.

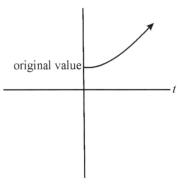

Note: **B** and **D** are linear graphs.
A, though appearing to be an exponential graph, is more like a quadratic, since the value for x in an exponential graph will not return a value of zero for the y-intercept.

10. B

John has two choices in financing his car.

Lease
($307.50/mo)(48 mo) + $12 850 = $27 610

Buy
($557.25/mo)(48 mo) = $26 748

Savings of buying vs. leasing
= $27 610 – $26 748 = $862

11. A

Upon entering the information into lists and performing exponential regression, we find coefficients $a = 23\ 061.46$ and $b = 0.855\ 9$, for the general equation, $y = ab^x$

For each year, the value of John's car is 85.6% the previous year's value. So John's car loses 14.4%/year.

NR2. **3, 2, 1**

In order to find the return for each bank, we enter the interest rate in decimal form in matrix Q. We enter the investment type in matrix R. Multiplying Q and R gives our total return for each bank.

$$
\begin{array}{ll}
\text{Matrix } Q & \text{Matrix } R \\
\begin{bmatrix} 0.076 & 0.08 & 0.118 \\ 0.08 & 0.073 & 0.12 \\ 0.083 & 0.075 & 0.128 \end{bmatrix} \times \begin{bmatrix} 700 \\ 500 \\ 400 \end{bmatrix} = \begin{bmatrix} 140.4 \\ 140.5 \\ 146.8 \end{bmatrix} \begin{array}{l} 1 \\ \text{Banks } 2 \\ 3 \end{array}
\end{array}
$$

The banks, from highest overall return to lowest are 3, 2, and 1.

12. **A**

Here, we need to find the total cost of each option.

Method 1
Monthly payments
Cost = ($770.30/mon)(12 mo/yr)(25 yr)
     = $231 090

Method 2
Weekly payments
Cost = ($177.40/week)(52 week/yr)(25 yr)
     = $230 620

The amount saved is
$$
\begin{array}{r}
\$231\ 090.00 \\
- \$230\ 620.00 \\
\hline
\$470.00
\end{array}
$$

13. **D**

In order to find the savings of buying a vehicle over leasing, we need to calculate the total cost of the lease. We can then determine the difference in cost.

Lease:
(483)(36)
= $17 388 + Purchase option ($16 362)
= $33 750

Buy: $32 500

Difference: $33 750 – $32 500 = $1 250

14. **D**

In order to compare, we must find the total cost of each mortgage. Then, we can find the savings advantage of the 15-year mortgage over the 20-year mortgage.

20 years: ($1 011.80)(20)(12) = $242 832

15 years: ($1 152.80)(15)(12) = $207 504

Difference: $35 328

15. **C**

Rate of return is the observed percentage growth in an investment portfolio.

Type	Invested (%)	Amount ($)	Profit	Return
GIC	20%	$4 000	4%	$160.00
Blue-Chip	50%	$10 000	9.25%	$925.00
High-Risk	30%	$6 000	–7.5%	–$450.00
Totals	100%	$20 000		$635.00

$$\% \text{ growth} = \frac{635}{20\ 000} = 0.031\ 75 = 3.2\%$$

To calculate the % growth, or rate of return, we use the TVM Solver on the TI-83 Calculator.

The present value of our investment (PV) is $20 000.

Our future value (FV) is $20 635.00

The average rate of return to the nearest tenth of a percentage is 3.2%.

16. **B**

See the solution to the previous question (multiple choice number 15).
The investor's total return for the first year is $635.00

Copyright Protected

Not for Reproduction

17. D

Susan's total investment portfolio, with the bonus, is $35 000.
$0.4 \times \$35\,000 = \$14\,000$

Susan's fixed income investment needs to be $14 000 in order to comprise 40% of her total investment.

$\$14\,000 - \$9\,600 = \$4\,400$.

She needs to add $4 400.

18. B

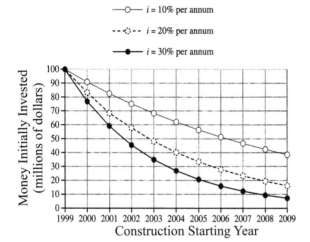

- ○ — $i = 10\%$ per annum
- ◁ — $i = 20\%$ per annum
- ● — $i = 30\%$ per annum

Money Initially Invested (millions of dollars)

Construction Starting Year

From an examination of the graph, we can see that to obtain a given amount of money for any construction starting year, as the interest rate increases the money initially invested decreases.

For example, we can see from the above graph that if $100 million is needed in the year 2004, the amount of initial investments at various interest rates in 1999 are:

at 10% about 57 million,
at 20% about 40 million, and
at 30% about 28 million.

As the interest rate increases, to obtain $100 million in 2004, the amount that needs to be initially invested decreases. Hence, choice **B** is correct and choice **A** is incorrect.

The graph also shows that for any interest rate, the relationship between money initially invested and construction starting year is an exponential one and not quadratic or linear. Hence, choices **C** and **D** are incorrect.

19. A

From the graph given in the previous solution, we can see that to have $100 million in the year 2006, the following amounts need to be invested in 1999 at interest rates of 10% and 20%:

at 10% about $51 million, and
at 20% about $28 million.

That is, the difference in initial investments is $51 million – $28 million = $23 million = $23 000 000.

20. C

If $1 is deposited into an annuity at the beginning of each month at a 12% annual rate compounded monthly—i.e. at a monthly rate of 1%—the column corresponding to 1% in the amount of an Annuity Table gives us amounts received at the end of various periods.

We are asked to find out if $1 309.32 is deposited at the beginning of each month, how many months it will take for the annuity to become $46 000?

This is the same as finding out how many months it will take for $1 deposited every month to become

$$\frac{\$46\,000}{\$1\,309.32} = \$35.132\,741.$$

By looking at the column corresponding to 1%, we see that it will take 30 months for this to happen.

21. C

We can use the formula $A = P(1 + i)^n$, where A is the accumulated amount, P is the principal amount, i is the interest rate per compounding period, and n is the number of compounding periods, to solve this problem. From the information in the question, we are given that the principal amount is $2 000 000, the interest rate is 3%, and there are 70 compounding periods (1985 – 1915). By substitution, we get

$A = 2\ 000\ 000(1 + 0.03)^{70}$
$A = 2\ 000\ 000(7.917\ 821\ 912...)$
$A = 15\ 835\ 643.82$
$A = 15\ 836\ 000$ (to the nearest thousand)

This question can also be done with the solver.

```
N = 70
I = 3
PV = 2 000 000
PMT = 0
FV = ? $15 835
643
P/Y = 1
C/Y = 1
END
```

22. B

From the information given in the question, we can use the formula $A = P(1 + i)^n$ to solve this problem. Recall that A is the accumulated amount, P is the principal amount, i is the interest rate per compounding period, and n is the number of compounding periods. Substituting the values given in the question, we get:

$32\ 000\ 000 = 2\ 000\ 000(1 + i)^{160}$
[divide both sides by 2 000 000]

$16 = (1 + i)^{160}$
[take the 160th root of both sides]

$\sqrt[160]{16} = (1 + i)$
$1.017\ 4... = 1 + i$
$i = 0.017\ 4... = 1.74...\%$

Recall that i is the interest rate per compounding period. To find the annual rate, multiply by 2.

$1.74...\% \times 2 = 3.5\%$
(rounded to the nearest tenth percent)

This question can also be done with the solver.

```
N = 80 × 2
I = ? 3.495 9
PV = 2 000 000
PMT = 0
FV = 32 000 000
P/Y = 2
C/Y = 2
END
```

23. C

If John invests an additional $1 000 at the beginning of year 4 at 4.1%, then he will earn $1 000 × 0.041 = $41 in interest, on the $1 000, in the fourth year.

He will have a total of
$1 000 + $41 = $1 041 in addition to his regular closing balance.

Therefore, his total investment would be worth:
regular closing balance + value of additional investment
$5 871.82 + $1 041.00 = $6 912.82

Written Response

1. **a)** *What does the value 33 in matrix A represent?*

Solution

There are 33 buses in the parking lot on Saturday.

b) *Use matrix multiplication to calculate the revenue for each of the three days. Write a statement that describes the result of this multiplication.*

Solution

$$\begin{bmatrix} 85 & 12 \\ 43 & 17 \\ 102 & 33 \end{bmatrix} \times \begin{bmatrix} 8 \\ 22 \end{bmatrix} = \begin{bmatrix} 944 \\ 718 \\ 1\,542 \end{bmatrix}$$

The revenue is $944, $718, and $1 542 for Thursday, Friday, and Saturday, respectively.

c) *Use matrix operations to calculate an increase of 10% in the daily parking price. Show all calculation.*

Solution

$$1.10 \times \begin{bmatrix} 8 \\ 22 \end{bmatrix} = \begin{bmatrix} 8.8 \\ 24.2 \end{bmatrix}$$

The new parking price is $8.80 for cars and $24.20 for buses.
or

$$0.1 \times \begin{bmatrix} 8 \\ 22 \end{bmatrix} = \begin{bmatrix} 0.8 \\ 2.2 \end{bmatrix}$$

The parking prices will increase by $0.80 for cars and $2.20 for buses.

d) *How much more money would the owner have made on Saturday as a result of a 10% price increase?*

Solution

$$\begin{bmatrix} 85 & 12 \\ 43 & 17 \\ 102 & 33 \end{bmatrix} \times \begin{bmatrix} 8 \\ 22 \end{bmatrix} \times 1.10 = \begin{bmatrix} 85 & 12 \\ 43 & 17 \\ 102 & 33 \end{bmatrix} \times \begin{bmatrix} 8.8 \\ 24.2 \end{bmatrix}$$

$$= \begin{bmatrix} 1\,038.4 \\ 789.8 \\ 1\,696.2 \end{bmatrix}$$

or

$$1.1 \times \begin{bmatrix} 944 \\ 718 \\ 1\,542 \end{bmatrix} = \begin{bmatrix} 1\,038.4 \\ 789.8 \\ 1\,696.2 \end{bmatrix}$$

New revenue = $1 696.20
Orig. revenue = $1 542.00

$1 696.20 – $1 542 = $154.20
The increase in revenue on Saturday is $154.20.

2. **a)** *Determine the total monthly revenue for each plant.*

Solution

Acoustic Guitar Plant:
Revenue = 120 ($500) + 75
   ($1 500)
   = $172 500.00

Electric Guitar Plant:
Revenue = 251 ($510) + 109
   ($750)
   = $209 760.00

b) *Determine the monthly profit for each plant.*

Solution

AGP: 172 500 – 120(60 + 145)
– 75 (128 + 275) – 40 000 = $77 675.00

EGP: 209 760 – 251 (35 + 210)
– 109 (93 + 290) – 28 000 = $78 518.00

The monthly profit for the acoustic guitar plant is $77 675.00 and $78 518.00 for the electric guitar plant.

c) *Calculate the monthly profit*

- *per acoustic guitar*
- *per electric guitar*

Solution

Acoustic guitar: $\dfrac{77\ 675}{195} = \$398.33$

Electric Guitar: $\dfrac{78\ 518}{360} = \$218.11$

The company makes a profit of $398.33/mo from each acoustic guitar, and $218.11/mo from each electric guitar

d) *The company is experiencing financial difficulty and wishes to close one plant. Which plant should be closed? Explain your answer.*

Solution

Each of the following answers is sufficient:

The company should close the acoustic guitar plant because it makes the lowest monthly profit.

The company should close the electric guitar plant because it makes the lowest profit per guitar.

3. We are given that $5 000 is the principal and 7% is the interest rate, i.e., 0.07.

The interest earned in year 1
= $5 000 × 0.07 = $350

So, the closing balance for year 1 is
$5 000 + $350 = $5 350

The interest earned in year 2
= $5 350 × 0.07 = $374.50

So, the closing balance for year 2 is
$5 350 + $374.50 = $5 724.50

The interest earned in year 3
= $5 724.50 × 0.07 = $400.72
So, the closing balance for year 3 is
$5 724.50 + $400.72 = $6 125.22

The interest earned in year 4
= $6 125.22 × 0.07 = $428.77

Hence, the closing balance for year 4 is
$6 125.22 + $428.77 = $6 553.99

This gives us the table;

Year	Opening Balance ($)	Interest Rate (%)	Interest Earned ($)	Closing Balance ($)
1	5 000.00	7	350.00	5 350.00
2	5 350.00	7	374.50	5 724.50
3	5 724.50	7	400.72	6 125.22
4	6 125.22	7	428.77	6 553.99

Not for Reproduction

ANSWERS AND SOLUTIONS
UNIT TEST 3—FINANCE

1. C	5. B	9. A	NR2. 4.2%
2. D	6. B	10. B	12. B
3. A	7. A	11. B	13. D
4. C	8. C	NR1. $320.30	

1. C

The formula that belongs in cell E9 must combine the opening balance of the year with the interest earned, but at the same time it must reflect the fact that the individual is making payments back to the lending institution. This can be summarized as E9 = B9 + C9 – D9.

2. D

The formula in cell C9 is intended to calculate the interest earned on the loan per period. It needs to refer to the cell to the left of it and to the interest rate that is held in cell B4. When it is copied, it should continue to refer to the cell to the left and to B4. It should also take into account the number of compounding periods. To do this, it should be: C12 = B12 * $B$4 / $B$5. The '$' is an absolute reference that guarantees that when those cells are copied, they refer to the same cell.

3. A

To determine the amount that the couple will pay in interest over the period of their loan, we first need to determine how much they will pay total. Every month they pay $750.00 for 25 years. This comes to:

$25 \times 12 \times \$750.00 = \$225\ 000.$

Bearing in mind that they only borrowed $150 000, everything above and beyond this is interest. This means that:

$\$225\ 000 - \$150\ 000 = \$75\ 000.$

They paid $75 000 in interest.

4. C

Bear in mind that, in the previous question, we found that the total amount paid was $225 000. If the rent they would owe was $550.00/month, then we only need to divide to determine the number of months that they could rent the house with that money. After that, we only need to divide the number by 12 to get the number of years.

$$\frac{\$225\ 000}{\$550} = 409.09, \frac{409.09}{12} = 34.09.$$

This means 34 years.

5. B

To answer this question, we simply need to find the sum of the monthly expenses. To find the amount that should be spent on water, we need to divide $260 by 2.

$$\$875 + \$85 + \$115 + \frac{\$260}{2} + \$43.50 = \$1\ 248.50.$$

6. B

To find the average rate of depreciation, first we need to enter the time and the value of the car into your calculator and perform an exponential regression.

$y = (24\ 403.64)(0.875)^x$

From this we see that each year, the car only keeps about 87.5% of the value it had in the previous year. If we have 87.5% left, we lost 12.5%. The rate of depreciation is therefore 12.5%.

7. A

To compare which vehicles hold their values the best we need to perform an exponential regression on each of the vehicles.

SUV $y=(0.897)(0.882)^x$
Minivan $y=(0.866)(0.846)^x$
Sports Car $y=(0.832)(0.814)^x$
Sedan $y=(0.876)(0.780)^x$

The vehicle with the highest retention is the SUV. It holds about 88.2% of its value each year.

8. C

To determine how much he will spend, all that is required is to multiply the monthly payment by the number of months.
$673.15 × 48 = $32 311.20.

9. A

To determine the difference in overall cost we need to first determine the total cost for both options.

Option A:
$2 500 + $673.15 × 48 = $34 811.20

Option B:
$2 500 + $456.24 × 48 + $12 380.05
= $36 779.57

Difference:
$36 779.57 – $34 811.20 = $1 968.37

10. B

To find the average rate of return, enter the chart into the calculator and perform an exponential regression.

$y = (5\ 103.84)(1.034)^x$

From this, we can see that the value of the investment is 3.4% greater with each year.

11. B

The total return on the investment in the fifth year can be determined by subtracting the initial investment from the final value in the fifth year.

$5 986.86 – $5 000 = $986.86

NR1. $320.30

To determine the total return at the end of the year, we first need to determine the return for each investment.

Investments	Amount	Rate of Return	Return
A	$1 500	4.5%	$67.50
B	$2 300	5.7%	$131.10
C	$750	−2.3%	−$17.25
D	$1 250	6.1%	$76.25
E	$1 900	3.3%	$62.70
Total:	$7 700		$320.30

NR2. 4.2%

To determine the total rate of return, take the total return and divide it by the total amount invested.

$$\frac{\$320.30}{\$7\ 700} \times 100 = 4.2\%$$

Copyright Protected

12. B

Since we have the total value of the portfolio at the end what we need to do is find all the individual returns and the total investment and subtract these from the total to get the missing value. This can be used to find the missing rate of return.

Investments	Amount	Rate of Return	Return
A	$450	6%	$27.00
B	$730	4%	$29.20
C	$590	x%	$29.50
D	$610	4.5%	$27.45
Total	$2 380		$113.15

$$\frac{\$29.50}{\$590} \times 100 = 5\%$$

13. D

The total return for the year was determined in the previous question by adding up the total investment and subtracting it from the total value of the portfolio at the end of the year.

Copyright Protected

ANSWERS AND SOLUTIONS – UNIT REVIEW
CYCLIC, RECURSIVE, AND FRACTAL PATTERNS

1. B	8. D	NR3. 4	16. C	20 C
2. A	9. D	12. A	17. A	21. A
3. A	10. B	13. C	18. D	NR7. 75
4. C	NR1. 22.9	NR4. 733	19. D	WR1. See Solution
5. A	11. B	14. D	NR5. 2.5	WR2. See Solution
6. D	NR2. 21	15. C	NR6. 192	WR3. See Solution
7. C				

1. B

Using sine regression, we get:

L_1	L_2
0	2
4	10
6	15.66
8	18
12	10
16	2

Be sure the MODE is set to Radians

Stat, calc C:SinReg, SinRegL$_1$L$_2$Y$_1$

$y = a*\sin(bx + c) + d$

$a = 8.02$
$b = 0.39$
$c = 1.57$
$d = 10.0$

Therefore, the equation is
$h = 8\sin(0.39t – 1.57) + 10$

2. A

The vehicle is traveling 30° west of north, which we can also write as N 30°W.

3. A

This problem requires a general understanding of sinusoidal functions. These two functions differ in max/min values or amplitude, and cycle or period.

4. C

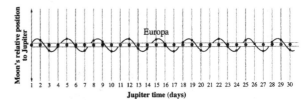

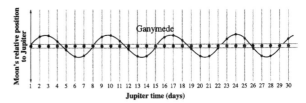

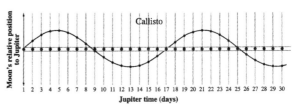

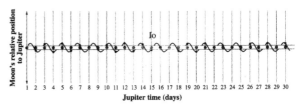

The graphs in the diagram are similar in appearance to a sine function and are graphed on the same scale. The graph with the greatest vertical oscillation has the greatest amplitude.

Of the graphs of the four moons, the graph corresponding to Callisto oscillates the most vertically—hence, has the greatest amplitude.

5. **A**

The graph with the shortest period is the one which is most compressed horizontally.

The graph corresponding to the moon Io is the most compressed horizontally—hence, has the shortest period.

6. **D**

For the sine function $y = \sin\theta$, the amplitude is 1 and the period is $360°$.

For the general function $y = a\sin b\theta$

the amplitude is a, and the period is $\dfrac{360°}{b}$

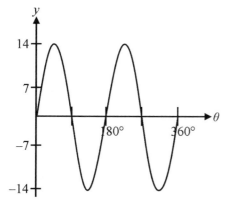

The graph shown above is that of a general sine function of the form $y = a\sin b\theta$.

In the above graph the maximum value is $M = 14$ and the minimum value $m = -14$, i.e. there is an oscillation of 14 units above the θ-axis and 14 units below the θ-axis.

Hence, the amplitude $a = 14$.

We can see that the graph repeats itself every $180°$, i.e. the period $\dfrac{360°}{b} = 180°$.

Therefore, $b = \dfrac{360°}{180°} = 2$. That is, the equation that produces the above graph is $y = 14\sin 2\theta$.

7. **C**

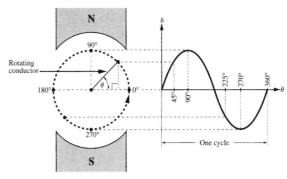

We can see from the figure that the amplitude of the sine wave, i.e. the height of the wave, at $\theta = 90°$, is equal to the radius of the rotating conductor at $\theta = 90°$.

Therefore, if the radius of the rotating conductor is larger, the amplitude of the sine wave increases.

8. **D**

The graph of $y = a\sin bx$ is shown. The amplitude of the graph is a, the maximum value is $M = +10$, and minimum value is $m = -10$.

Therefore, the amplitude is

$$a = \frac{M - m}{2} = \frac{10 - (-10)}{2} = \frac{20}{2} = 10$$

9. **D**

This again tests our knowledge of functions. If the height, y, is given as a function of time, x, as in $y = 5.7\sin(0.31x) + 7.9$, then to find the points when the height of the chair is 15 m, we look for points where $y = 15$.

10. B

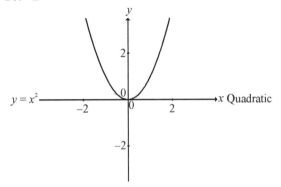

$y = x^2$ — Quadratic

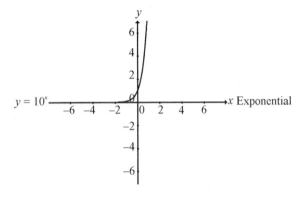

$y = 10^x$ — Exponential

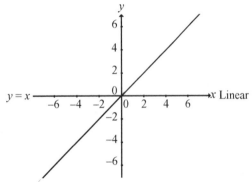

$y = x$ — Linear

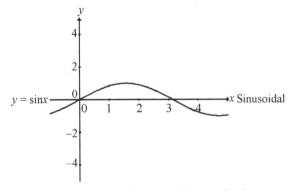

$y = \sin x$ — Sinusoidal

The most appropriate graph is quadratic as the curve most nearly follows the basic equation $y = x^2$.

NR1. 22.9

Here, we are given a function and asked to find its value at D (Day) = 186. Since we are using real numbers and not degrees in our function, we must change the calculator mode to radians. We then solve through substitution.

$$
\begin{aligned}
A &= 23.553\sin(0.017D - 1.364) - 0.003 \\
&= 23.553\sin(0.017(186) - 1.364) - 0.003 \\
&= 23.553(0.974\ 3) - 0.003 \\
&= 22.945 \\
&\sim 22.9
\end{aligned}
$$

11. B

This tests transformation of sinusoidal functions.

Recall $f(x) = a\sin(bx + c) + d$

Amplitude $= a$ max value $= d + a$

Period $= \dfrac{2\pi}{b}$ min value $= d - a$

                     middle value $= d$

The answer is **B**, 8 m.

Copyright Protected

NR2. **21**

The partial graph of the function
$f(\theta) = a\sin(\theta + c) + d$ is shown below.

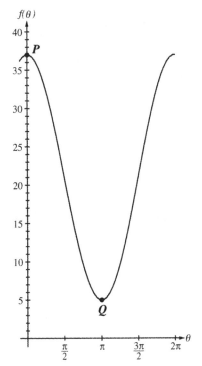

The graph has a maximum at $P(0,37)$ and a
minimum at $Q(\pi,5)$.

From the graph shown above the maximum
value of $f(\theta)$ is $M = 37$, and the minimum
value of $f(\theta)$ is $m = 5$. The value of "d" in
the function, $f(\theta)$ $a\sin(\theta + c) + d$, can be
calculated by using the formula
$$d = \frac{M+m}{2} = \frac{37+5}{2} = \frac{42}{2} = 21.$$

NR3. **4**

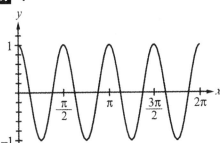

The period of the graph of $y = \cos bx$ is $\dfrac{2\pi}{b}$.

In the graph shown above, the period is $\dfrac{\pi}{2}$.

Therefore, $b = \dfrac{2\pi}{\dfrac{\pi}{2}} = 2\pi \times \dfrac{2}{\pi} = 4.$

12. **A**

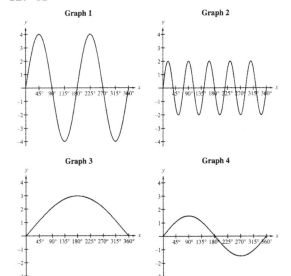

The amplitudes of the four graphs shown
are

graph 1: 4
graph 2: 2
graph 3: 3,
graph 4: about 1.7

We are given that the louder the sound, the
greater the amplitude of its sound wave.
Therefore, graph 1 corresponds to the
loudest sound.

13. C

When this data is entered in a list and plotted on a calculator, it forms a sinusoidal curve. It would most appropriately be modelled by a sinusoidal regression.

NR4. 733

This problem requires us to enter the given information into two lists. A quadratic regression can then be performed.

14. D

After entering this information into two lists and performing a quadratic regression, we find

$a = -29.85$
$b = 298.25$
$c = 607.96$

For school year, 2, we use $x = 2$ in
$$y = ax^2 + bx + c$$
$$= (-29.85)(2)^2 + (298.25)(2) + (607.96)$$
$$= 1\ 085.06$$

Since we cannot have a fraction of a student, the correct answer is 1 085.

15. C

The numbers in the water intake column
600, 800, 1 000,...

form an arithmetic sequence with the first term $a = 600$ and a common difference of $d = t_2 - t_1 = t_3 - t_2 = 200$.

Using this information, we can calculate the day on which the athlete takes 2 000 mL of water by using the formula for the nth term of an arithmetic sequence $t_n = a + (n - 1)d$
Substituting $t_n = 2\ 000$, $a = 600$, and $d = 200$ we get:
$2\ 000 = 600 + (n - 1)\ 200P$
$= 600 + 200n - 200$

$2\ 000 = 400 + 200n$
$200n = 2\ 000 - 400 = 1\ 600$
$$n = \frac{1600}{220} = 8.$$

Now let us consider the sequence of numbers in the column for training time:
2, 1.8, 1.62,...
This is a geometric sequence with the first term $t_1 = a = 2$ and a common ratio of
$$r = \frac{t_2}{t_1} = \frac{1.8}{2} = 0.9, \frac{t_3}{t_2} = \frac{1.62}{1.8} = 0.9$$

Hence, we can find the training time of the athlete on the eighth day; i.e., the day on which she takes 2 000 mL of water, by using the formula for the general term of a geometric sequence: $t_n = ar^{n-1}$.

$$t_8 = 2(0.9)^{8-1} = 2(0.9)^7 \doteq 0.96 \text{ hours}$$

16. C

To calculate the surface area of a cube with one open side, we find the area of one side and multiply by the number of covered sides: 5. To find the surface area of the smallest cube, first find the length of one of the sides of the smallest cube.

From the diagram, we can see that there are 3 cubes. The length of a side of the largest cube is 15 cm. The length of a side of the next cube is $15 x \times \frac{2}{3} = 10$.

The length of a side of the smallest cube is
$10 x \times \frac{2}{3} = 6.\overline{666}$.

$$\text{Area of one side} = (6.\overline{6})^2$$
$$= 44.\overline{444} \text{ cm}^2$$
$$SA = 5(44.4\overline{4})$$
$$\doteq 222.2 \text{ cm}^2$$

17. A

In each diagram, bisecting the sides of each square increases the number of squares four fold. This pattern may be continued to the fifth iteration as follows.

Iteration Number	Number of Squares
0	1
1	4
2	16
3	64
4	256
5	1 024

The number of smallest-sized squares in iteration five is 1 024.

18. D

We can model this pattern as in question 18 by pairing iteration number with side length. Because each iteration means bisecting the sides of each square, subsequent iterations will produce a sequence of halved side lengths.

Iteration Number	Side Length (cm)
0	4
1	2
2	1
3	$\frac{1}{2}$
4	$\frac{1}{4}$
5	

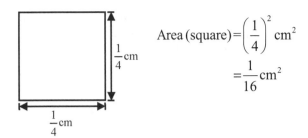

$$\text{Area (square)} = \left(\frac{1}{4}\right)^2 \text{cm}^2$$
$$= \frac{1}{16} \text{cm}^2$$

19. D

A golf ball regains 60% of its original height after each bounce. The general form of this function can be written as $100 \times (0.6)^n$, where n is the number of bounces.

Since we are given that $n = 3$, the height of the ball after the third bounce is

$$100 \times (0.6)^3$$
$$= 100 \times 0.216 = 21.6$$

NR5. 2.5

This problem requires knowledge and use of patterns.

Side	Total Area	Shaded Area
2 cm	2 cm × 2cm = 4 cm^2	$\frac{1}{2}$ × 4 cm^2 = 2 cm^2

In order to find the area of the second shaded (smaller) square, we first calculate the length of the diagonal.

$$a^2 + b^2 = c^2$$
$$c^2 + 2^2 + 2^2$$
$$c^2 = 8$$
$$c = \sqrt{8} = 2\sqrt{2}$$

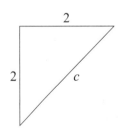

Copyright Protected

The second square is drawn using the mid point of the diagonal. We can calculate the length of the side of the smallest square.

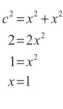 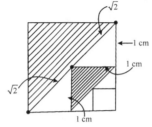

$$c^2 = x^2 + x^2$$
$$2 = 2x^2$$
$$1 = x^2$$
$$x = 1$$

Therefore, the area of the shaded small triangle is

$$A = \frac{1}{2}(1 \times 1) = 0.5 \, cm^2$$

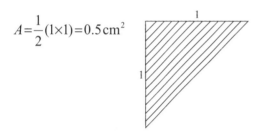

Therefore, the total shaded area is
$2 \, cm^2 + 0.5 \, cm^2 = 2.5 \, cm^2$.

NR6. 192

Here, our problem is to find the total perimeter given certain increments of perimeter. In iteration 3, we increase the perimeter by 48. Our total perimeter is the previous perimeter + 48.
$= 144 + 48 = 192$

20. C

The following steps may be used on the TI-83 calculator. Enter the iteration number {0, 1, 2} into L_1 and the total perimeter {81, 108, 144} into L_2. Calculating the exponential regression by selecting
stat → calc → in Reg and pressing Enter, returns our exponential equation.

$$y = 81(1.\overline{3})^{10}$$
$$= 1\,438.38$$
$$\approx 1\,438 \, cm \, (to \, the \, nearest \, cm).$$

21. A

From the information in the question, we have to calculate the area of a rectangle, after a reduction of each side by 15%. First, calculate the new dimensions of each side.

Original width   = 3.5 cm
percent reduction   = 15% = 0.15
3.5 × 0.15   = 0.525 cm
     (amount of reduction)

New width = 3.5 cm – (3.5 cm × 0.15)
     = 3.5 cm – 0.525 cm
     = 2.975 cm

Original length   = 4.0 cm
percent reduction   = 15% = 0.15
4.0 × 0.15   = 0.6 cm
     (amount of reduction)

New length   = 4.0 cm – (4.0 cm × 0.15)
     = 4.0 cm – 0.6 cm
     = 3.4 cm

Area of the picture   = $w \times l$
     = 2.975 cm × 3.4 cm
     = 10.115 cm^2
     ≈ 10.1 cm^2

NR7. 75

We must first determine the time difference between each successive clock. This is found by taking the number of minutes past noon on the second clock and subtracting the number of minutes past noon on the clock before it.

Therefore, if we look at the chart, the time difference between clocks 1 and 2 is 10 minutes, between clocks 2 and 3 is 15 minutes, and between clocks 3 and 4 is 20 minutes.

The sequence 10, 15, 20 shows an increase of 5 minutes over the previous interval. The difference between clocks 3 and 4 was 20, so adding 5 more minutes means that the next interval will be 25 minutes. Adding 25 minutes to the last clock means that the next clock in the sequence will be 75 minutes past noon.

The following table illustrates this information.

Clock Number	Time	Difference
1	12:05	
		10 min
2	12:15	
		15 min
3	12:30	
		20 min
4	12:50	

Therefore, correct to the nearest whole number, the answer is 75.

Written Response

1. **a)** *Input the data above into two of your calculator lists, and graph the data with the window settings*

  • *X:* [0, 30, 5]
  • *Y:* [0, 9, 1]

Plot the information from your graphing calculator on the coordinate plane below.

b) *Perform an exponential regression on the data and sketch this regression model on the coordinate plane on the previous page.*

State the exponential regression equation in the form $y = ab^x$. Round the values of a and b to the nearest hundredth.

Solution

$y = 8.25(0.89)^x$

c) *What do the variables x and y represent in the context of this question?*

Solution

x represents the wire gauge
y represents the diameter of the wire (in mm)

d) *Determine the diameter of wire for a 40 gauge wire, to the nearest hundredth of a millimeter.*

Solution

The diameter of wire for a 40 gauge wire is 0.08 mm

e) *Use your graphing calculator to perform an exponential regression on this data. Compare the graph of this relationship with the graph relating wire gauge and diameter.*

Solution

Both are exponential functions. The first function falls to the right, while the second function rises to the right. The *y*-intercept of the first function is 8.25, and *y*-intercept of the second function is 228.5.

2. a) *Complete the chart.*

Side Length	Total Number of Posts
3 m	4
6 m	8
9 m	12
12 m	16
15 m	**20**
18 m	**24**

b) *Calculate the total number of posts required to completely enclose the 420 m × 420 m plot of land. Support your answer mathematically.*

Solution

Perform a linear regression to obtain $y \dfrac{4}{3}x$, where x = side length and y = total number of posts.

$$y = \frac{4}{3}(420)$$
$$y = 560$$

The owner will require 560 posts to enclose the lot of land.

c) *Calculate the total cost of materials required for this project by completing the table below. Show your work.*

Solution

Material Costs			
Item	**Quantity**	**Unit Cost**	**Total Cost**
Posts	**571**	$10.20	**$5 824.20**
Barbed Wire	**12**	**$40.00**	**$480.00**
Fence Staples	1 box	$50.00	$50.00
Paint (4 L cans)	**7**	**$19.50**	**$136.50**
		Subtotal	**$6 490.70**
		GST (6%)	**$389.44**
		Total Cost	**$6 880.14**

Posts:
560 + 11 = 571
571 posts

Cans of Paint:
$$\frac{571 \text{ posts} \times 0.577\,\text{m}^2}{48\,\text{m}} = 6.86$$
7 cans of paint

Barbed Wire:
420 × 4 × 3 + 22 = 5 062 m
$$\frac{5\,062}{440} = 11.5$$

12 rolls of barbed wire

Copyright Protected

3. Complete the chart below by indicating the number of glass pieces required for tiers 2, 3, and 4, and by indicating the total number of glass pieces required for a chandelier consisting of 2, 3, 4, or 5 tiers.

Solution

Tier Number (n)	Number of glass pieces in n^{th} tier	Total number of glass pieces in a chandelier with n tiers
1	1	1
2	3	4
3	9	13
4	27	40
5	81	121

The cost for each glass piece is $1.75. Determine the cost of the glass pieces required for a 7-tiered chandelier.

Solution

Tier Number (n)	Number of glass pieces in n^{th} tier	Total number of glass pieces in a chandelier with n tiers
1	1	1
2	3	4
3	9	13
4	27	40
5	81	121
6	243 (81 × 3)	121 + 243 = 364
7	729 (243 × 3)	364 + 729 = 1 093

Therefore, the cost is $1 912.75

The manufacturer of the glass pieces has determined that the width of each piece is normally distributed about a mean of 4.00 cm with a standard deviation of 0.05 cm. Any piece with a width less than 3.90 cm or more than 4.10 cm cannot be used for a chandelier. If 100 000 glass pieces are selected at random for chandeliers, how many pieces from this initial selection will not meet the size requirement?

Solution

$$z = \frac{x - \mu}{\sigma}$$
$$z = \frac{4.1 - 4}{0.05} = 2$$
$$z = \frac{3.9 - 4}{0.05} = -2$$

The rejected number of glass pieces is 100 000 × 2 × 0.022 8 = 4 560.

Copyright Protected

ANSWERS AND SOLUTIONS—UNIT TEST 4— CYCLIC, RECURSIVE AND FRACTAL PATTERNS

1. C	**4. D**	**8. B**	**11. A**
NR1. 0.42	**5. C**	**9. C**	**12. C**
2. B	**6. D**	**NR2. 31.25**	**NR3. 58 447.66 cm^3**
3. C	**7. D**	**10. B**	**WR1. See Solution**
			WR2. See Solution

1. C

The only pattern here that is self-similar and increases in complexity is **C**. The patterns in **A** and **D** are not self-similar. The pattern in **B** does not get more complicated with each iteration.

NR1. 0.42

There are two ways that this problem can be approached. First, one can enter the table into their calculator and perform a sinusoidal regression. The value of b can then be read right off the calculator.

$y = 10.00\sin(0.42x - 3.14) + 30$

This can also be done by using the formula $b = \dfrac{2\pi}{\text{Period}}$. The period of the graph can be read off the chart. It is 15 seconds. This means that $b = \dfrac{2\pi}{15} = 0.42$.

2. B

We need to enter the table of values into the calculator to perform a sinusoidal regression.

$y = 70.01\sin(0.63x) + 639.99$

Once we know the equation, we can enter 7 into the variable and evaluate the expression for the pitch of the siren. This is interpolation because we have the values on either side of the value in question.

3. C

Once we have the regression equation from the previous question we only need to graph the regression equation along with $y = 639.96$. Once these two are graphed, we need to only find the first point of intersection that occurs after $x = 20$. This occurs where $x = 25$.

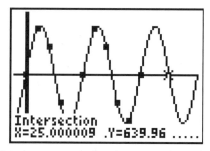

This is extrapolation because the value that we are looking for is outside of the given values.

4. D

In this question we can determine the values of a and b from inspecting the graph and using the formula $b = \dfrac{2\pi}{\text{Period}}$. We notice that the distance from the median at $y = 8$ of the graph to its maximum value where $y = 14$. This is a difference of 6, and thus the amplitude of the graph. Therefore we know that $a = 6$. In addition, we can see that the period of this graph is 12. In other words, it takes 12 units along the x-axis for the pattern to repeat. If we substitute this into the formula for the value of b, we get that

$b = \dfrac{2\pi}{12} = 0.52$.

5. C

The vertical displacement can be determined by comparing the median of the graph to the x-axis. Because the median of the graph is 8, we know that the graph has been shifted 8 units up.

6. D

The maximum and minimum values of the graph can be determined by using the values of the amplitude, a, and vertical displacement, d. The maximum value is the sum of these two and the minimum value is the difference between them.

Therefore:

Maximum = Displacement + Amplitude
$\qquad$ = 1 + 3 = 4

Minimum = Displacement + Amplitude
$\qquad$ = 1 − 3 = −2

7. D

To determine the period of the function, we only need the b-value from the equation, which in this case is $\dfrac{\pi}{3}$. The formula we need is $Period = \dfrac{2\pi}{b}$. Now we substitute in the value and solve for b.

We find that $Period = \dfrac{2\pi}{\left(\dfrac{\pi}{3}\right)}$

$$Period = 2\pi\left(\frac{3}{\pi}\right) = 6.$$

To determine which direction the graph had been shifted, we need to investigate the value of c in the equation. We see here that $c = -2$, which means that the graph has been shifted to the right.

8. B

With each iteration, the number of new squares increases by a power of two. On the 5th iteration, the number of new squares will be $2^5 = 32$.

9. C

The data displays a repetitive pattern which makes the sinusoidal model the most appropriate.

NR2. 31.25

Enter the table of values into the lists in the calculator and perform an exponential regression to get the equation $y = 2\,000(0.125)^x$. Once you have the equation, you simply enter 2 into the variable and evaluate for the number of grams of material left. $y = 2\,000(0.125)^2 = 31.25$.

10. B

To find the number of dollar increases in price that corresponds to the \$5 760 first enter the data into the calculator and perform a quadratic regression.

$$y = -10x^2 + 100x + 6\,000$$

Graph this function on the calculator and graph the line $y = 5\,760$. Find the point of intersection between the two graphs. The x-coordinate of the point of intersection is the number of dollar increases in price that correspond to a revenue of \$5 760.

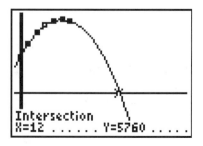

From this, we see that the owner needs to increase his price by $12 to generate a revenue of $5 760 and this corresponds to a ticket price of $32.

11. A

With each iteration, the number of new line segments increases by a factor of 3, but the length of each line segment drops by a fifth. By the 6th iteration, we have multiplied the original length by a power of $\left(\dfrac{3}{5}\right)$ six times.

$$length = 625\left(\dfrac{3}{5}\right)^6$$

12. C

The original area of the first square is $\left(\dfrac{1}{2}\right)(48\,cm)(96\,cm) = 2\,304\,cm^2$. In each case, the length of the base changes by a factor of $\left(\dfrac{1}{2}\right)$ and the length of the height changes by a factor of $\left(\dfrac{1}{2}\right)$.

When we incorporate both of these in the calculation of the new areas, the total change factor for the area with each iteration is $\left(\dfrac{1}{2}\right)\left(\dfrac{1}{2}\right) = \left(\dfrac{1}{4}\right)$. Keeping in mind that with each new iteration, there is a factor of 3 new triangles introduced. We can see that the area for each new iteration is a multiple of $\left(\dfrac{3}{4}\right)$.

On the nth iteration, the new area is

$$2\,304\left(\dfrac{3}{4}\right)^n = 2\,304(0.75)^n.$$

NR3. **58 447.66 cm³**

To determine the total volume of the fractal all we need to do is to fill in the chart.

Iteration Number	Number of New Cones	Radius of the New Cones (cm)	Volume of New Cones (cm³)	Total Volume of New Cones (cm³)	Total Volume (cm³)
0	1	27	41 223.98	41 223.98	41 223.98
1	8	9	1 526.81	12 214.51	53 438.49
2	64	3	56.55	3 619.11	57 057.61
3	512	1	2.09	1 072.33	58 129.94
4	4 096	0.33	0.08	317.73	58 447.66

Written Response

1. Enter in the data into the calculator and create a scatterplot.

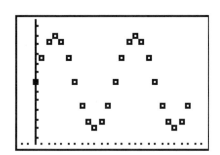

x: [12.3, 25.3, 1]
y: [0.3, 13.7, 1]

The window settings were determined by using ZoomStat on the calculator.
To find the equation of the line of best fit, we perform a sinusoidal regression.
The equation we find is
$y = 4.98\sin(0.52x + 0) + 7.00$
$y = 4.98\sin(0.52x) + 7$

2. First enter the data into the calculator to both find the regression equation and plot the data.

The regression equation is
$y = 2\,000.01(1.06)x$.

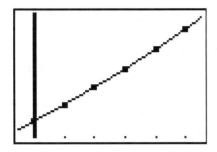

x: [–0.5, 5.5, 1]
y: [1 895.62, 2 718.38, 1]

To determine when the lake will be at capacity, we need to determine how many fish it can hold. To do this, we divide the total area of the lake by the area required for each fish.

$$\frac{204\,800}{64} = 3\,200$$

This means the lake can hold 3 200 fish. Enter this into the calculator as the second function. Graph both and find the point of intersection.

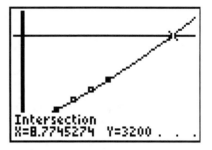

x: [–0.5, 10, 1]
y: [1 895.62, 3 500, 1]

From here, we see that it will take 8.8 years for the lake to reach its maximum.

Copyright Protected

ANSWERS AND SOLUTIONS
UNIT REVIEW—VECTORS

1. C	5. A	9. D	NR3. 828	14. A
2. A	6. A	NR1. 17.7	11. B	15. B
3. C	7. A	NR2. 135	12. C	16. B
4. D	8. C	10. C	13. D	NR4. 16.8

1. C

Two vectors are equal only if they have the same magnitude and direction.

2. A

A vector quantity has both magnitude and direction. Time is not considered a vector as it has only one direction.

3. C

A scalar quantity has only a magnitude (no direction).
Note: Position is also called displacement.

4. D

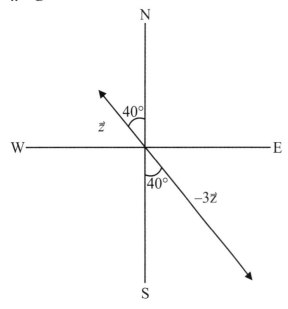

We are given $\vec{z} = 70$ km/h N 40° W. Therefore $-3\,\vec{z}$ means that velocity has been increased by a factor of 3 in the opposite direction. Direction reversal is indicated by the negative sign.

$-3(70$ km/h N 40° W)
$= -210$ km/h N 40° W or 210 km S 40° E

5. A

We add vectors by using the head-to-tail method. The resultant vector is drawn from the tail of the first to the head of the last.

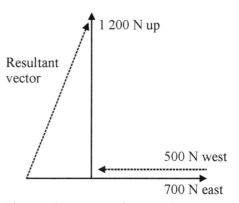

The resultant vector is up and east.

6. A

Using the head-to-tail method of adding vectors, we organize them as in **A**.

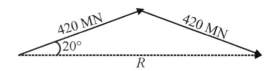

Not for Reproduction

7. A

To solve this problem, we must break down the vector describing the plane's travel into north/south and east/west components and use trigonometry to solve for the amount by which the plane's travel is changed.

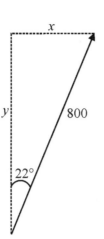

$\cos 22° = \dfrac{y}{800}$

$y = 741.75\,\text{km/h}$

$\sin 22° = \dfrac{x}{800}$

$x = 299.69\,\text{km/h}$

Wind blowing directly east at 110 km/h adds to the east/west components of the plane's travel.

East/West Component = 299.69 + 110
= 409.69 km/h

$\tan \theta = \dfrac{409.69}{741.75}$

$\theta = 28.9°$

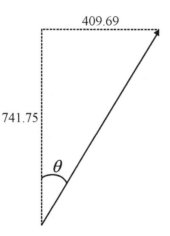

The angle by which the plane's travel has been altered is

$28.9° - 22°$
$= 6.9°$
$\approx 7°$

8. C

We must break down each force vector into its components and directions.

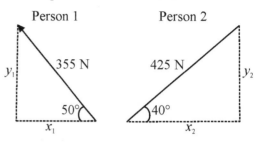

$y_1 = 355 \sin 50°$ $y_2 = 425 \sin 40°$
    $= 271.95\,\text{N}$ $= 273.18\,\text{N}$

$x_1 = 355 \sin 50°$ $x_2 = 425 \sin 40°$
    $= 228.19\,\text{N}$ $= 325.57\,\text{N}$

Assign left '−' and right '+'

Therefore, $x_1 = -228.19$ and $x_2 = +325.57$

To solve for the resultant vector, first add each component.

Vertical $= y_1 + y_2 = 271.95 + 273.18$
                    $= 545.13\,\text{N}$
Horizontal $= x_1 + x_2 = -228.19 + 325.57$
                    $= 97.38\,\text{N}$

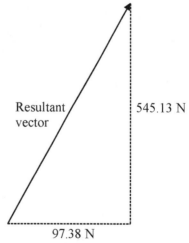

Solve using Pythagorean Theorem.

Resultant vector $= \sqrt{545.13^2 + 97.38^2}$

Resultant vector $= 553.76\,\text{N}$
                 $\approx 554\,\text{N}$

9. D

If a force is along the positive *x*-axis and another force is along the negative *y*-axis, the resultant vector will be in quadrant IV

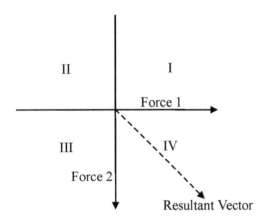

NR1. 17.7

To find the angle of the resultant vector, we use trigonometry associated with right triangles.

$$\tan\theta = \frac{8\,km/h}{25\,km/h}$$
$$\theta = 17.7°$$

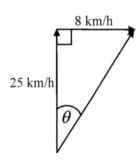

NR2. 135

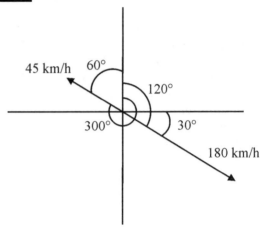

Since the plane is travelling directly into the wind, we can simply add the vectors.

$V_R = 180\,km/h - 45\,km/h$
$\quad = 135\,km/h$

10. C

The resultant force is obtained through adding the components of each initial force.

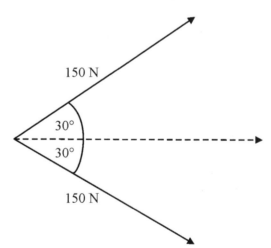

The vertical components are of equal size and opposite direction, so they will cancel each other out.

Copyright Protected

Horizontal Components

$$\text{Fido}\cos30°\ \frac{x_{\text{Fido}}}{150\,\text{N}}$$

$$\text{Spot}\cos30°=\frac{x_{\text{Spot}}}{150\,\text{N}}$$

$$x_{\text{Fido}}=(150\,\text{N})(\cos30°)=129.90\,\text{N}$$
$$x_{\text{Spot}}=(150\,\text{N})(\cos30°)=129.90\,\text{N}$$

Resultant force
= 129.90 N + 129.90 N ≈ 260 N

NR3. **828**

$\vec{F}_{net}=0$
because
$\vec{a}=0$
(constant
velocity)

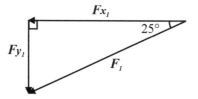

- components of $\vec{F}_1$ and $\vec{F}_2$ parallel to the back of the boat must be equal, therefore, $F_1=F_2$.
- vertical components must add up to 700 N

$$F_1=\sin25.0°+F_2\sin25.0°=700\,\text{N}$$
$$2F_1\sin25.0°=700\,\text{N}$$
$$F_1=828\,\text{N}$$
$$F_2=F_1=828\,\text{N}$$

The y-component (vertical) is calculated using sin25°, in this case.

11. B

We can see that since $60°+30°=90°$, the Pythagorean Theorem is applicable here. A vector diagram with vectors added tip–to–tail is useful.

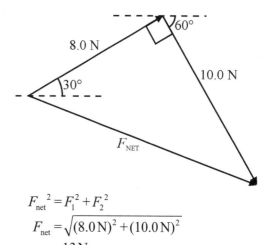

$$F_{net}{}^2=F_1^2+F_2^2$$
$$F_{net}=\sqrt{(8.0\,\text{N})^2+(10.0\,\text{N})^2}$$
$$=13\,\text{N}$$

Note: The question asks for magnitude only, so no direction is needed here.

12. C

$$\theta=30°+x$$
$$\tan\theta=\frac{10.0\,\text{N}}{8.0\,\text{N}}$$
$$=1.25$$
$$\theta=51°$$
$$x=51°-30°$$
$$=21°\text{ south of east}$$

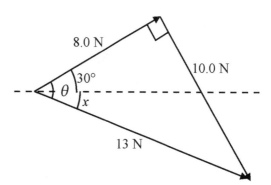

[Be sure your calculator is in degree mode.]

Copyright Protected

13. D

We solve this problem by breaking the vector into horizontal and vertical components. We then add the components.

Find the resultant vector using the Pythagorean's Theorem.

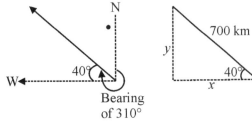

$$\sin 40° = \frac{y}{700}$$
$$y = 449.95 \text{ km}$$

$$\cos 40° = \frac{x}{700}$$
$$x = 536.23 \text{ km}$$

The horizontal component is increased by 100 km.

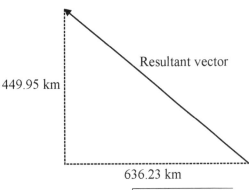

$$\text{Resultant Vector} = \sqrt{636.23^2 + 449.95^2}$$
$$= 779.26 \text{ km}$$

14. A

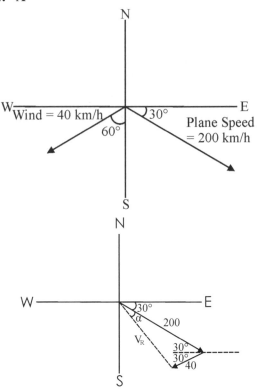

Place vectors head-to-tail

Now, we have a triangle with two known side lengths and contained angle. Solve using the Cosine Law.

$$C^2 = A^2 + B^2 - 2AB \cos c$$
$$= 200^2 + 40^2 - 2(200)(40) \cos 60°$$
$$C = 183 \text{ km}$$

For direction, we use the Law of Sines.

$$\frac{\sin \alpha}{40} = \frac{\sin 60°}{183}$$
$$\alpha = 10.9°$$

$$\text{Direction} = 10.9° + 30°$$
$$= 40.9°$$

Therefore, the answer is 183 km E 41°S

15. B

To find the resultant vector, we must first solve for the plane's speed. We then use the Pythagorean Theorem to solve for the resultant vector's velocity.

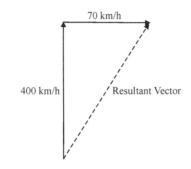

$$\text{Time (hours)} = \frac{45\,\text{min}}{60\,\text{min/h}}$$
$$= 0.75\,\text{h}$$

$$\text{Velocity} = \frac{\text{distance}}{\text{time}}$$
$$= \frac{300\,\text{km}}{0.75\,\text{h}}$$
$$= 400\,\text{km/h}$$

Resultant vector $= \sqrt{400^2 + 70^2}$

Resultant vector $= 406.08\,\text{km/h} \approx 406\,\text{km/h}$

16. B

This is a 2-D problem requiring us to break the vectors into their x, y components. Once this is done, we can add their components and assemble a resulting vector.

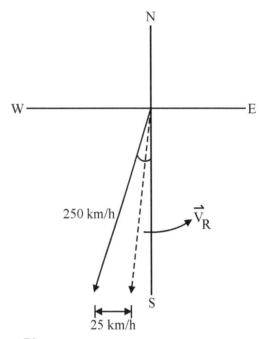

Plane
(250 km/h) (sin25°) = 105.65 km/h west
(250 km/h) (cos25°) = 226.58 km/h south

Wind
25 km/h east

Resultant velocity (105.65 – 25) km/h west
= 80.65 km/h west

north–south velocity is unchanged.

$$V_R = \sqrt{(80.65)^2 + (226.58)^2}$$
$$= 240.51\,\text{km/h}$$
$$V_R \approx 240\,\text{km/h}$$

NR4. 16.8

This is a 3-D problem requiring us to add vector components to assemble a resultant vector. From this resultant vector, we can find the change in direction due to wind.

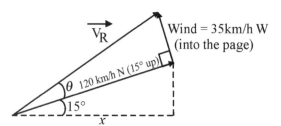

First, find the plane's horizontal velocity

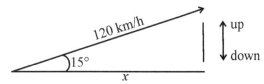

Plane

$x = 120\cos 15°$

$\quad = 115.91$ km/h

Then, find the direction the plane must aim to fly north.

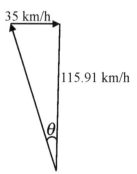

Find the change in direction due to wind.

$$\tan\theta = \frac{35\,\text{km/h}}{115.91\,\text{km/h}}$$

$$\theta = \tan^{-1}\left(\frac{35}{115.91}\right)$$

$$\quad = 16.8°$$

The pilot should aim the plane 16.8° west of north.

Copyright Protected

Not for Reproduction

ANSWERS AND SOLUTIONS
UNIT TEST 5—VECTORS

1. D	NR1. 1.06	NR2. 188°	8. A	11. A
2. B	4. D	6. D	9. B	12. D
3. B	5. B	7. C	10. C	WR1. See Solution
				WR2. See Solution
				WR3. See Solution

1. D

A vector quantity has a magnitude and a direction. Option **D** is the only option that incorporates both.

2. B

A scalar quantity is one that has only a magnitude and no direction.

3. B

In the data given, the car is moving at 220 km/hr directly east. This combination gives us the vector quantity.

NR1. **1.06**

To determine the new velocity of the car, we need to determine what 6% of its old velocity is. This amounts to multiplying the old velocity by 0.06. Since we are increasing the velocity of the car by 6%, we then need to add 100% of the old velocity to the 6% found previously. This amounts to multiplying the old velocity by 1.06.

4. D

When a vector is multiplied by a negative scalar, only the direction of the vector is changed. The vector points in the exact opposite direction. To achieve this with the direction notation, all that is required is to change the directions given to their exact opposites. In this case [N 30°E] becomes [S 30°W].

5. C

In this case, the ship gets $\frac{3}{4}$ of the way towards the ship in distress. This leaves only $\frac{1}{4}$ of the displacement vector left.

This scalar multiple only affects the magnitude of the vector and not the direction. This leaves us with 50 km [080°].

Copyright Protected

NR2. 188

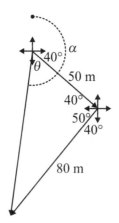

Based on the data given the angle between east and the first vector is 40°. The angle between the second angle and south is 40°. When we calculate the resulting angle between the two given vectors, we find that it is 90°. Since this is a right angle triangle, we can use the inverse tangent to find the value of θ. Once we have this value, we simply need to add it to the bearing of the first vector to determine the bearing of the resultant.

$\theta = \tan^{-1}\left(\dfrac{80}{50}\right)$ $\alpha = 130° + 58°$

$\theta = 58°$ $\alpha = 188°$

6. D

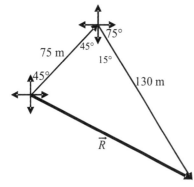

First we need to use the diagram to add the vectors together head to tail. Once this is done, we use the properties of parallel lines and angles to find the angle between the two vectors. In this case, we need to add 45° to 15° to determine that the total angle between them is 60°.

7. C

To add two forces together we generally use the parallelogram method of vector addition. The scenario described yields the following diagram.

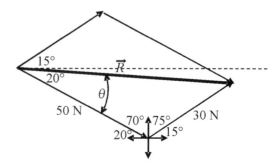

We can see that the angle between the two vectors must be 145°. At this point, we can use the Cosine Law to determine the magnitude of the resultant vector as follows:

$\left|\vec{R}\right| = \sqrt{30^2 + 50^2 - 2(30)(50)\cos(145°)}$

$\left|\vec{R}\right| = 76.5$

Now we can use the Sine Law to determine the angle made by the 50 N vector and the resultant at the origin of the system as follows:

$\dfrac{\sin\theta}{30} = \dfrac{\sin 145°}{76.5}$

$\sin\theta = \dfrac{30\sin 145°}{76.5}$

$\theta = 13°$

Now if we take that 13° and subtract it from the angle at which the first vector is pointing away from the horizontal, we find that the resultant is point at 20° − 13° = 7° below the horizontal.

Not for Reproduction

8. A

To evaluate $\vec{u} - \vec{v}$ is the same as evaluating $\vec{u} = (-\vec{v})$, which is the same as adding 5 N [320°] and −(8 N [030°]), the second of which is equivalent to 8 N [210°].

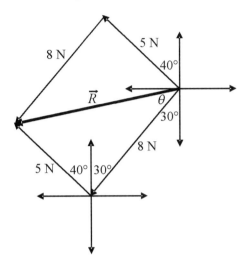

The vectors can then be added using the parallelogram method of vector addition. The angle between the two vectors is 70°, and this is found by applying the properties of angles and parallel lines. We can then use the Cosine Law to determine the magnitude of the resultant as follows:

$$|\vec{R}| = \sqrt{5^2 + 8^2 - 2(5)(8)\cos 70°}$$
$$|\vec{R}| = 7.85 \text{ N}$$

Using this value, we can use the Sine Law to determine the angle the resultant makes with the first vector (θ in the diagram).

$$\frac{\sin\theta}{5} = \frac{\sin 70°}{7.85}$$
$$\sin\theta = \frac{5\sin 70°}{7.85}$$
$$\theta = 37°$$

Now if we add this value to the bearing of the first vector, we can find the bearing of the resultant.

$$210° + 37° = 247°$$

9. B

Since the scenario provides us with a right triangle, we need only apply basic trigonometry to determine the magnitude and direction of the resultant. To find the magnitude of the resultant requires only the application of the Pythagorean Theorem.

$$|\vec{R}| = \sqrt{6^2 + 4^2}$$
$$|\vec{R}| = 7.2 \text{ km/h}$$

Now to determine the direction at which the canoeist is traveling we only need to find the value of θ, and use the correct notation to communicate the total resultant.

$$\theta = \tan^{-1}\left(\frac{4}{6}\right)$$
$$\theta = 34°$$

When we put this together, we get $\vec{R} = 7.2 \text{ km/h} [\text{N}34°\text{E}]$.

10. C

First we need to use the diagram to determine the angle between the two vectors provided.

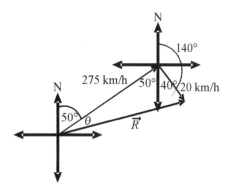

Because the angle between the two vectors is 90°, we can use basic trigonometry to determine the magnitude and direction of the resultant. By using the Pythagorean Theorem, we can determine the magnitude of the resultant as follows:

$$|\vec{R}| = \sqrt{275^2 + 20^2}$$
$$|\vec{R}| = 275.7 \, \text{km/h}$$

After this we can use the inverse tangent function to determine the value of θ. This value can then be added to the bearing of the first angle to determine the bearing of the resultant.

$$\theta = \tan^{-1}\left(\frac{20}{275}\right)$$
$$\theta = 4°$$

This means that the total bearing of the resultant vector must be [054°].

11. A

The resultant vector, $\overrightarrow{AD}$, is the one that points towards the lower right as indicated in the following diagram.

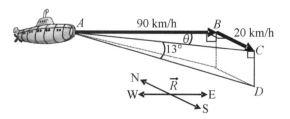

To answer this question, we need only take advantage of the fact that each surface of the shape outlined above is a right triangle.

From the information in triangle ABC, we can determine the length of AC using the Pythagorean Theorem as follows:

$$|\vec{R}| = \sqrt{90^2 + 20^2}$$
$$|\vec{R}| = 92.2 \, \text{km/h}$$

Now using this information and the 13° angle indicated in triangle ACD, we can find the length of AD using the cosine ratio as follows:

$$\cos 13° = \frac{92.2}{AD}$$
$$AD \cos 13° = 92.2$$
$$AD = \frac{92.2}{\cos 13°}$$
$$AD = 94.6 \, \text{km/h}$$

Finally, to determine the value of θ indicated in the diagram, we need only use the inverse tangent function as follows:

$$\theta = \tan^{-1}\left(\frac{20}{90}\right)$$
$$\theta = 13°$$

Copyright Protected

12. D

To find the difference between two vectors we add the negative of the second to the first. To find the negative of a vector graphically means that the vector must point in the opposite direction. The second vector is 5 m [W50°S]. The vector that represents the negative of this vector is 5 m [E50°S]. Graphically, this looks like

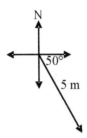

The only option where the second vector is represented this way is in the following diagram.

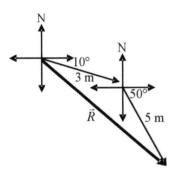

1. To use the parallelogram method, we need only fill in the information about the angles and the magnitude of the vectors that is missing from the diagram that is already provided.

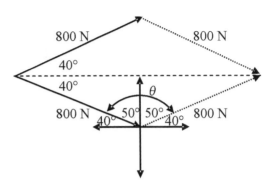

Now we need to apply the Cosine Law to determine the magnitude of the resultant vector as follows.

$$\left|\vec{R}\right|=\sqrt{800^2+800^2-2(800)(800)\cos100°}$$

$$\left|\vec{R}\right|=1\,225.7\,\text{N}$$

Due to the symmetry of the scenario, the resultant vector will be directly along the horizontal line indicated in the illustration. Because the tree requires 1 200 N of force to move it, the horses will indeed be able to move the tree with an excess of 25.7 N.

Copyright Protected

2. The first thing we need to do is to draw a diagram of the scenario so that we can better understand the geometry. We also need to use our understanding of parallel lines and angles to determine the angle in-between the given vectors.

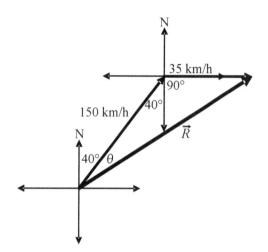

Now using the Cosine and Sine Laws we can determine the magnitude of the resultant vector and its bearing.

$$\left|\vec{R}\right| = \sqrt{150^2 + 35^2 - 2(150)(35)\cos(130°)}$$

$$\left|\vec{R}\right| = 174.6 \text{ km/h}$$

Using this value and the Sine Law we can determine the value of θ in the question. When this angle is added to the bearing of the first vector, we will have the bearing of the resultant.

$$\frac{\sin\theta}{35} = \frac{\sin 130°}{174.6}$$

$$\sin\theta = \frac{35\sin 130°}{174.6}$$

$$\theta = 9°$$

This means that the resultant velocity of the helicopter is 174.6 km/h [049°].

3. To determine the magnitude of the resultant displacement vector, we need to break this question into right triangles that are perpendicular to each other. Let us label the vertices of the diagram as follows.

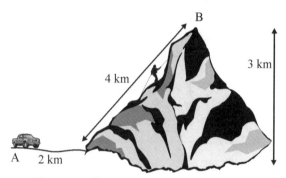

First we will determine the magnitude of the vector that points from A to D using the Pythagorean Theorem.

$$\left|\overrightarrow{AD}\right| = \sqrt{2^2 + 3^2}$$

$$\left|\overrightarrow{AD}\right| = 3.6 \text{ km}$$

Knowing this, we can determine the length of the vector joining A to B, by applying the Pythagorean Theorem to the right triangle ADB.

$$\left|\overrightarrow{AB}\right| = \sqrt{3.6^2 + 4^2}$$

$$\left|\overrightarrow{AB}\right| = 5.4 \text{ km}$$

This gives us the magnitude of the displacement vector. To determine the angle that this vector makes with the horizontal, we only need to use basic trigonometry.

We can use the inverse tangent function on the data we calculated for triangle ADB as follows.

$$\theta = \tan^{-1}\left(\frac{4}{3.6}\right)$$

$$\theta = 48°$$

Thus the total displacement vector from A to B is 5.4 km at an angle of elevation of 48°.

ANSWERS AND SOLUTIONS
UNIT REVIEW—DESIGN

NR1. 1 120	**NR2. 60.0**	**11. C**	**16. A**
1. D	**6. C**	**12. C**	**17. B**
2. B	**7. C**	**NR3. 58**	**18. C**
3. D	**8. A**	**13. A**	**WR1. See Solution**
4. C	**9. A**	**14. D**	
5. D	**10. B**	**15. D**	

NR1. 1 120

The number of the campsites that the owner can develop must not exceed the dimensions of the land plot. Also, only 70% of the land plot must be developed.

Since sites are 5 m × 10 m, then you can put

$$\frac{400\,m}{10\,m} = 40\,sites$$

$$\frac{200\,m}{5\,m} = 40\,sites$$

$$= 1\,600\,sites$$

Total possible sites = 40 × 40 = 1 600 sites.

However, only 70% of total amount of land can be developed;

Maximum number of sites = (0.7)(1 600)
= 1120 sites

1. D

The cost to produce one can of maple syrup depends on how much syrup one can holds.

$$\text{volume } (v) = h\pi r^2$$
$$h = 13 \text{ cm} \quad r = 5 \text{ cm}$$
$$= (13)\pi(5)^2$$
$$= 1\,021.02 \text{ cm}^3$$

or 1 021.02 mL (as 1 cm³ = 1 mL given in the problem)

Total cost = volume × cost/mL
= 1 021.02 mL × $0.02/mL
= $20.42

2. B

This problem requires us to calculate the dimensions of a hay stack that will fit in a farm shed. We are told the orientation of the bales and that only full bales may be used. The stack dimensions are found from the shed dimensions.

$$\text{Length} = \frac{20 \text{ m}}{1.4 \text{ m}} = 14.3 = 14 \text{ bales}$$

$$\text{Width} = \frac{10 \text{ m}}{0.6 \text{ m}} = 16.7 = 16 \text{ bales}$$

$$\text{Height} = \frac{5\,m}{0.6\,m} = 8.3 = 8 \text{ bales}$$

$$\text{Number of bales} = l \times w \times h$$
$$= 14 \times 16 \times 8$$
$$= 1\,792 \text{ bales}$$

3. D

From the information given, the glass forms a cone with a radius of 5 cm and a height of 18 cm.

The formula for volume of a cone is

$V = \frac{1}{3}\pi r^2 h.$

$V = \frac{1}{3}\pi \left(\frac{10 \text{ cm}}{2}\right)^2 \times 18 \text{ cm}$

$V \doteq \frac{1}{3} \times 3.14 \times 25 \text{ cm}^2 \times 18 \text{ cm}$

$V = 471 \text{ cm}^3$

4. C

The glass in this question is a cone with a radius of 5 cm, the height to 9 cm. We can use the formula for the volume of a cone to determine how much liquid the glass holds.

$V = \frac{1}{3}\pi r^2 h$

$V = \frac{1}{3}\pi \left(\frac{10 \text{ cm}}{2}\right)^2 9 \text{ cm}$

(remember that the height of the cone is $\frac{1}{2}$ the total height of the glass)

$V \doteq \frac{1}{3} \times 3.14 \times 25 \text{ cm}^2 \times 9 \text{ cm}$

$V \doteq 236 \text{ cm}^3$

(rounded to the nearest whole number)

5. D

The roof of the tent forms a pyramid with a square base. The walls form a rectangular prism. We can determine the volume of the prism and the volume of the pyramid separately, and then add the two volumes.

Volume of base = length × width × height

$V_{base} = 4 \times 4 \times 3$

$V_{base} = 48 \text{ m}^3$

The formula for the volume of a pyramid is

$V = \frac{1}{3}lwh,$ where l is the length, w is the width, and h is the height.

$V_{top} = \frac{4 \times 4 \times 3}{3}$

$V_{top} = 16 \text{ m}^3$

Volume of tent = Volume of prism + Volume of pyramid

$V = 48 \text{ m}^3 + 16 \text{ m}^3 \qquad\qquad V = 64 \text{ m}^3$

NR2. 60.0

Recall that the formula for volume of a cylinder is $V = \pi r^2 h$, where r is the radius of the base and h is the height of the cylinder.

Therefore, $106 \text{ m}^3 = \pi \left(\frac{1.5 \text{ m}}{2}\right)^2 h$

$\left(\text{remember that } r = \frac{d}{2}\right)$

(use the approximation 3.14 for π)

$106 \text{ m}^3 = 3.14 \times 0.562\ 5 \text{ m}^2 h$
$\doteq 1.766\ 25 \text{ m}^2 h$

Dividing both sides by $1.766\ 25 \text{ m}^2$, we get

$\frac{106}{1.766\ 25} = h$

$60.014 \text{ m} \doteq h$

Rounded to one decimal place, $h = 60.0 \text{ m}$

6. C

To find the cost of production for a can requires us to first calculate the height of the cylinder. We can use this to find the surface area then the resulting cost given the unit price of $0.000 5/cm^2.

$$\text{Volume}=\pi r^2 h$$
$$355=\pi(3)^2 h \qquad (1\ \text{mL}=1\ \text{cm}^3)$$
$$h=12.562\,\text{cm}$$

$$\text{SA}\ 2\pi r^2 +2\pi rh$$
$$=2\pi(3)^2 +2\pi(3)(12.562)$$
$$=18\pi+75.372\pi$$
$$=293.34\ \text{cm}^2$$

$$\text{Cost}=(293.34\,\text{cm}^2)(\$0.000\ 5/\text{cm}^2)$$
$$=\$0.146\ 67/\text{can}$$

7. C

The cost of material to resurface a highway requires us to find the volume needed. After calculating the volume needed, we can find the cost, given the unit price $900/m^3.

$$\text{Volume}=l\times w\times h$$
$$=25\times6\times0.15$$
$$=22.5\ \text{m}^3$$
$$\text{Cost}=(22.5\ \text{m}^3)(\$900/\text{m}^3)$$
$$=\$20\ 250$$

8. A

For this cylinder, we must solve for the radius. Upon finding a radius, we can solve for the surface area and subsequently for the total cost.
$$\text{Volume}=\pi r^2 h$$
$$5\ 000\ \text{L}=\pi r^2 15$$
$$\pi r^2 =333.33$$
$$r^2 =106.10$$
$$r=10.3\ \text{m}$$

$$SA=2\pi r^2 +2\pi rh$$
$$=2\pi(10.3)^2 +22\pi(10.3)(15)$$
$$=(1\ 666.58+970.75)\ \text{m}^2$$
$$=1\ 637.33\ \text{m}^2$$

$$\text{Cost}=(1\ 637.33\ \text{m}^2)(\$30/\text{m}^2)$$
$$=\$49\ 119.90$$

9. A

Volume for a cylinder is:

$$v=\pi rh$$
$$=\pi(0.3)^2(0.8)$$
$$=0.226\ 195\ \text{m}^2$$

Volume for the electrical box:

$$v=l\times w\times h$$
$$=0.2\,\text{m}\times0.2\,\text{m}\times0.1\text{m}$$
$$=0.004\ \text{m}^3$$

Total amount of concrete

$$=0.226\ 19\ \text{m}^3 -0.004\ \text{m}^3$$
$$=0.222\ 19\ \text{m}^3$$

$$\text{Total cost}=(0.222\ 19\ \text{m}^3)\ (\$134/\text{m}^3)$$
$$=\$29.77$$

10. B

The total cost is the sum of the components
2 elbows $= 2(\$5.15)$ $= \$10.30$
1 trap $= 1(\$8.40)$ $= \$8.40$
straight pipe $= 4.95$ m
$\times (\$4.05/\text{m})$ $= \$20.05$

$\$10.30 + \$8.40 + \$20.05 = \$38.75$

11. C

The cost for carpet in the room, not including the fireplace area is as follows.

$$\text{Total area} = (10\,\text{ft})(12\,\text{ft})$$
$$= 120\,\text{ft}^2$$

$$\text{Fireplace area} = \frac{1}{2}bh$$
$$= \frac{1}{2}(3)(3)$$
$$= 4.5\,\text{ft}^2$$

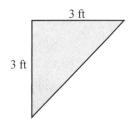

$$\text{Required area} = 120\,\text{ft}^2 - 4.5\,\text{ft}^2$$
$$= 115.5\,\text{ft}^2$$

$$\text{Total cost} = (\$2.48/\text{ft}^2)(115.5\,\text{ft}^2)$$
$$= \$286.44$$

12. C

This is a question regarding budget. One must pay particular attention to the amount of paint.

Paint cost = (3 gal)($31/gal) = $93
The cost of all items is $3 096.

A: $3 096 – $478 = $2 618   ✗
B: $3 096 – $280 – $117 = $2 639 ✗
C: $3 096 – $504 – $93 = $2 499 ✓
D: $3 096 – $478 – $93 = $2 525 ✗

The only arrangement that would cost below $2 500 is **C**.

NR3. 58

If the budget is $120.00, then the amount of money left over for lettering is
$120.00 – $86.59 – $20.00 = $13.41

13.41 ÷ 0.23, rounded down, is 58.

13. A

To cover Frank's cost and make a 200% profit, we first add up his costs for making one package of marbles.

Cost per marble = 1.2¢ + 1.5¢
                = 2.7¢/marble

Cost of one package =
(2.7¢/marble)(100 marbles) + 30¢
= 300¢ or = $3.00

A 200% profit means that production costs of $3.00 are charged plus twice that amount for profit. The answer then is $9.00.

14. D

Here, we need to find the area of glass needed for this particular frame.

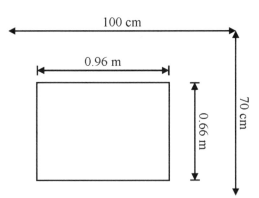

$$\text{Area} = l \times w$$
$$= (0.96\,\text{m})(0.66\,\text{m})$$
$$= 0.633\,6\,\text{m}^2$$

$$\text{Total cost} = \text{area} \times \text{cost/m}^2$$
$$= 0.633\,6\,\text{m}^2 \times 41.82/\text{m}^2$$
$$= \$26.50$$

Copyright Protected

15. D

Here, we must find the surface area of the cylinder, then use cost/m^2 to estimate its total cost.

$$SA = h2\pi r \quad + \quad 2\pi r^2 \qquad h = 6\,\text{m}$$
$$\text{(curved side area)} \quad \text{(area of 2 ends)} \quad r = 2\,\text{m}$$

$$= (6)(2\pi)(2) + 2\pi(2)^2$$
$$= 24\pi + 8\pi = 100.53\,\text{m}^2$$

$$\begin{aligned}\text{Total cost} &= \text{area} \times \text{cost/m}^2 \\ &= 100.53\,\text{m}^2 \times \$2.08/\text{m}^2 \\ &= \$209.10 \end{aligned}$$

16. A

To calculate the volume of any box, we use $v = l \times w \times h$.

However, with the given information, we must calculate the dimensions of the box once it is assembled.

length $= 20 - 2x$
width $= 15 - 2x$
height $= x$
$v = x(20 - 2x)(15 - 2x)$

17. B

The area of the cardboard that is **removed** is half the area of the cardboard; i.e. $\frac{1}{2}(16)(12) = 96$. The dimensions of the cardboard that is removed are $l = (16 - 2x)$ cm and $w = (12 - 2x)$ cm.

Therefore,

$$96 = lw = (16 - 2x)(12 - 2x)$$
$$96 = 192 - 16(2x) - 12(2x) + 4x^2$$
$$4x^2 - 56x + 96 = 0$$

Dividing both sides by 4
$$x^2 - 14x + 24 = 0$$

To solve for x, factor the equation as
$$x^2 - 14x + 24 = (x - 12)(x - 2) = 0$$
$$x = 12 \text{ or } x = 2$$

$x = 12$ cm is not a meaningful solution as
$l = 16 - 2x = 16 - 24 = -8$, and
$w = 12 - 2x = 12 - 24 = -12$

l and w cannot be negative numbers. Therefore, $x = 2$ cm.

18. C

We are given that each crate has a volume of 1.24×10^1 m^3. The total available space is 1.488×10^3 m^3. To determine how many crates will fit, simply divide the available space by the space required by each crate.

$$\text{number of crates} = \frac{\text{Total space}}{\text{space/crate}} = \frac{1.488 \times 10^3 \text{ m}^3}{1.24 \times 10^1 \text{ m}^3}$$

Both values are in scientific notation.

We can divide these by using the following steps:
1.488 Exp 3 ÷ 1.24 Exp 1 = 120

Convert this to scientific notation.
$120 = 1.2 \times 10^2$

We can also change the original values to numbers in standard form first, then divide.

$$1.488 \times 10^3 \text{ m}^3 = 1\,488\,\text{m}^3$$
$$1.24 \times 10^1 \text{ m}^3/\text{crate} = 12.4\,\text{m}^3/\text{crate}$$

$$\frac{1\,488\,\text{m}^3}{12.4\,\text{m}^3/\text{crate}} = 120\,\text{crates}$$

Convert this back to scientific notation
$120 = 1.2 \times 10^2$

To check, simply multiply the number of crates by the volume per crate.

$$120 \text{ crates} \times 1.24 \times 10^1 \text{ m}^3 = 1\,488\,\text{m}^3.$$

Copyright Protected

Written Response

1. a) *Explain the relationship between the values in columns A and B.*

Solution

The sum of each row of columns A and B yields 500 ft² (the total floor of the living room and dining room).

b) *Show, by writing a statement or a formula, how the value in cell E9 ($5 515) was calculated. Make reference to other cells in row 9.*

Solution

Cell C9 is calculated by multiplying A9, the total area of hardwood, by $12.50. Cell D9 is calculated by multiplying B9, the total area of carpet, by $7.25. Cell E9 is then calculated by adding cells C9 and D9 to find the total cost of flooring for the given areas of carpet and hardwood.

or

E9 = A9 * 12.50 + B9 * 7.25

or

C9 = A9 * 12.50
D9 = B9 * 7.25
C9 + D9 = E9

or

C9 + D9 = E9

c) *If the family is to remain within their budget, what is the maximum area of hardwood that they can place into this living room/dining room area?*

Solution

To remain within budget, the maximum area of hardwood is a 13 ft by 20 ft piece or 260 ft².

d) *What is the total cost for this plan?*

Solution

Option l:
The family could have 250 ft² of each carpet and hardwood for a total cost of $4 937.50

Option 2: reference row 14
260 ft² of hardwood and 240 ft² of carpet for a total cost of $4 990.00

Option 3: reference row 15
240 ft² of hardwood and 260 ft² of carpet for a total cost of $4 885.00

Will the family remain within their budget? Explain.

Solution

The total cost is less than $5 000.00, so the family will remain within their budget.

ANSWERS AND SOLUTIONS
UNIT TEST 6—DESIGN

1. A	4. D	NR2. $0.02	7. B
2. C	5. D	6. C	WR1. See Solution
3. B	NR1. 575	NR3. $2.55	

1.   A

The cost of fencing requires that we first calculate the perimeter of Matt's property. This requires that we add up the lengths of the sides as follows.

$$P = 70\,m + 50\,m + 70\,m + 30\,m + 40\,m$$
$$+ 40\,m + 40\,m$$
$$= 340\,m$$

Next we multiply the perimeter by the cost per unit length.

$$Cost = (340\,m)(\$6.50/m) = \$2\,210.00$$

2.   C

To determine the property tax that Matt will have to pay, we need to first determine the area of Matt's property and multiply it by the cost per unit area. To determine the area, we need to find the area of the rectangular portion of his property, the triangular area of this property and the square portion of this property.
Then we add up these values.

$$A = (50\,m)(70\,m) + \left(\frac{1}{2}\right)(40\,m)(30\,m) + (40\,m)(40\,m)$$

$$A = 5\,700\,m^2$$

Now if we multiply the area by the cost per unit area, we will determine the amount that Matt will pay in property taxes.

$$T = (5\,700\,m^2)(\$0.45/m^2)$$
$$T = \$2\,565.00$$

3.   B

To determine the price of the ice cream that will fill the container, we first need to determine the volume of the hemispherical container. To do this, we simply need to find the volume of a sphere with the same radius as the container and divide it by two.

$$V = \left(\frac{4}{3}\right)\pi r^3 \qquad \frac{V}{2} = \frac{7\,238.23\,cm^3}{2}$$

$$V = \left(\frac{4}{3}\right)\pi(12\,cm)^3 \qquad \frac{V}{2} = 3\,619.11\,cm^3$$

$$V = 7\,238.23\,cm^3$$

After this, the volume is multiplied by the cost per unit volume.

$$(3\,619.11\,cm^3)(\$0.002/cm^3) = \$7.24$$

4.   D

To determine the cost of the felt to cover the container we need to determine the surface area of the container and multiply this by the cost per area of the felt.

$$SA = 2\pi r^2 + 2\pi rh$$
$$SA = 2\pi(3\,cm)^2 + 2\pi(3\,cm)(4\,cm)$$
$$SA = 131.95\,cm^2$$

Now we multiply this value by the cost per unit area, $0.03/cm^2.

$$(131.95\,cm^2)(\$0.03/cm^2) = \$3.96$$

5. D

To determine the cost of the banner, we need to first determine the area of the banner and multiply this by the cost of the material per unit area. Then we need to determine the number of letters required and multiply this by the cost per letter.

The area can be determined by dividing the banner into a rectangle and two triangles. First, convert all the lengths to meters.

$$A = (0.5\,\text{cm})(3.0\,\text{m}) + (0.5)(0.5\,\text{m})(0.3\,\text{m})$$
$$+ (0.5)(0.5\,\text{m})(0.3\,\text{m})$$
$$A = 1.65\,\text{m}^2$$

There are 18 letters that need to be embroidered and each costs $0.80. The total can be determined by

$$C = (1.65\,\text{m}^2)(1.30/\text{m}^2) + 19(\$0.80/\text{letter})$$
$$C = \$17.35$$

NR1. **575**

To determine the number of cans that can be made, we need to determine how many circular tops we can cut from the sheet along the length and along the width of the sheet of tin. The diameter of the can is to be 5 cm, or 0.05 m.
Since the sheet is 2 m wide, we can punch

out $\dfrac{2\,\text{m}}{0.05\,\text{m}} = 40$ circles. We must also

determine how many we can punch out along the length by dividing the length by

the diameter to find $\dfrac{3\,\text{m}}{0.05\,\text{m}} = 60$.

This means we can make 40 × 60 = 2 400 can bottoms. We must now do a similar thing with the side of the can. Taking a rectangular shape and wrapping it around the ends of the can form the side of the can. This shape will have dimensions equal to 0.13 m by 0.025 m × π = 0.08 m.

We can cut these rectangular pieces out of the sheet of tin either lengthwise or width wise. If we line these up lengthwise, we find that we can cut out

$$\dfrac{3\,\text{m}}{0.13\,\text{m}} = 23.07$$

or 23 pieces along the length and

$$\dfrac{2\,\text{m}}{0.08\,\text{m}} = 25.5$$

or 25 pieces along the width.
(Remember that we can only consider whole pieces, not the fractional pieces.)
This yields 23 × 25 = 575.

The other way we can do this is along the width of the piece. We can cut out

$$\dfrac{3\,\text{m}}{0.08\,\text{m}} = 38.2$$

or 38 pieces along the width and

$$\dfrac{2\,\text{m}}{0.13\,\text{m}} = 15.4$$

or 15 pieces along the length.
This yields 38 × 15 = 570.

Since the number of sides can be maximized using the first method and we aren't limited by the number of bottoms that can be punched out, we can make 575 cans.

NR2. **$0.02**

Based on the number of cans that we created in the previous question, we need only to divide the total cost of the sheets by the number of cans we can create.

$$\dfrac{2 \times \$7.00}{575} = \$0.02$$

Copyright Protected

6. C

To determine the cost of the paint, we first need to determine the total surface area of the wall that can be painted. We take the total area and subtract the window and door. Then we multiply this value by two because we want to put two coats of paint on the wall. Divide this total area by the area that can be covered by each can and remember to round up to the next whole can that will be necessary.
Finally, multiply this number by the cost of each can.

$$A = 2((9)(20) - (2.5)(4) - (7)(2.5))$$
$$A = 305 \, \text{ft}^2$$

$$\text{Number of cans} = \frac{305 \, \text{ft}^2}{36 \, \text{ft}^2} = 8.47$$

This number must be rounded up to 9 full cans to complete the wall. If each can costs $12.00, then the total cost will be $108.00.

NR3. $2.55

To determine how much the couple can afford to spend per tile, we first need to determine how much is left over to spend on tiles by subtracting what needs to be spent on the toilet, tub and sink. Next, we need to find the number of tiles that are necessary to cover the specified area. Finally, we can divide the cost by the number of tiles.

$$\$2\,000 - \$900 - \$220 - \$320 = \$560$$

Therefore they have $560 left to spend on the tiles. Since the area around the tub is 60" high and the tiles are 6" squares they can be placed 10 tiles high around the tub. Along the back of the tub, the wall is also 60" long, and so we can place 10 tiles along the length of the tub. This means there will be 100 tiles along the back of the tub. Since the sides of the tub are 32", it will require more than 5 tiles to cover this width. We will assume that it requires 6 tiles along the width. Remembering that the tiles can be placed 10 high, this means we have an additional 60 tiles on both sides of the tub giving a total of 220 tiles necessary. If we divide the leftover money by the number of tiles that are required, we see that the couple can afford to spend $\dfrac{\$560}{220} = \$2.55$ per tile.

7. B

To answer this problem, we first need to set up an equation that will calculate the cost of the material for the silo as a function of the height of the silo. Then we will use algebra to solve for the height. Since we do not need the bottom of the silo, our formula for the surface area of a cylinder can be edited down to $SA = \pi r^2 + 2\pi r h$. If we multiply this by the cost per unit area, and substitute in the value for the radius, we get an expression for the total cost of the material. If we set this equal to the budgeted amount we can solve for the height.

$$\$270 = (\$3.00/\text{m}^2)(\pi(2\,\text{m})^2 + 2\pi(2\,\text{m})h)$$

$$\frac{\$270}{\$3.00/\text{m}^2} = \pi(2\,\text{m})^2 + 2\pi(2\,\text{m})h$$

$$\frac{\$270}{\$3.00/\text{m}^2} - \pi(2\,\text{m})^2 = 2\pi(2\,\text{m})h$$

$$\frac{\dfrac{\$270}{\$3.00/\text{m}^2} - \pi(2\,\text{m})^2}{2\pi(2\,\text{m})} = h$$

$$6.2\,\text{m} = h$$

Copyright Protected

Written Response

1. a) The different factors of the volume equation are x, $50 - 2x$, and $\dfrac{150-2x}{2}$. The first factor, x, refers to the size of the squares that were cut out of the pieces of tin around which the remaining flaps of tin will be folded up. This means that x becomes the height of the box. The factor, $50 - 2x$, is showing us that the width of the piece of tin has had corners cut out of both ends, but it still refers to the width of the resulting box. The final factor $\dfrac{150-2x}{2}$, can only refer to the length of the box. The factor is being divided by two, because part of the presence of a fold that will eventually become the lid of the box.

b) If we enter the given equation into the calculator and use the following window settings, we only need to use the "maximum" function in the CALC menu to find the maximum volume of the box.

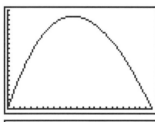

```
WINDOW
 Xmin=0
 Xmax=25
 Xscl=1
 Ymin=0
 Ymax=21000
 Yscl=1000
 Xres=1
```

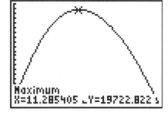

```
Maximum
X=11.285405  Y=19722.822
```

Therefore the maximum volume of the box will be 19 722.82 cm^3 This will occur when $x = 11.29$ cm. As a result, the height of the box will be 11.29 cm. The width of the box will be $50 - 2(11.28) = 27.43 \text{ cm}$.

The length of the box will be $\dfrac{150 - 2(11.28)}{2} = 63.71 \text{ cm}$.

c) The surface area of the box can be calculated by finding the surface area of each of the boxes sides and adding them together. Since each side has an equal partner on the other side of the box, we need only calculate the area of three sides and multiply this result by 2 to find the surface area of the entire box.

The left side of the box has an area equal to $A = x(50 - 2x)$. The front of the box has an area equal to $A = x\left(\dfrac{150-2x}{2}\right)$, and the area for the top of the box is $A = (50 - 2x)\left(\dfrac{150-2x}{2}\right)$. If we put these all together and multiply by 2, the result is

$$A = 2\left[x(50-2x) + x\left(\dfrac{150-2x}{2}\right) + (50-2x)\left(\dfrac{150-2x}{2}\right)\right]$$

or we can simplify this by cancelling out a common factor of two from the factor, $\dfrac{150-2x}{2}$, to get the final expression

$$A = 2(x(50-2x) + x(75-x) + (50-2x)(75-x))$$

KEY STRATEGIES

FOR

SUCCESS ON EXAMS

Copyright Protected

NOTES

Not for Reproduction

 # *KEY* STRATEGIES FOR SUCCESS ON EXAMS

There are many different ways to assess your knowledge and understanding of course concepts. Depending on the subject, your knowledge and skills are most often assessed through a combination of methods which may include performances, demonstrations, projects, products, and oral and written tests. Written exams are one of the most common methods currently used in schools. Just as there are some study strategies that help you to improve your academic performance, there are also some test writing strategies that may help you to do better on unit test and year-end exams. To do your best on any test, you need to be well prepared. You must know the course content and be as familiar as possible with the manner in which it is usually tested. Applying test writing strategies may help you to become more successful on exams, improve your grades, and achieve your potential.

📖 STUDY OPTIONS FOR EXAM PREPARATION

Studying and preparing for exams requires a strong sense of self-discipline. Sometimes having a study buddy or joining a study group

- helps you to stick to your study schedule
- ensures you have others with whom you can practice making and answering sample questions
- clarifies information and provides peer support

It may be helpful to use a combination of individual study, working with a study buddy, or joining a study group to prepare for your unit test or year-end exam. Be sure that the study buddy or group you choose to work with is positive, knowledgeable, motivated, and supportive. Working with a study buddy or a study group usually means you have to begin your exam preparation earlier than you would if you are studying independently.

Tutorial classes are often helpful in preparing for exams. You can ask a knowledgeable student to tutor you or you can hire a private tutor. Sometimes school jurisdictions or individual schools may offer tutorials and study sessions to assist students in preparing for exams. Tutorial services are also offered by companies that specialize in preparing students for exams. Information regarding tutorial services is usually available from school counsellors, local telephone directories, and on-line search engines.

Copyright Protected

📖 EXAM QUESTION FORMATS

There is no substitute for knowing the course content. To do well in your course you need to combine your subject knowledge and understanding with effective test writing skills. Being familiar with question formats may help you in preparing for quizzes, unit tests, or year-end exams. The most typical question formats include multiple choice, numerical response, written response, and essay. The following provides a brief description of each format and suggestions for how you might consider responding to each of the formats.

MULTIPLE CHOICE

A multiple choice question provides some information for you to consider and then requires you to select a response from four choices, often referred to as distracters. The distracters may complete a statement, be a logical extension or application of the information. In preparing for multiple choice questions you may wish to focus on:

- studying concepts, theories, groups of facts or ideas that are similar in meaning; compare and contrast their similarities and differences; ask yourself "How do the concepts differ?", "Why is the difference important?", "What does each fact or concept mean or include?", and "What are the exceptions?"

- identifying main ideas, key information, formulas, concepts, and theories, where they apply and what the exceptions are

- memorizing important definitions, examples, and applications of key concepts

- learning to recognize **distracters** that may lead you to apply plausible but incorrect solutions, and **three and one splits** where one answer is obviously incorrect and the others are very similar in meaning or wording

- using active reading techniques such as underlining, highlighting, numbering, and circling important facts, dates, basic points

- making up your own multiple choice questions for practice

NUMERICAL RESPONSE

A numerical response question provides information and requires you to use a calculation to arrive at the response. In preparing for numerical response questions you may wish to focus on:

- memorizing formulas and their applications

- completing chapter questions or making up your own for practice

- making a habit of **estimating the answer** prior to completing the calculation

- paying special **attention to accuracy** in computing and the use of significant digits where applicable

WRITTEN RESPONSE

A written response question requires you to respond to a question or directive such as "explain", "compare", contrast". In preparing for written response questions you may wish to focus on:

- ensuring your response answers the question

- recognizing directing words such as "list", "explain", and "define"

- providing concise answers within the time limit you are devoting to the written response section of the exam

- identifying subject content that lends itself to short answer questions

ESSAY

An essay is a lengthier written response requiring you to identify your position on an issue and provide logical thinking or evidence that supports the basis of your argument. In preparing for an essay you may wish to focus on:

- examining issues that are relevant or related to the subject area or application of the concept

- comparing and contrasting two points of view, articles, or theories

- considering the merits of the opposite point of view

- identifying key concepts, principles, or ideas

- providing evidence, examples, and supporting information for your viewpoint

- preparing two or three essays on probable topics

- writing an outline and essay within the defined period of time you will have for the exam

- understanding the "marker's expectations"

Copyright Protected

📖 *KEY* TIPS FOR ANSWERING COMMON EXAM QUESTION FORMATS

Most exams use a variety of question formats to test your understanding. You must provide responses to questions ranging from lower level, information recall types to higher level, critical thinking types. The following information provides you with some suggestions on how to prepare for answering multiple choice, written response, and essay questions.

MULTIPLE CHOICE

Multiple choice questions often require you to make fine distinctions between correct and nearly correct answers so it is imperative that you:

- begin by answering only the questions for which you are certain of the correct answer

- read the question stem and formulate your own response before you read the choices available

- read the directions carefully paying close attention to words such as "mark *all* correct", "choose the *most* correct", and "choose the *one best* answer"

- use active reading techniques such as underlining, circling, or highlighting critical words and phrases

- watch for superlatives such as "all", "every", "none", "always" which indicate that the correct response must be an undisputed fact

- watch for negatives such as "none", "never", "neither", "not" which indicate that the correct response must be an undisputed fact

- examine all of the alternatives in questions which include "all of the above" or "none of the above" as responses to ensure that "all" or "none" of the statements apply *totally*

- be aware of distracters that may lead you to apply plausible but incorrect solutions, and 'three and one splits' where one answer is obviously incorrect and the others are very similar in meaning or wording

- use information from other questions to help you

- eliminate the responses you know are wrong and then assess the remaining alternatives and choose the best one

- guess if you are not certain

Not for Reproduction

WRITTEN RESPONSE

Written response questions usually require a very specific answer. In answering these questions you should:

- underline key words or phrases that indicate what is required in your answer such as "three reasons", "list", or "give an example"

- write down rough, point-form notes regarding the information you want to include in your answer

- be brief and only answer what is asked

- reread your response to ensure you have answered the question

- use the appropriate subject vocabulary and terminology in your response

- use point form to complete as many questions as possible if you are running out of time

ESSAY

Essay questions often give you the opportunity to demonstrate the breadth and depth of your learning regarding a given topic. In responding to these questions it may be helpful to:

- read the question carefully and underline key words and phrases

- make a brief outline to organize the flow of the information and ideas you want to include in your response

- ensure you have an introduction, body, and conclusion

- begin with a clear statement of your view, position, or interpretation of the question

- address only one main point or key idea in each paragraph and include relevant supporting information and examples

- assume the reader has no prior knowledge of your topic

- conclude with a strong summary statement

- use appropriate subject vocabulary and terminology when and where it is applicable

- review your essay for clarity of thought, logic, grammar, punctuation, and spelling

- write as legibly as you can

- double space your work in case you need to edit it when you proof read your essay

- complete the essay in point form if you run short of time

Copyright Protected

📖 *KEY* Tips for Responding to Common 'Directing' Words

There are some commonly used words in exam questions that require you to respond in a predetermined or expected manner. The following provides you with a brief summary of how you may wish to plan your response to exam questions that contain these words.

- ◆ **Evaluate** (to assess the worth of something)
  - ‣ Determine the use, goal, or ideal from which you can judge something's worth
  - ‣ Make a value judgment or judgments on something
  - ‣ Make a list of reasons for the judgment
  - ‣ Develop examples, evidence, contrasts, and details to support your judgments and clarify your reasoning

- ◆ **Discuss** (usually to give pros and cons regarding an assertion, quotation, or policy)
  - ‣ Make a list of bases for comparing and contrasting
  - ‣ Develop details and examples to support or clarify each pro and con
  - ‣ On the basis of your lists, conclude your response by stating the extent to which you agree or disagree with what is asserted

- ◆ **Compare and Contrast** (to give similarities and differences of two or more objects, beliefs, or positions)
  - ‣ Make a list of bases for comparing and contrasting
  - ‣ For each basis, judge similarities and differences
  - ‣ Supply details, evidence, and examples that support and clarify your judgment
  - ‣ Assess the overall similarity or difference
  - ‣ Determine the significance of similarity or difference in connection with the purpose of the comparison

- ◆ **Analyze** (to break into parts)
  - ‣ Break the topic, process, procedure, or object of the essay into its major parts
  - ‣ Connect and write about the parts according to the direction of the question: describe, explain, or criticize

- ◆ **Criticize** (to judge strong and weak points of something)
  - ‣ Make a list of the strong points and weak points
  - ‣ Develop details, examples, and contrasts to support judgments
  - ‣ Make an overall judgment of quality

- ◆ **EXPLAIN** (to show causes of or reasons for something)
  - ▸ In Science, usually show the process that occurs in moving from one state or phase in a process to the next, thoroughly presenting details of each step
  - ▸ In Humanities and often in Social Sciences, make a list of factors that influence something, developing evidence for each factor's potential influence

- ◆ **DESCRIBE** (to give major features of something)
  - ▸ Pick out highlights or major aspects of something
  - ▸ Develop details and illustrations to give a clear picture

- ◆ **ARGUE** (to give reasons for one position and against another)
  - ▸ Make a list of reasons for the position
  - ▸ Make a list of reasons against the position
  - ▸ Refute objections to your reasons for and defend against objections to your reasons opposing the position
  - ▸ Fill out reasons, objections, and replies with details, examples, consequences, and logical connections

- ◆ **COMMENT** (to make statements about something)
  - ▸ Calls for a position, discussion, explanation, judgment, or evaluation regarding a subject, idea, or situation
  - ▸ Is strengthened by providing supporting evidence, information, and examples

- ◆ **DEMONSTRATE** (to show something)
  - ▸ Depending upon the nature of the subject matter, provide evidence, clarify the logical basis of something, appeal to principles or laws as in an explanation, or supply a range of opinion and examples

- ◆ **SYNTHESIZE** (to invent a new or different version)
  - ▸ Construct your own meaning based upon your knowledge and experiences
  - ▸ Support your assertion with examples, references to literature and research studies

(Source: http://www.counc.ivic.ca/learn/program/hndouts/simple.html)

Copyright Protected

📖 TEST ANXIETY

Do you get test anxiety? Most students feel some level of stress, worry, or anxiety before an exam. Feeling a little tension or anxiety before or during an exam is normal for most students. A little stress or tension may help you rise to the challenge but too much stress or anxiety interferes with your ability to do well on the exam. Test anxiety may cause you to experience some of the following in a mild or more severe form:

- "butterflies" in your stomach, sweating, shortness of breath, or a quickened pulse

- disturbed sleep or eating patterns

- increased nervousness, fear, or irritability

- sense of hopelessness or panic

- drawing a "blank" during the exam

If you experience extreme forms of test anxiety you need to consult your family physician. For milder forms of anxiety you may find some of the following strategies effective in helping you to remain calm and focused during your unit tests or year-end exams.

- Acknowledge that you are feeling some stress or test anxiety and that this is normal

- Focus upon your breathing, taking several deep breaths

- Concentrate upon a single object for a few moments

- Tense and relax the muscles in areas of your body where you feel tension

- Break your exam into smaller, manageable, and achievable parts

- Use positive self-talk to calm and motivate yourself. Tell yourself, "I can do this if I read carefully/start with the easy questions/focus on what I know/stick with it/. . ." instead of saying, "I can't do this."

- Visualize your successful completion of your review or the exam

- Recall a time in the past when you felt calm, relaxed, and content. Replay this experience in your mind experiencing it as fully as possible.

Not for Reproduction

📖 *KEY* STRATEGIES FOR SUCCESS BEFORE AN EXAM – A CHECKLIST

Review, review, review. That's a huge part of your exam preparation. Here's a quick review checklist for you to see how many strategies for success you are using as you prepare to write your unit tests and year-end exams.

KEY Strategies for Success Before an Exam	*Yes*	*No*
Have you been attending classes?		
Have you determined your learning style?		
Have you organized a quiet study area for yourself?		
Have you developed a long-term study schedule?		
Have you developed a short-term study schedule?		
Are you working with a study buddy or study group?		
Is your study buddy/group positive, knowledgeable, motivated and supportive?		
Have you registered in tutorial classes?		
Have you developed your exam study notes?		
Have you reviewed previously administered exams?		
Have you practiced answering multiple choice, numerical response, written response, and essay questions?		
Have you analyzed the most common errors students make on each subject exam?		
Have you practiced strategies for controlling your exam anxiety?		
Have you maintained a healthy diet and sleep routine?		
Have you participated in regular physical activity?		

📖 *KEY* STRATEGIES FOR SUCCESS DURING AN EXAM

Doing well on any exam requires that you prepare in advance by reviewing your subject material and then using your knowledge to respond effectively to the exam questions during the test session.
Combining subject knowledge with effective test writing skills gives you the best opportunity for success.
The following are some strategies you may find useful in writing your exam.

- ◆ Managing Test Anxiety
  - ▸ Be as prepared as possible to increase your self-confidence.
  - ▸ Arrive at the exam on time and bring whatever materials you need to complete the exam such as pens, pencils, erasers, and calculators if they are allowed.
  - ▸ Drink enough water before you begin the exam so you are hydrated.
  - ▸ Associate with positive, calm individuals until you enter the exam room.
  - ▸ Use positive self-talk to calm yourself.
  - ▸ Remind yourself that it is normal to feel anxious about the exam.
  - ▸ Visualize your successful completion of the exam.
  - ▸ Breathe deeply several times.
  - ▸ Rotate your head, shrug your shoulders, and change positions to relax.

- ◆ While the information from your crib notes is still fresh in your memory, write down the key words, concepts, definitions, theories, or formulas on the back of the test paper before you look at the exam questions.
  - ▸ Review the entire exam.
  - ▸ Budget your time.
  - ▸ Begin with the easiest question or the question that you know you can answer correctly rather than following the numerical question order of the exam.
  - ▸ Be aware of linked questions and use the clues to help you with other questions or in other parts of the exam.

If you "blank" on the exam, try repeating the deep breathing and physical relaxation activities first.
Then move to visualization and positive self-talk to get you going. You can also try to open the 'information flow' by writing down anything that you remember about the subject on the reverse side of your exam paper. This activity sometimes helps you to remind yourself that you <u>do</u> know something and you are capable of writing the exam.

Copyright Protected

📖 GETTING STARTED

MANAGING YOUR TIME

- Plan on staying in the exam room for the full time that is available to you.

- Review the entire exam and calculate how much time you can spend on each section. Write your time schedule on the top of your paper and stick as closely as possible to the time you have allotted for each section of the exam.

- Be strategic and use your time where you will get the most marks. Avoid spending too much time on challenging questions that are not worth more marks than other questions that may be easier and are worth the same number of marks.

- If you are running short of time, switch to point form and write as much as you can for written response and essay questions so you have a chance of receiving partial marks.

- Leave time to review your paper asking yourself, "Did I do all of the questions I was supposed to do?", "Can I answer any questions now that I skipped over before?", and "Are there any questions that I misinterpreted or misread?"

USING THE FIVE PASS METHOD

- **BROWSING STAGE** – Scan the entire exam noting the format, the specific instructions, marks allotted for each section, and which questions you will complete and which ones you will omit if there is a choice.

- **THE FIRST ANSWERING PASS** – To gain confidence and momentum, answer only the questions you are confident you can answer correctly and quickly. These questions are most often found in the multiple choice or numerical response sections of the exam. Maintain a brisk pace; if a question is taking too long to answer, leave it for the Second or Third Pass.

- **THE SECOND ANSWERING PASS** – This Pass addresses questions which require more effort per mark. Answer as many of the remaining questions as possible while maintaining steady progress toward a solution. As soon as it becomes evident the question is too difficult or is tasking an inordinate amount of time, leave it for the Third Answering Pass.

- **THE THIRD ANSWERING PASS** – During the Third Answering Pass you should complete all partial solutions from the first two Passes. Marks are produced at a slower rate during this stage. At the end of this stage, all questions should have full or partial answers. Guess at any multiple choice questions that you have not yet answered.

- **THE FINAL REVIEW STAGE** – Use the remaining time to review the entire exam, making sure that no questions have been overlooked. Check answers and calculations as time permits.

Copyright Protected

USING THE THREE PASS METHOD

- **OVERVIEW** – Begin with an overview of the exam to see what it contains. Look for 'easy' questions and questions on topics that you know thoroughly.

- **SECOND PASS** – Answer all the questions that you can complete without too much trouble. These questions help to build your confidence and establish a positive start.

- **LAST PASS** – Now go through and answer the questions that are left. This is when you begin to try solving the questions you find particularly challenging.

📖 KEY EXAM TIPS FOR SELECTED SUBJECT AREAS

The following are a few additional suggestions you may wish to consider when writing exams in any of the selected subject areas.

ENGLISH LANGUAGE ARTS

Exams in English Language Arts usually have two components, writing and reading. Sometimes students are allowed to bring approved reference books such as a dictionary, thesaurus, and writing handbook into the exam. If you have not used these references on a regular basis, you may find them more of a hindrance than a help in an exam situation. In completing the written section of an English Language Arts exam:

- plan your essay

- focus on the issue presented

- establish a clear position using a thesis statement to direct and unify your writing

- organize your writing in a manner that logically presents your views

- support your viewpoint with specific examples

- edit and proof read your writing

In completing the reading section of an English Language Arts exam:

- read the entire selection before responding

- use titles, dates, footnotes, pictures, introductions, and notes on the author to assist you in developing an understanding of the piece presented

- when using line references, read a few lines before and after the identified section

MATHEMATICS

In some instances, the use of calculators is permitted (or required) to complete complex calculations, modeling, simulations, or to demonstrate your use of technology. It is imperative that you are familiar with the approved calculator and the modes you may be using during your exam. In writing exams in mathematics:

- use appropriate mathematical notation and symbols

- clearly show or explain all the steps involved in solving the problem

- check to be sure you have included the correct units of measurement and have rounded to the appropriate significant digit

- use appropriate labelling and equal increments on graphs

SCIENCES

In the Sciences written response and open-ended questions usually require a clear, organized, and detailed explanation of the science involved in the question. You may find it helpful to use the acronym **STEEPLES** to organize your response to these types of questions. STEEPLES stands for **S**cience, **T**echnological, **E**cological, **E**thical, **P**olitical, **L**egal, **E**conomical, and **S**ocial aspects of the issue presented. In writing exams in the sciences:

- use scientific vocabulary to clearly explain your understanding of the processes or issues

- state your position in an objective manner

- demonstrate your understanding of both sides of the issue

- clearly label graphs, diagrams, tables, and charts using accepted conventions

- provide all formulas and equations

SOCIAL STUDIES, HISTORY, GEOGRAPHY

Exams in these courses of study often require you to take a position on an issue and defend your point of view. Your response should demonstrate your understanding of both the positive and negative aspects of the issue and be supported by well-considered arguments and evidence. In writing exams in Social Studies, History or Geography, the following acronyms may be helpful to you in organizing your approach.

- **SEE** – stands for **S**tatement, **E**xplanation, **E**xample. This acronym reminds you to couple your statement regarding your position with an explanation and then an example.

- **PERMS** – stands for **P**olitical, **E**conomic, **R**eligious or moral, **M**ilitary, and **S**ocietal values.
  Your position statement may be derived from or based upon any of these points of view.
  Your argument is more credible if you can show that recognized authorities such as leaders, theorists, writers or scientists back your position.

Copyright Protected

📖 SUMMARY

Writing exams involves a certain amount of stress and anxiety. If you want to do your best on the exam, *there is no substitute for being well prepared.* Being well prepared helps you to feel more confident about your ability to succeed and less anxious about writing tests. In preparing for unit or year-end exams remember to:

- use as many senses as possible in preparing for exams
- start as early as possible set realistic goals and targets
- take advantage of study buddies, study groups, and tutorials
- review previously used exams
- study with positive, knowledgeable, motivated, and supportive individuals
- practice the material in the format in which you are to be tested
- try to simulate the test situation as much as possible
- keep a positive attitude
- end your study time with a quick review and then do something different before you try to go to sleep on the night before the exam
- drink a sufficient amount of water prior to an exam
- stay in the exam room for the full amount of time available
- try to relax by focusing on your breathing

If you combine your best study habits with some of the strategies presented here, you may increase your chances of writing a strong exam and maximizing your potential to do well.

DIPLOMA EXAMINATION

A GUIDE TO WRITING THE DIPLOMA EXAMINATION

The *Diploma Examination* section contains all of the questions from the January 2002 diploma examination. The questions presented here are distinct from those in the Unit Review section. It is recommended that students work carefully through these exams as they are reflective of the format and difficulty **level of the final exam that students are likely to encounter**.

THE KEY contains detailed answers that illustrate the problem-solving process for every question in this section.

When writing practice exams, students are encouraged to simulate actual Diploma Exam conditions. This will help students become:

- *aware of the mental and physical stamina required to sit through an entire exam*
- *familiar with the exam format and how the course content is tested*
- *aware of any units or concepts that are troublesome or require additional study*
- *more successful in managing their review effectively*

To simulate the exam conditions, students should:

- *use an alarm clock or other timer to monitor the time allowed for the exam*
- *select a quiet writing spot away from all distractions*
- *place their picture ID on the desk or table where the exam is being written*
- *assemble the appropriate materials that are allowed for writing the exam such as pens, HB pencils, calculator, dictionary*
- *use "test wiseness" skills*
- *complete as much of the exam as possible within the allowable time*

In writing the practice exam, students should:

- *read instructions, directions, and questions carefully*
- *organize writing time according to the exam emphasis on each section*
- *highlight key words*
- *think about what is being asked*
- *plan their writing; once complete, proof for errors in content, spelling, grammar*
- *watch for bolded words such as most, least, best*
- *in multiple-choice questions, cross out any choices students know are incorrect*
- *if possible, review all responses upon completion of the exam*

JANUARY 2002 DIPLOMA EXAMINATION

Use the following information to answer the next question.

A box contains 6 blue balls and 4 red balls. Two balls are drawn from the box, one after the other, without replacement.

1. The actions described above will result in events that are

   A. dependent

   B. independent

   C. complementary

   D. mutually exclusive

Use the following information to answer the next question.

The numbers 1 through 5 are each written on a separate slip of paper, and the papers are placed in a box. The letters A, B, C, and D are each written on a separate slip of paper, and the papers are placed into a **different** box. Jodi draws one slip of paper from each box.

2. The number of elements in the sample space for this trial is

A. 51		B. 20	
C. 9		D. 2	

Use the following information to answer the next question.

A particular traffic light at the outskirts of a town is red for 30 s, green for 25 s, and yellow for 5 s in every minute.

3. The probability that the traffic light will **not** be green when a motorist first sees it is

   A. $\dfrac{1}{2}$ B. $\dfrac{1}{12}$

   C. $\dfrac{5}{12}$ D. $\dfrac{7}{12}$

Use the following information to answer the next question.

Given their previous performance, the probability of a particular baseball team winning any given game is $\dfrac{4}{5}$.

4. The probability that the team will win their next 2 games is

   A. $\dfrac{8}{5}$

   B. $\dfrac{16}{25}$

   C. $\dfrac{2}{5}$

   D. $\dfrac{1}{25}$

Use the following information to answer the next question.

The average individual score per round for each of several golfers on the 2000 PGA tour is recorded in the table below.

Name	Average	Name	Average
Mike Weir	70.4	Joe Durrant	70.9
Greg Chalmers	70.5	Tiger Woods	67.8
David Duval	69.4	Scott Dunlop	70.4

Numerical Response

1. The standard deviation, σ, of the golfers' average scores, to the nearest hundredth, is

_____.

Copyright Protected

Use the following information to answer the next question.

A medical researcher measured the body temperature of 700 people and found that the temperatures were normally distributed with a mean of 36.8°C and a standard deviation of 0.35°C.

5. The number of people expected to have a body temperature of 37.5°C or lower is

   A. 16

   B. 68

   C. 490

   D. 684

Use the following information to answer the next question.

A potato chip manufacturing company has found that the mean mass of potato chips in its bags is 65 g and the standard deviation is 7 g.

Numerical Response

2. The symmetric 95% confidence interval for the mass of potato chips in a bag, to the nearest whole number, is between 51 g and
_____ g.

Use the following information to answer the next question.

A boy pulls a wagon along level ground by exerting a force of 60 N at an angle of 32° to the horizontal, as shown in the diagram below.

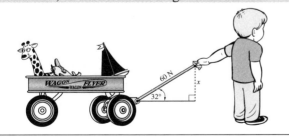

6. The magnitude of the vertical force, *x*, to the nearest tenth of a Newton, is

   A. 60.0 N   B. 50.9 N

   C. 32.0 N   D. 31.8 N

Use the following information to answer the next question.

Vector $\vec{a}$ has a bearing of 72°, as shown in the diagram below.

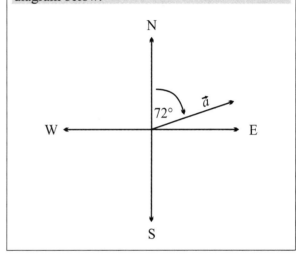

7. If vector $\vec{a}$ is multiplied by a negative scalar, then the new vector will have a bearing of

   A. 108°

   B. 144°

   C. 252°

   D. 288°

Copyright Protected

Use the following information to answer the next question.

A person is trying to sail a boat north across a river, but the boat is being pushed off-course by a 15 km/h current flowing toward the east, as shown below.

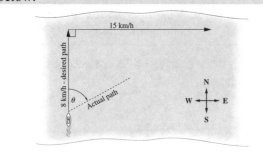

Use the following information to answer the next question.

Two forces act on a point P. The first force has a magnitude of 100 N. The second force has a magnitude of 80 N and is at an angle of 50° to the first force, as shown below.

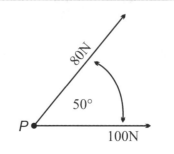

8. *Relative to the shore, the actual speed of the boat is ___i___ km/h, and relative to the desired path, the boat is travelling off-course by an angle, θ, of ___ii___ .*

The statement is completed by the information in row

	i	*ii*
A.	17	62°
B.	17	28°
C.	13	62°
D.	13	28°

9. The magnitude of the resultant force, to the nearest whole number is

A. 31 N

B. 128 N

C. 163 N

D. 180 N

10. Which of the following statements describes a vector quantity?

A. A car travelled north.

B. A car travelled at 100 km/h.

C. A car travelled north at 100 km/h.

D. A car travelled 200 km at 100 km/h.

Not for Reproduction

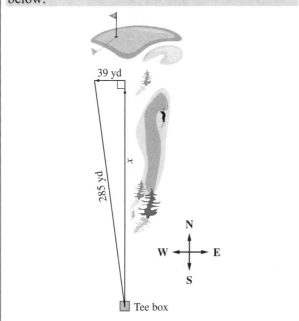

*Use the following information to answer
the next question.*

A golfer tees off and hits a drive. The 285 yd
drive is affected by a westerly wind that pushes
the ball 39 yd off-line, as shown in the diagram
below.

39 yd

285 yd

x

N

W ← → E

S

Tee box

11. If there had been no wind, then the distance,
    x, that the ball would have travelled is

   A. 246 yd

   B. 282 yd

   C. 288 yd

   D. 324 yd

*Use the following information to answer
the next question.*

Two tractors pull on a large block with a force
of 10 000 N each. Each of the tractors pulls at
an angle 20° from the direction that the block is
to move in, as shown below.

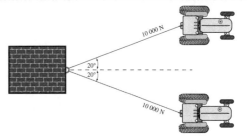

10 000 N

20°
20°

10 000 N

The force exerted by the tractors can be
modeled by the vector diagram shown below.

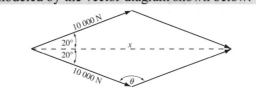

10 000 N

20°
20°

x

10 000 N

θ

Written Response – 10%

1. **a)** Determine the measure of angle θ in the
        vector diagram.

   b) Calculate the magnitude, x, of the
         resultant force that the tractors exert on
         the block.

   c) If a force of 18 000 N is required to
         move the block, will the tractors be able
         to do so? Explain and justify your
         answer mathematically.

Use the following information to answer the next two questions.

A student walks a total of 7 blocks from her home to school. Each block is 150 m long.

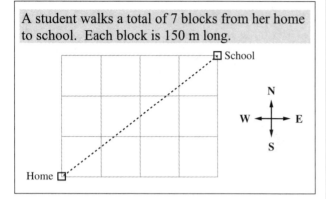

12. The direction and straight-line distance from the student's home to her school are, respectively,

    A. E 37°N and 750 m

    B. E 53°N and 750 m

    C. E 37°N and 1 050 m

    D. E 53°N and 1 050 m

13. The number of different paths that the student could choose to travel from home to school, if she travels only directly north and east, is

    A. 6

    B. 7

    C. 12

    D. 35

Use the following information to answer the next question.

The graduation council has been given the task of determining the menu for the graduation banquet. They have to select one salad, one main course, one side dish, one vegetable dish, and one dessert from the following choices.

Salad:	caesar, garden, tomato-herb, pasta
Main course:	chicken, beef, fish
Side dish:	rice, baked potato, mashed potato, French fries, pasta
Vegetable:	peas, corn, carrots, mixed vegetables, broccoli
Dessert:	cheesecake, pudding, ice cream, pie

Numerical Response

3. The number of possible menu combinations is _____.

Use the following information to answer the next question.

The table below shows the number of vehicles parked in a downtown parking lot over a three-day period.

	Cars	Buses	Bicycles
Thursday	72	6	7
Friday	81	2	2
Saturday	94	3	12

The charge for cars is $6, the charge for buses is $15, and there is no charge for bicycles. The total revenue for each of the three days can be determined from the product of the two matrices below.

$$\begin{bmatrix} 72 & 6 & 7 \\ 81 & 2 & 2 \\ 94 & 3 & 12 \end{bmatrix} \times \begin{bmatrix} 6 \\ 15 \\ 0 \end{bmatrix}$$

14. From this matrix operation, it can be determined that the revenue from

    A. cars on Thursday was $522

    B. all vehicles on Saturday was $609

    C. all vehicles on Thursday was $516

    D. buses over the three days was $516

Use the following information to answer the next question.

A paperboy who delivers papers on his bike can travel only on the trails represented in the diagram below.

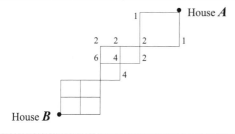

The number beside a vertex indicates the number of trails that lead to that vertex.

15. The number of different trails that the paperboy can take to get from house *A* to house *B* without backtracking is

    A. 36

    B. 60

    C. 72

    D. 120

Use the following information to answer the next question.

A Matrix Equation

$$\begin{bmatrix} -3 & 11 \\ 2 & 8 \end{bmatrix} + 3\begin{bmatrix} a & b \\ c & d \end{bmatrix} = \begin{bmatrix} 0 & 26 \\ 35 & 14 \end{bmatrix}$$

Numerical Response

4. In this equation, the value of *c* is _____.

16. On which of the following matrices can addition be performed?

    A. $\begin{bmatrix} a & b & c \\ d & e & f \end{bmatrix}$ and $\begin{bmatrix} g \\ h \end{bmatrix}$

    B. $\begin{bmatrix} a & b & c \\ d & e & f \end{bmatrix}$ and $\begin{bmatrix} g & h \\ i & j \\ k & l \end{bmatrix}$

    C. $\begin{bmatrix} a & b & c \\ d & e & f \end{bmatrix}$ and $\begin{bmatrix} a & b \\ c & d \end{bmatrix}$

    D. $\begin{bmatrix} a & b & c \\ d & e & f \end{bmatrix}$ and $\begin{bmatrix} g & h & i \\ j & k & l \end{bmatrix}$

Use the following information to answer the next question.

A researcher discovered mould growing in a petri dish in her laboratory.

When first observed, the mould covered only 12.5% of the dish's surface. After 24 hours, the surface area of the mould doubled in size, as shown in the table below.

Time (h)	Area covered (%)
0	12.5
24	25

Numerical Response

5. If the mould continues to grow at the same rate, the petri dish will be covered with mould after _____ hours.

Use the following information to answer the next two questions.

The diagrams below show the first two iterations of a fractal pattern. In each consecutive iteration, 8 new circles are drawn around the circles created in the previous iteration.

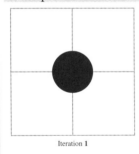
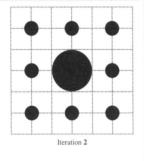

Iteration 1   Iteration 2

17. The total number of **new** circles created in iteration 3 will be

A. 17	**B.** 64
C. 72	**D.** 81

Use the following additional information to answer the next question.

The diameter of the new circle created by each of the first four iterations is shown in the table below.

Iteration	1	2	3	4
Diameter in units	2	0.667	0.222	0.074

This data can be modelled by an exponential regression equation in the form $y = a \times b^x$

18. The diameter, to the nearest thousandth of a unit, of each new circle created by iteration 7 would be

A. 0.003 units	**B.** 0.008 units
C. 0.025 units	**D.** 0.518 units

Use the following information to answer the next question.

A group of biologists studied the population of wolves in an area in northern Canada.
The biologists found that the number of wolves was directly related to the number of caribou found in the study area. The wolf population for the period of the study is shown in the table below.

Year	Wolf Population
Base year (0)	400
1	548
2	800
3	1 168

Written Response – 10%

2. **a)** State the exponential regression equation for this data in the form $y = ab^x$. Round the value of a to the nearest whole number and the value of b to the nearest hundredth.

b) The biologists found that a herd of approximately 17 800 caribou was needed to sustain 650 wolves. If the wolf population continued increasing at the same rate as it did in years 0 to 3 of the study, how many caribou would be required to sustain the wolf population in year 4?

Use the following additional information to answer the next part of the question.

The area the biologists studied was approximately 14 500 km^2, and they found the maximum population density of wolves to be 18 wolves/100 km^2.

c) • What is the maximum number of wolves that this area can sustain?

• If the wolf population continued increasing at the same rate as it did in years 0 to 3 of the study, how much time will have elapsed when this maximum number of wolves is reached?

Use the following information to answer the next question.

The highest tides on Earth occur in the Minas Basin in the Bay of Fundy, Nova Scotia, where tides can reach a maximum height of 16 m. The tidal heights over a particular period are graphed below.

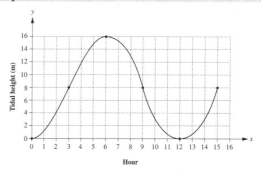

This graph can be represented by the sinusoidal function $y = a \times \sin(0.52x - 1.57) + d$

19. The value of d in the sinusoidal function is

A. 0

B. 8

C. 12

D. 16

Use the following information to answer the next three questions.

The function
$y = 17.14 \sin (0.48 x - 1.75) + 7.11$,
where x represents the number of the month, models the average monthly temperature, in degrees Celsius, for Edmonton.

20. The amplitude of this function is

    A. 0.48°C

    B. 1.75°C

    C. 7.11°C

    D. 17.14°C

21. The maximum average temperature in Edmonton can be found by adding 17.14°C and

    A. 7.11°C

    B. 0.48°C

    C. 1.75°C

    D. −1.75°C

22. Using her calculator set in radian mode, a tourist is able to determine that the average monthly temperature in Edmonton for month 8 (August) is

    A. 1.8°C

    B. 7.11°C

    C. 22.0°C

    D. 25.1°C

Use the following information to answer the next question.

A manufacturer wishes to determine the cost of producing a plastic garbage container. The lid of the container is in the shape of a hemisphere, and it is attached to a closed-bottom cylinder, as shown in the diagram below. The opening for the garbage swings shut when not in use.

The surface area of the container can be determined by using the formula
$SA = \pi r^2 + 2\pi rh + 2\pi r^2$
The plastic required to produce the container costs $0.000 6/cm².

23. The cost of the plastic required to produce one garbage container is

    A. $7.68

    B. $11.07

    C. $15.36

    D. $29.22

Use the following information to answer the next question.

The surface area to be repainted on an older model car is 17 m². The paint costs $42.50 per can, including tax, and each can will cover 2.75 m². Paint must be purchased in whole cans.

24. The total cost to purchase the number of cans of paint required is

A. $297.50

B. $263.50

C. $262.73

D. $240.83

Use the following information to answer the next question.

The manufacturer of hollow plastic cones wishes to calculate the profit on the sale of a cone with the dimensions shown below. It costs $0.08/in² to produce this cone. The cone will be sold for $5.99.

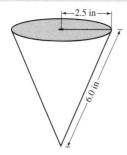

The surface area of this cone can be calculated using the formula $SA = \pi rs$. where r is the radius and s is the slant height.

25. The profit made on the sale of one cone will be

A. $0.48   **B.** $1.55

C. $2.22   **D.** $5.91

Use the following information to answer the next question.

The Duffys have a grain bin on their farm. The bin, which is made in the shape of a cylinder and a cone, has the dimensions shown below.

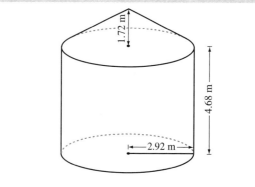

26. The maximum volume of this bin is

A. 57.14 m³   **B.** 125.36 m³

C. 140.72 m³   **D.** 171.43 m³

Use the following information to answer the next question.

The Hacketts are planning to pour a concrete driveway. The driveway will be 6.25 m by 7.0 m by 0.10 m deep, and the concrete pads will be bordered with brick, as shown in the diagram below.

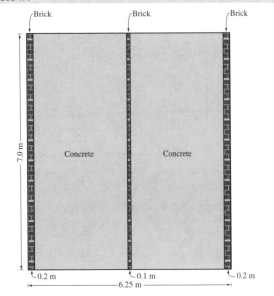

To determine the cost of the concrete, the Hackett's must first calculate its **volume**.

27. If concrete costs $142.25/m^3$, the total cost of the concrete portion of the driveway will be

    A. $572.56
    B. $531.66
    C. $286.28
    D. $124.77

Use the following information to answer the next question.

The Jones bought a new house for $149 700. As a result of economic growth in the area, the value of their house increased at an average rate of 8%/a for 5 years.

28. The value of their house after the 5 years, to the nearest dollar, was

    A. $219 958
    B. $209 580
    C. $198 754
    D. $161 676

Use the following information to answer the next question.

A student entered the data for a $17 000 loan, compounded monthly at 6%/a, on the computer spreadsheet shown below.

	A	B	C	D	E
1			Loan Amortization Table		
2					
3	Interest Rate =	0.06	Year =	5	
4	Number of payments =	60	Compound =	12	
5	Principal =	17 000			
6	Payment =	327			
7					
8	Payment	Outstanding Balance	Payment to Interest	Payment to Principal	Principal Owed
9	1	=$B$5	=B9*($B$3/$D$4)	=$B$6–C9	=B9–D9
10	2	=E9	=B10*($B$3/$D$4)	=$B$6–C10	=B10+D10

Numerical Response

6. The value of cell C9, to the nearest dollar, is $ _____.

Use the following information to answer the next two questions.

Owen invested $2 000 three years ago. During this time, he has been tracking the investment by recording its value at the end of each year.

Year	Value
0	$2 000.00
1	$2 160.00
2	$2 309.04
3	$2 477.98

29. The average annual rate of return on this investment, to the nearest tenth of a percentage, is

    A. 0.7%/a
    B. 1.1%/a
    C. 1.2%/a
    D. 7.4%/a

30. The total **return** on this investment after year 3 is

A. $168.94

B. $477.98

C. $6 947.02

D. $8 947.02

Use the following information to answer the next question.

A person purchases a new car for $21 500.00. He takes out a four-year loan at 7%/a, compounded monthly. The following spreadsheet shows the entries for the first two monthly payments.

	A	B	C	D	E	F
1	Month	Current Balance	Interest Charged	Balance with Interest	Payment	New Balance
2	1	$21 500.00	$125.42	$21 625.42	$514.84	$21 110.58
3	2	$21 110.58	$123.15	$21 233.73	$514.84	$20 718.89

31. Which of the following formulas would have been used to calculate the new balance at the end of month 2?

A. = D3 – C3

B. = B3 + E3

C. = D3 – E3

D. = D3 + E3

Use the following information to answer the next question.

Mike is planning to purchase a sofa and chair set for his new apartment. He is considering the following two options.

Option One: "rent-to-own" with a down payment of $179.99 and 24 monthly payments of $58.50

Option Two: purchase the set outright for $1 099.00 (including taxes)

32. The difference in total cost between the two options, to the nearest dollar, is

A. $125   B. $193

C. $305   D. $485

Use the following information to answer the next question.

A couple plans to purchase a home. They will take out a 25-year mortgage for $146 000 at 7.0%/a, compounded semi-annually. The monthly payments on this mortgage will be $1 022.61.

33. The total amount of interest, to the nearest dollar, that the couple will pay on this mortgage is

A. $306 783

B. $160 783

C. $25 565

D. $12 271

Copyright Protected

Use the following information to answer the next question.

In 1998, a truck dealership sold 300 blue trucks, 100 green trucks, and 200 red trucks. In 1999, sales of blue trucks decreased by 10%, sales of green trucks increased by 20%, and sales of red trucks increased by 30%. This situation can be modeled by the matrix operation shown below.

$$\begin{bmatrix} 0.9 & 0 & 0 \\ 0 & 1.2 & 0 \\ 0 & 0 & 1.3 \end{bmatrix} \times \begin{bmatrix} 300 \\ 100 \\ 200 \end{bmatrix} = \begin{bmatrix} & & \\ & & \\ & & \end{bmatrix}$$

Written Response – 15%

3. **a)** Calculate the product of the matrices above.

b) How many green trucks were sold in 1999?

c) Assume that the pattern continues. Use matrix multiplication to determine the sales for each colour of truck in the year 2000.

Use the following additional information to answer the next part of the question.

In 1998, of all vehicles sold at a different vehicle dealership, 800 were trucks and 600 were sport utility vehicles (SUVs).

In 1999, 8% of the truck owners traded in their trucks for new SUVs, and 22% of the SUV owners traded in their SUVs for new trucks.

No SUV or truck owner switched to a different type of vehicle and no owner of other types of vehicles switched to an SUV or a truck.

d) • Represent this information by completing the 2×2 matrix below, and then perform the matrix multiplication.

$$\begin{bmatrix} 800 & 600 \end{bmatrix} \times \begin{bmatrix} \underline{} & 0.08 \\ 0.22 & \underline{} \end{bmatrix}$$

• Explain what the product of the matrix multiplication in the bullet above means in this context.

Not for Reproduction

ANSWERS AND SOLUTIONS
JANUARY 2002 DIPLOMA EXAMINATION

1. A	15. B	21. A	29. D
2. B	NR4. 11	22. C	30. B
3. D	16. D	23. B	31. C
4. B	NR5. 72	24. A	32. D
NR1. 1.04	17. B	25. C	33. B
5. D	18. A	26. C	WR3. See Solution
NR2. 79	WR2. See Solution	27. A	
6. D	19. B	28. A	
7. C	20. D	NR6. 85	

1. A

The number of possibilities for choosing the first ball is 10. The number of possibilities for choosing the second ball is 9. Because choosing the first ball affects the second choice, these actions are considered dependent.

2. B

The number of choices from the first box is 5. The number of choices from the second box is 4. Thus, according to the Fundamental Counting Principle, the number of ways we can select is $4 \times 5 = 20$.

3. D

The light is not green for 35 seconds for every minute. We write the probability as

$$p = \frac{35}{40}$$
$$= \frac{7}{12}$$

4. B

The probability of the team winning the first game is $\frac{4}{5}$. The probability of them winning the second game is $\frac{4}{5}$ as well.

Thus the probability of the team winning both games is $\frac{4}{5} \times \frac{4}{5} = \frac{16}{25}$.

NR1. 1.04

This problem requires us to enter the data into a list and performing a 1-Var. Statistics calculation to find the standard deviation. Enter the data by pressing STAT → EDIT. Then press STAT → CALC → 1-Var Stats. We find $\sigma = 1.04$.

5. D

The data follow a normal distribution, so we can use a z-score to approximate the number of people with a body temperature of 37.5°C or lower. We can solve this one of two ways.

1. Using the data tables provided, we find the z-score probabilities, then approximate population.

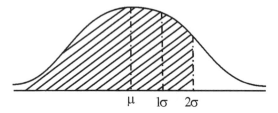

$$z = \frac{x - \mu}{\sigma}$$
$$= \frac{37.5 - 36.8}{0.35}$$
$$= 2$$

Probability = 0.977 3
number of people $= (700)(0.977\ 3)$
$= 684$

2. With the TI-83 calculator, use the Shade Norm command and the appropriate window settings, use –5 as a lower bound.

Enter Shadenorm (–5, 2).
We find the probability is 0.977 3.
number of People = (700) (0.977 3)
$= 684$

NR2. 79

The symmetric 95% confidence interval includes data within 2 standard deviation of the mean. We are given the lower boundary as 51. From the formula sheet, 95% confidence interval $= \mu \pm 1.96\sigma$

The upper boundary is:

upper boundary $= 65 + 1.96 \times 7$
$= 78.65$

6. D

This problem requires us to break the diagonal force into its components. We find the vertical component as follows.

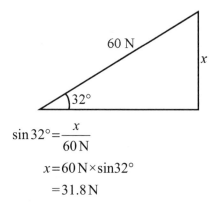

$$\sin 32° = \frac{x}{60\,\text{N}}$$
$$x = 60\,\text{N} \times \sin 32°$$
$$= 31.8\,\text{N}$$

7. C

If a vector is multiplied by a negative scalar, the vector's direction is reversed. Since $\vec{a}$ will point in the opposite direction, its new bearing is

bearing $= 72° + 180°$
$= 252°$

8. A

Vectors are added by placing them head-to-tail. We then use Pythagorean's Theorem to solve for the resultant vector. Here, the vectors are already placed head-to-tail.

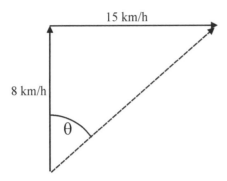

15 km/h

8 km/h

θ

$R^2 = 15^2 + 8^2$ $\tan\theta = \dfrac{15}{8}$

$R = \sqrt{15^2 + 8^2}$ $\theta = 61.9°$

$= 17$ km/h $\approx 62°$

9. C

In order to add these vectors, we place them head-to-tail. Then we use the cosine law to solve for the magnitude of the resultant vector.

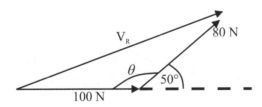

V_R 80 N

θ   50°

100 N

$\theta = 180° - 50°$

$= 130°$

$c^2 = a^2 + b^2 - 2ab\cos c$

$V_R^{\,2} = 80^2 + 100^2 - 2(80)(100)\cos 130°$

$V_R = 163$ N

10. C

A vector is a quantity that has both magnitude and direction.

11. B

This diagram outlines a right angle triangle. We can use the Pythagorean Theorem to solve for the unknown length.

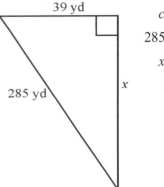

39 yd

285 yd

x

$c^2 = a^2 + b^2$

$285^2 = 39^2 + x^2$

$x^2 = 285^2 - 39^2$

$x = \sqrt{79\ 704}$

$= 282$ yd.

Written Response

1. a) Determine the measure of angle θ in the vector diagram.

Solution
$\theta = 180 - 40$
$\theta = 140°$

b) Calculate the magnitude, x, of the resultant force that the tractors exert on the block.

Solution
$x = \sqrt{10\ 000^2 + 10\ 000^2 - 2(10\ 000)^2\cos 140°}$
$x = 18\ 793.85$

The tractors exert a force of 18 794 N.

c) If a force of 18 000 N is required to move the block, will the tractors be able to do so? Explain and justify your answer mathematically.

Solution :
Yes, the tractors exceed the required force by 794 N.

Copyright Protected

12. A

The student's path is shown through a right angle triangle. We can then solve for the diagonal distance using the Pythagorean Theorem.

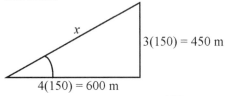

$$c^2 = a^2 + b^2$$
$$x^2 = 450^2 + 600^2$$
$$x = \sqrt{450^2 + 600^2}$$
$$= 750\,\text{m}$$

$$\tan\theta = \frac{450}{600}$$
$$\theta = \tan^{-1}\left(\frac{450}{600}\right)$$
$$\theta = 37°$$

The student's path is 37° North of East. We write this as E 37° N.

13. D

The number of different paths she could choose is the addition of the number of choices at each node or intersection. The choices follow this pattern.

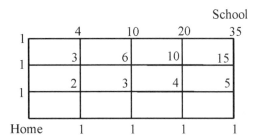

NR3. 1 200

The number of possible menu combinations is the number of choices for each course multiplied by the number of courses. This is by the Fundamental Counting Principle.

Salad = 4
Main course = 3
Side dish = 5
Vegetable = 5
Dessert = 4

number of combinations $= 4 \times 3 \times 5 \times 5 \times 4$
$= 1\ 200$

14. B

We enter the information into matrix A and matrix B. We then multiply them and have a new matrix C.

$$\begin{array}{l} \text{Thursday} \\ \text{Friday} \\ \text{Saturday} \end{array}\begin{bmatrix} 522 \\ 516 \\ 609 \end{bmatrix}$$

From this matrix, we find the total revenue for each day.

15. B

The number of different trails from A to B forms a pattern already developed in the problem. Since it has already been started for us, we continue as follows.

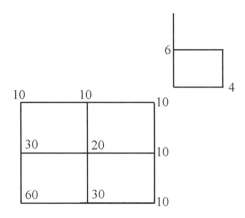

NR4. 11

Consider the equation corresponding to c.

$2 + 3c = 35$,
$3c = 35 - 2 = 33$
$c = \dfrac{33}{3} = 11$

Therefore, the value of c is 11.

16. D

We can only add or subtract matrices with the same dimensions.

NR5. 72

This is an exponential pattern in which the mould doubles in size every 24 hours.

0	12.5%
24 h	25%
48 h	50%
72 h	100%

The petri dish will be covered in mould after 72 hours.

17. B

The number of new circles in each iteration follows an exponential pattern as follows,

NewCircle:	8^0	8^1	8^2
Iteration:	1	2	3

In iteration 3, we have 64 new circles.

18. A

This pattern we are told, follows an exponential regression pattern. We can solve for this pattern using this regression type in our calculator. Enter the information into the lists and press STAT → 0. Exp Reg.

We are shown $y = a \times b^x$
$a = 6.004\,5$
$b = 0.333$

Then, we use $x = 7$, to solve for the seventh iteration.

$y = (6.004\,5)(0.333^7)$
≈ 0.003

Written Response

2. a) State the exponential regression equation for this data in the form $y = ab^x$.
Round the value of a to the nearest whole number and the value of b to the nearest hundredth.

Solution:
$y = 392(1.43)^x$

b) The biologists found that a herd of approximately 17 800 caribou was needed to sustain 650 wolves. If the wolf population continued increasing at the same rate as it did in years 0 to 3 of the study, how many caribou would be required to sustain the wolf population in year 4?

Solution:

Using Rounded Values:	Using Calculated Values:
$y=392(1.43)^4$ $y=1\,639.193\,476$ $\dfrac{17\,800}{650}=\dfrac{caribou}{1\,639.193\,476}$ Caribou $=44\,888.682\,88$ The caribou should number 44 889.	Graph the exponential regression and $y=1\,639.193\,476$ use the CALL function to determine the value of y when $x=4$.

c) What is the maximum number of wolves that this area can sustain?

Solution:
$$\frac{14\,500}{100}\times18=2\,610$$

The area can sustain 2 610 wolves.

If the wolf population continued increasing at the same rate as it did in years 0 to 3 of the study, how much time will have elapsed when this maximum number of wolves is reached?

Solution:
1. Graph $y=392.44\ldots(1.43\ldots)x$
2. Graph $y=2\,610$
3. Use INTERSECT function on calculator when $y=2\,610$, $x=5.273\ldots$

The wolf population will reach the maximum sustainable population during year 5.

19. B

The variable, "d", in the general sinusoidal equation $y=a\sin(bx+c)+d$ describes the median value.

Here, d is 8.

20. D

Translation of sinusoidal functions follows the general equation $y=a\sin(bx+c)+d$, where a determines the amplitude.

For this function,
$y=17.14\sin(0.48x-1.75)+7.11$.
The amplitude is 17.14.

21. A

For the general equation
$y=a\sin(bx+c)+d$, d is the median value.
The maximum value is found by adding the median and amplitude.

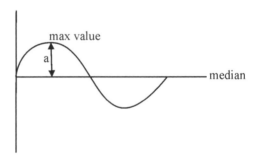

Max value $=17.14+7.11$

22. C

The average monthly temperature in Edmonton is determined by

$$y=17.14\sin(0.48x-1.75+7.11)$$
$$=17.14\sin(0.48(8)-1.75)+7.11$$
$$=17.14\sin(2.09)+7.11$$
$$=17.14\sin(0.868)+7.11$$
$$=22.0°C$$

* Remember to set the mode to radians.

Copyright Protected

23. B

The cost of plastic is found by first calculating the total plastic used through the surface area formula provided. We then use the cost/cm to find the total cost.

$$SA = \pi r^2 + 2\pi rh + 2\pi r^2$$
$$= \pi(25)^2 + 2\pi(25)(80) + 2\pi(25)^2$$
$$= 1\,963.5 + 12\,566.4 + 3\,927$$
$$= 18\,456.9 \text{ cm}^2$$

$$Cost = (18\,456.9 \text{ cm}^2)(\$0.000\,6/\text{cm}^2)$$
$$= \$11.07$$

24. A

To find the total cost, we must find the total number of cans of paint required.
We round this number up to the nearest whole number, as we cannot purchase only part of a can.

$$\#cans = \frac{17 \text{ m}^2}{2.75 \text{ m}^2}$$
$$= 6.18$$
$$\approx 7$$
$$Total = (7)(\$42.50)$$
$$cost = \$297.50$$

25. C

Here, we find the amount of material required, and then calculate the cost using the cost per square inch.

$$SA = \pi rs$$
$$= \pi(2.5)(6.0)$$
$$= 47.12 \text{ in}^2$$

$$Cost = (47.12 \text{ in}^2)(\$0.008/\text{in}^2)$$
$$= \$3.77$$

$$Profit = Selling \, Price - \$3.77$$
$$= \$5.99 - \$3.77$$
$$= \$2.22$$

26. C

Volume for this structure is found by calculating the volume for the cylinder and then calculating the volume for the cone on top.

$$Cone \; V = \frac{1}{3}\pi r^2 h$$
$$= \frac{1}{3}\pi(2.92)^2(1.72)$$
$$= 15.36 \text{ m}^3$$

$$Cylinder \; V = \pi r^2 h$$
$$= \pi(2.92)^2(4.68)$$
$$= 125.36 \text{ m}^3$$

$$Max \, Volume = 15.36 \text{ m}^3 + 125.36 \text{ m}^3$$
$$= 140.72 \text{ m}^3$$

27. A

To calculate the volume of concrete needed, we need to take into account the brick borders.

width = 6.25 m – 0.2 m – 0.1 m – 0.2 m
= 5.75 m

volume = 5.75 m × 7.0 m × 0.10 m
= 4.03 m

The total cost is found through the given cost/m^3

cost = (4.03 m^3)(\$142.25/m^3)
= \$572.56

28. A

This problem uses the financial application on the TI-83 to predict the value of a house after 5 years.

TVM Solver
N = 5
I % = 8
PV = 149 700
PMT = 0
FV = $219 958.41
P/Y = 1
C/Y = 1
PMT = END

NR6. 85

The value of C9 is found through the given formula

C9 = B9 * ($B $3/$D $4)
  = (17 000) (0.06/12)
  = $85

29. D

For average annual rate of return, we use the TVM-Solver on the TI-83 calculator.

N = 3
I% = 7.40
PV = 2 000
PMT = 0
FV = –2 477.98
P/Y = 1
C/Y = 1
PMT: END (Begin)

30. B

The total return is the amount of money earned.

This is $2 477.98 – $2 000 = $477.98

31. C

The new balance is found by subtracting the payment from the balance with interest.

32. D

To find the difference in cost, we must find the total cost of each.

Option One: $179.99 + 24 ($58.50)
       = $179.99 + $1 404
       = $1 583.99

Option Two: $1 099

Difference = $1 583.99 – $1 099
       = $484.99
       ≈ $485

33. B

The total amount of interest is found by first calculating the total amount paid. We then subtract the value of the home.

Total cost = ($1 022.61) (25) (12)
       = $306 783

Interest   = $306 783 – $146 000
       = $160 783

Copyright Protected

Written Response

3. **a)** *Calculate the product of the matrices above.*

Solution

$$\begin{bmatrix} 0.9 & 0 & 0 \\ 0 & 1.2 & 0 \\ 0 & 0 & 1.3 \end{bmatrix} \times \begin{bmatrix} 300 \\ 100 \\ 200 \end{bmatrix} = \begin{bmatrix} 270 \\ 120 \\ 260 \end{bmatrix}$$

b) *How many green trucks were sold in 1999?*

Solution
$100 \times 1.2 = 120$ green trucks sold.

c) *Assume that the pattern continues. Use matrix multiplication to determine the sale for each colour of truck in the year 2000.*

Solution

$$\begin{bmatrix} 0.9 & 0 & 0 \\ 0 & 1.2 & 0 \\ 0 & 0 & 1.3 \end{bmatrix} \times \begin{bmatrix} 270 \\ 120 \\ 260 \end{bmatrix} = \begin{bmatrix} 243 \\ 144 \\ 338 \end{bmatrix}$$

Sales of blue trucks will be 243, green trucks will be 144, and red trucks will be 338.

d) *Represent the information by completing the 2 × 2 matrix below, and perform the matrix multiplication.*

$$\begin{bmatrix} 800 & 600 \end{bmatrix} \times \begin{bmatrix} \underline{} & 0.08 \\ 0.22 & \underline{} \end{bmatrix}$$

Solution

$$\begin{bmatrix} 800 & 600 \end{bmatrix} \times \begin{bmatrix} 0.92 & 0.08 \\ 0.22 & \underline{0.78} \end{bmatrix} = \begin{bmatrix} 868 & 532 \end{bmatrix}$$

• *Explain what the product of the matrix multiplication in the bullet above means in this context.*

Solution
In 1999, 868 people owned trucks bought from the dealership, and 532 owned SUVs bought from the dealership.

Copyright Protected

NOTES

Data
Booklet

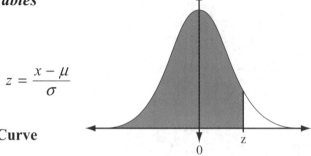

$$z = \frac{x - \mu}{\sigma}$$

Areas under the Standard Normal Curve

z	0.09	0.08	0.07	0.06	0.05	0.04	0.03	0.02	0.01	0.00
−3.4	0.0002	0.0003	0.0003	0.0003	0.0003	0.0003	0.0003	0.0003	0.0003	0.0003
−3.3	0.0003	0.0004	0.0004	0.0004	0.0004	0.0004	0.0004	0.0005	0.0005	0.0005
−3.2	0.0005	0.0005	0.0005	0.0006	0.0006	0.0006	0.0006	0.0006	0.0007	0.0007
−3.1	0.0007	0.0007	0.0008	0.0008	0.0008	0.0008	0.0009	0.0009	0.0009	0.0010
−3.0	0.0010	0.0010	0.0011	0.0011	0.0011	0.0012	0.0012	0.0013	0.0013	0.0013
−2.9	0.0014	0.0014	0.0015	0.0015	0.0016	0.0016	0.0017	0.0018	0.0018	0.0019
−2.8	0.0019	0.0020	0.0021	0.0021	0.0022	0.0023	0.0023	0.0024	0.0025	0.0026
−2.7	0.0026	0.0027	0.0028	0.0029	0.0030	0.0031	0.0032	0.0033	0.0034	0.0035
−2.6	0.0036	0.0037	0.0038	0.0039	0.0040	0.0041	0.0043	0.0044	0.0045	0.0047
−2.5	0.0048	0.0049	0.0051	0.0052	0.0054	0.0055	0.0057	0.0059	0.0060	0.0062
−2.4	0.0064	0.0066	0.0068	0.0069	0.0071	0.0073	0.0075	0.0078	0.0080	0.0082
−2.3	0.0084	0.0087	0.0089	0.0091	0.0094	0.0096	0.0099	0.0102	0.0104	0.0107
−2.2	0.0110	0.0113	0.0116	0.0119	0.0122	0.0125	0.0129	0.0132	0.0136	0.0139
−2.1	0.0143	0.0146	0.0150	0.0154	0.0158	0.0162	0.0166	0.0170	0.0174	0.0179
−2.0	0.0183	0.0188	0.0192	0.0197	0.0202	0.0207	0.0212	0.0217	0.0222	0.0228
−1.9	0.0233	0.0239	0.0244	0.0250	0.0256	0.0262	0.0268	0.0274	0.0281	0.0287
−1.8	0.0294	0.0301	0.0307	0.0314	0.0322	0.0329	0.0336	0.0344	0.0351	0.0359
−1.7	0.0367	0.0375	0.0384	0.0392	0.0401	0.0409	0.0418	0.0427	0.0436	0.0446
−1.6	0.0455	0.0465	0.0475	0.0485	0.0495	0.0505	0.0516	0.0526	0.0537	0.0548
−1.5	0.0559	0.0571	0.0582	0.0594	0.0606	0.0618	0.0630	0.0643	0.0655	0.0668
−1.4	0.0681	0.0694	0.0708	0.0721	0.0735	0.0749	0.0764	0.0778	0.0793	0.0808
−1.3	0.0823	0.0838	0.0853	0.0869	0.0885	0.0901	0.0918	0.0934	0.0951	0.0968
−1.2	0.0985	0.1003	0.1020	0.1038	0.1056	0.1075	0.1093	0.1112	0.1131	0.1151
−1.1	0.1170	0.1190	0.1210	0.1230	0.1251	0.1271	0.1292	0.1314	0.1335	0.1357
−1.0	0.1379	0.1401	0.1423	0.1446	0.1469	0.1492	0.1515	0.1539	0.1562	0.1587
−0.9	0.1611	0.1635	0.1660	0.1685	0.1711	0.1736	0.1762	0.1788	0.1814	0.1841
−0.8	0.1867	0.1894	0.1922	0.1949	0.1977	0.2005	0.2033	0.2061	0.2090	0.2119
−0.7	0.2148	0.2177	0.2206	0.2236	0.2266	0.2296	0.2327	0.2358	0.2389	0.2420
−0.6	0.2451	0.2483	0.2514	0.2546	0.2578	0.2611	0.2643	0.2676	0.2709	0.2743
−0.5	0.2776	0.2810	0.2843	0.2877	0.2912	0.2946	0.2981	0.3015	0.3050	0.3085
−0.4	0.3121	0.3156	0.3192	0.3228	0.3264	0.3300	0.3336	0.3372	0.3409	0.3446
−0.3	0.3483	0.3520	0.3557	0.3594	0.3632	0.3669	0.3707	0.3745	0.3783	0.3821
−0.2	0.3859	0.3897	0.3936	0.3974	0.4013	0.4052	0.4090	0.4129	0.4168	0.4207
−0.1	0.4247	0.4286	0.4325	0.4364	0.4404	0.4443	0.4483	0.4522	0.4562	0.4602
−0.0	0.4641	0.4681	0.4721	0.4761	0.4801	0.4840	0.4880	0.4920	0.4960	0.5000

Copyright Protected

Areas under the Standard Normal Curve

z	0.00	0.01	0.02	0.03	0.04	0.05	0.06	0.07	0.08	0.09
0.0	0.5000	0.5040	0.5080	0.5120	0.5160	0.5199	0.5239	0.5279	0.5319	0.5359
0.1	0.5398	0.5438	0.5478	0.5517	0.5557	0.5596	0.5636	0.5675	0.5714	0.5753
0.2	0.5793	0.5832	0.5871	0.5910	0.5948	0.5987	0.6026	0.6064	0.6103	0.6141
0.3	0.6179	0.6217	0.6255	0.6293	0.6331	0.6368	0.6406	0.6443	0.6480	0.6517
0.4	0.6554	0.6591	0.6628	0.6664	0.6700	0.6736	0.6772	0.6808	0.6844	0.6879
0.5	0.6915	0.6950	0.6985	0.7019	0.7054	0.7088	0.7123	0.7157	0.7190	0.7224
0.6	0.7257	0.7291	0.7324	0.7357	0.7389	0.7422	0.7454	0.7486	0.7517	0.7549
0.7	0.7580	0.7611	0.7642	0.7673	0.7704	0.7734	0.7764	0.7794	0.7823	0.7852
0.8	0.7881	0.7910	0.7939	0.7967	0.7995	0.8023	0.8051	0.8078	0.8106	0.8133
0.9	0.8159	0.8186	0.8212	0.8238	0.8264	0.8289	0.8315	0.8340	0.8365	0.8389
1.0	0.8413	.8438	0.8461	0.8485	0.8508	0.8531	0.8554	0.8577	0.8599	0.8621
1.1	0.8643	0.8665	0.8686	0.8708	0.8729	0.8749	0.8770	0.8790	0.8810	0.8830
1.2	0.8849	0.8869	0.8888	0.8907	0.8925	0.8944	0.8962	0.8980	0.8997	0.9015
1.3	0.9032	0.9049	0.9066	0.9082	0.9099	0.9115	0.9131	0.9147	0.9162	0.9177
1.4	0.9192	0.9207	0.9222	0.9236	0.9251	0.9265	0.9279	0.9292	0.9306	0.9319
1.5	0.9332	0.9345	0.9357	0.9370	0.9382	0.9394	0.9406	0.9418	0.9429	0.9441
1.6	0.9452	0.9463	0.9474	0.9484	0.9495	0.9505	0.9515	0.9525	0.9535	0.9545
1.7	0.9554	0.9564	0.9573	0.9582	0.9591	0.9599	0.9608	0.9616	0.9625	0.9633
1.8	0.9641	0.9649	0.9656	0.9664	0.9671	0.9678	0.9686	0.9693	0.9699	0.9706
1.9	0.9713	0.9719	0.9726	0.9732	0.9738	0.9744	0.9750	0.9756	0.9761	0.9767
2.0	0.9772	0.9778	0.9783	0.9788	0.9793	0.9798	0.9803	0.9808	0.9812	0.9817
2.1	0.9821	0.9826	0.9830	0.9834	0.9838	0.9842	0.9846	0.9850	0.9854	0.9857
2.2	0.9861	0.9864	0.9868	0.9871	0.9875	0.9878	0.9881	0.9884	0.9887	0.9890
2.3	0.9893	0.9896	0.9898	0.9901	0.9904	0.9906	0.9909	0.9911	0.9913	0.9916
2.4	0.9918	0.9920	0.9922	0.9925	0.9927	0.9929	0.9931	0.9932	0.9934	0.9936
2.5	0.9938	0.9940	0.9941	0.9943	0.9945	0.9946	0.9948	0.9949	0.9951	0.9952
2.6	0.9953	0.9955	0.9956	0.9957	0.9959	0.9960	0.9961	0.9962	0.9963	0.9964
2.7	0.9965	0.9966	0.9967	0.9968	0.9969	0.9970	0.9971	0.9972	0.9973	0.9974
2.8	0.9974	0.9975	0.9976	0.9977	0.9977	0.9978	0.9979	0.9979	0.9980	0.9981
2.9	0.9981	0.9982	0.9982	0.9983	0.9984	0.9984	0.9985	0.9985	0.9986	0.9986
3.0	0.9987	0.9987	0.9987	0.9988	0.9988	0.9989	0.9989	0.9989	0.9990	0.9990
3.1	0.9990	0.9991	0.9991	0.9991	0.9992	0.9992	0.9992	0.9992	0.9993	0.9993
3.2	0.9993	0.9993	0.9994	0.9994	0.9994	0.9994	0.9994	0.9995	0.9995	0.9995
3.3	0.9995	0.9995	0.9995	0.9996	0.9996	0.9996	0.9996	0.9996	0.9996	0.9997
3.4	0.9997	0.9997	0.9997	0.9997	0.9997	0.9997	0.9997	0.9997	0.9997	0.9998

Copyright Protected

Applied Mathematics 30 Data Tables

Cost and Design

$$A = \pi r^2$$

$$A = 4\pi r^2$$

$$A = 2\pi r^2 + 2\pi r h$$

$$A = \pi r^2 + \pi r s$$

$$A = \frac{h(b_1 + b_2)}{2}$$

$$A = \frac{b \times h}{2}$$

$$A = b \times h$$

$$V = \frac{4}{3} \pi r^3$$

$$V = \pi r^2 h$$

$$V = B \times h \text{, where } B \text{ is the area of the base}$$

$$V = \frac{1}{3} \pi r^2 h$$

$$V = \frac{B \times h}{3} \text{, where } B \text{ is the area of the base}$$

Graphing **Calculator** Window Format

$$x: [x_{min}, x_{max}, x_{scl}]$$

$$y: [y_{min}, y_{max}, y_{scl}]$$

Trigonometry and Vectors

$$\frac{a}{\sin A} = \frac{b}{\sin B} = \frac{c}{\sin C}$$

$$a^2 = b^2 + c^2 - 2bc \times \cos A$$

$$\cos A = \frac{b^2 + c^2 - a^2}{2bc}$$

Statistics and Probability

$$\mu = np$$

$$\sigma = \sqrt{np(1 - p)}$$

$$z = \frac{x - \mu}{\sigma}$$

$$P(A \text{ or } B) = P(A) + P(B)$$

$$P(A \text{ and } B) = P(A) \times P(B)$$

Regression Models

$$y = a \times \sin(bx + c) + d$$

$$\text{period} = \frac{2\pi}{b}$$

$$y = ax^2 + bx + c$$

$$y = ax + b$$

$$y = a \times b^x$$

ORDERING INFORMATION

All School Orders

School Authorities are eligible to purchase these resources by applying the Learning Resource Credit Allocation (LRCA – 25% school discount) on their purchase through the Learning Resources Centre (LRC). Call LRC for details.

THE KEY *Study Guides* are specifically designed to assist students in preparing for unit tests, final exams, and provincial examinations.

KEY Study Guides – $29.95 each plus G.S.T.

SENIOR HIGH		JUNIOR HIGH	ELEMENTARY
Biology 30	Biology 20	Language Arts 9	Language Arts 6
Chemistry 30	Chemistry 20	Math 9	Math 6
English 30-1	English 20-1	Science 9	Science 6
English 30-2	Math 20 (Pure)	Social Studies 9	Social Studies 6
Math 30 (Pure)	Physics 20		
Math 30 (Applied)	Social Studies 20	Math 8	Math 4
Physics 30		Math 7	Language Arts 3
Social Studies 30	English 10-1		Math 3
Social Studies 33	Math 10 (Pure)		
	Science 10		
	Social Studies 10		

Student Notes and Problems (SNAP) Workbooks contain complete explanations of curriculum concepts, examples, and exercise questions.

SNAP Workbooks – $29.95 each plus G.S.T.

SENIOR HIGH		JUNIOR HIGH	ELEMENTARY
Chemistry 30	Chemistry 20	Math 9	Math 6
Math 30 Pure	Math 20 Pure	Science 9	Math 5
Math 30 Applied	Math 20 Applied	Math 8	Math 4
Math 31	Physics 20	Math 7	Math 3
Physics 30	Math 10 Pure		
	Math 10 Applied		
	Science 10		

Visit our website for a "tour" of resource content and features at
www.castlerockresearch.com

Research Corp

#2340, 10180 – 101 Street
Edmonton, AB Canada T5J 3S4
e-mail: learn@castlerockresearch.com

Phone: 780.448.9619
Toll-free: 1.800.840.6224
Fax: 780.426.3917

2006 (3)

Castle Rock Research Corp

THE KEY	QUANTITY
Biology 30	
Chemistry 30	
English 30-1	
English 30-2	
Math30 (Pure)	
Math 30 (Applied)	
Physics 30	
Social Studies 30	
Social Studies 33	
Biology 20	
Chemistry 20	
English 20-1	
Math 20 (Pure)	
Physics 20	
Social Studies 20	
English 10-1	
Math 10 (Pure)	
Science 10	
Social Studies 10	
Science 9	
Math 20 (Pure)	
Math 31	
Math 30 (Applied)	
Language Arts 6	
Math 7	
Math 8	
Science 9	
Social Studies 9	
Math 9	
Language Arts 9	
Social Studies 6	
Science 6	
Math 6	
Language Arts 6	
Math 7	
Social Studies 6	
Science 6	
Math 4	
Math 3	
Language Arts 3	

SNAP WORKBOOKS	QUANTITY	
Notes and Problems/ Student Notes and Problems	Workbooks	Solutions Manuals
Chemistry 30		
Chemistry 20		
Physics 30		
Physics 20		
Math 30 Pure		
Math 30 Applied		
Math 31		
Math 20 Pure		
Math 20 Applied		
Math 10 Pure		
Math 10 Applied		
Science 10		
Science 9		
Math 9		
Math 8		
Math 7		
Math 6		
Math 5		
Math 4		
Math 3		

TOTALS
KEYS
WORKBOOKS
SOLUTION MANUALS

Learning Resources Centre

Castle Rock Research is pleased to announce an exclusive distribution arrangement with the Learning Resources Centre (LRC). Under this agreement, schools can now place all their orders with LRC for order fulfillment. As well, these resources are eligible for applying the Learning Resource Credit Allocation (LRCA), which gives schools a 25% discount off LRC's selling price. Call LRC for details.

Orders may be placed with LRC by
telephone: (780) 427-5775
fax: (780) 422-9750
internet: www.lrc.learning.gov.ab.ca
or mail: 12360 - 142 Street NW
Edmonton, AB T5L 4X9

Learning Resources Centre

PAYMENT AND SHIPPING INFORMATION

Name: _____

School Telephone: _____

SHIP TO
School: _____

Address: _____

City: _____ Postal Code: _____

PAYMENT
☐ by credit card
VISA/MC Number: _____
Name on Card: _____ Expiry Date: _____
☐ enclosed cheque
☐ invoice school P.O. number: _____

#2340, 10180 – 101 Street, Edmonton, AB T5J 3S4   Tel: 780.448.9619   Fax: 780.426.3917
email: learn@castlerockresearch.com   Toll-free: 1.800.840.6224

www.castlerockresearch.com

2006 (4)